CREATING Theater

Trinity University Press

San Antonio

CREATING
Theater

by **Ruth Byers**

From idea through performance with children and teens

The Paul Baker Studies in Theater, No. 2

Printed by Von Boeckmann-Jones, Austin, Texas
Typesetting by G&S Typesetters, Austin, Texas

To the students and teachers
who have shared the experience
of creative playwriting.

ACKNOWLEDGMENTS

This book reflects sixteen years of exposure to the ideas and teachings of Paul Baker. First as a student and then as a member of his staff, I take great pride in acknowledging the tremendous influence of his philosophy of theater and concepts of creative work. The freedom that he provides his associates in teaching is equaled only by his interest and concern with developing creative talent. I am indebted to him and to the Board of Directors of the Dallas Theater Center for the time given to complete this book.

I am grateful also to others: to Gene McKinney, Louise Mosley, and Claudette Gardner for their helpful suggestions in preparing the manuscript; to Mrs. Sarah Eastman for giving clarity to my later drafts; to Laura Barber for skillfully editing the final manuscript; and to Mrs. Adelynne Pope, managing editor of Trinity University Press, for her many valuable suggestions and her patient, careful attention to every detail in the production of this book.

I would like to thank Curt Davison for his technical assistance in the design and layout of the book, and to express my appreciation to the following photographers whose pictures are included: Lo Jordan and Ian Films, Windy Drum, Georgette de Bruchard, Arlo Kaspar, Howard Karlsburg, and Yoichi Aoki.

I especially want to thank my husband Ernest for his constant encouragement and help in preparing this material.

In recognition of those teachers and students whose plays and comments I have included or mentioned in the text, all royalties received from production rights granted on their plays will go to a student-teacher scholarship fund for graduate study in Teen-Children's Theater at the Dallas Theater Center.

FOREWORD

One of my most vivid game memories is of playing checkers with my father. I can still hear father's voice—demanding, authoritative, triumphant—saying to me across the checker board, "Your move, son." I can remember the fear and trepidation which ran through me as I pushed an insignificant checker forward and was immediately inundated by father's triple-move. Father always won, needless to say. I have hated checkers ever since. This attitude of triumphant and unassailable mastery of a subject is too often the main stance and posture of teachers. This stance is further reinforced by the methodized and often lifeless use of lesson plans—preconceived results, progress reports, countless tests and measurements.

There is a very difficult, hazy, undefined area between the teacher who allows freedom and discovery to be an essential corner block for his teaching method, and the lazy, permissive, unimaginative, sloppy teacher who hides lack of any form or plan behind a paper-thin popularity approach. Hence, the school administrators have mostly clung to the methodized, measurable type of lesson planning. Too often their standardized teacher becomes the type who kills the very quality in the student which she seeks to develop—creative thought—by shouting in a hundred authoritative ways like my father, "Your move," and implying "You are so dumb you are sure to fail." It seems to me that Ruth Byers has gotten to the heart of the matter in this book, *Creating Theater*. She has drawn on years of alive and vital experience with children and teen-agers to indicate a method of approach and a freedom of application in developing creative activity with students. This is an almost impossible area to describe—for the description of a method for stimulating an atmosphere out of which creative work can evolve is getting close to the essential spiritual center of the teacher herself. The act is inspirational and almost indefinable. The qualities are those which a master painter, musician, and scientist bring to their work——those qualities which set the work aside as living, exciting, moving. Hence, the proof of this type of inspired teaching described here lies in the product——the students——and the secondary products selected for this book, the plays.

All through the text Ruth Byers has shown again and again that the teacher is part of the study group, excited and stimulated along with its other members by every discovery——trusting that the imaginations and insight coming into the group play will find many ways to develop an idea into a skit, poem, or production. The group must have the freedom to move in any direction and to exist in an area of formless chaos for considerable time. The teacher's main contribution is to keep from shouting "your move" ever, to wait and grow with the group, having faith—— faith that out of their mass of undirected ideas, sounds, colors, words, movement, texture, rhythm, will evolve a work. Ruth Byers has explained this complex creative act. The act equally applies to any learning area——science, religion, English, theater, art——as long as the teacher is willing to give up his egotistical prerogative implied in the challenging demand——"your move, son"——and allow a freedom and joy in discovery.

Ruth Byers also implies the development of a craft after the time for freedom of new ideas has solidified into some form. This craft will have grown from a study of various historical forms of theater and art beginning with Primitive, Egyptian, and Greek. After an emotional and spiritual insight into the periods has become a living reality to the group, reference points and appreciation for form and craft may grow. History then becomes living matter. An interest, an appreciation for the life of other times, embroidered in line, color, movement, texture, word, rhythm, space, spans eons of dusty facts and focuses the group insight on the periods in immediate modern perspective. In this approach the Egyptians have immediate dialogue with the lines and forms, the rhythm and sound of Picasso, or of the Beatles.

Most important of all throughout this suggested activity is the individual growth of the young artist, his ability to rely on his own inner activity and to have the confidence to share that activity with others in the work group. He finds that even the smallest imaginative picture can become an important contribution to the group effort, that later the inspired group effort, given form, can communicate to others, can become a play——a performance. This is the beginning of the foundation for the development of a young artist's viewpoint and expression——a foundation for the beginning artist's belief in the value, importance, and necessity of his own creative, productive self.

Paul Baker

CONTENTS

INTRODUCTION

This book is written for the teacher interested in providing students with fresh experiences in creativity which lead to play creation, writing, and production. I have attempted to briefly describe the continuous, integrated process of creating theater from the first expression of original ideas to a performance and the completion of a written script. This has been the core of my work and teaching in Teen-Children's Theater for the past thirteen years. The need for this summary has grown with the development of a graduate program in Teen-Children's Theater where student teachers experiment with this method of teaching and play creation while working in a program for several hundred students between the ages of eight and eighteen. First at the Baylor Theater and now at the Dallas Theater Center students this age have written over seventy-five original one-acts, three-acts, musicals, and television shows. They have written, designed, built, and presented original plays in various styles of classic drama including Greek, Roman, and Medieval. Inspiration for style and content has emanated from Primitive and Egyptian art, and plays have subsequently grown out of these studies. Plays in more contemporary styles of theater have also emerged. Many of these scripts have been preserved and presented over and over again by other classes. Although I refer to some of them in discussion, this book includes only nine. Selection was not arbitrary; nor does it imply value judgment of the scripts. The plays used best represent ideas projected in the text.

Creative playwriting is my own term for describing this prolific activity in the theater arts, for direction and purpose come through the process of play creation. The methods used for creating, writing, and producing original scripts are the subject of this book. Three specific ways of originating ideas are discussed: expression of a spontaneous idea during a creative activity,

which in turn generates inspiration for additional ideas; participation in ideation exercises designed to produce ideas immediately useful to playwriting; and studies in theater which use
periods of drama or styles of theater as teaching formats for
broader learning experiences. Emphasis focuses herein on ideation as a means for inventing playwriting material, but the discussion of how ideas develop into play scripts and subsequent
productions applies equally to any of the methods used to originate ideas. I regret that it was not possible to expand the section
on studies in theater. This has been the major emphasis of our
work and is an extensive subject. It has many avenues yet to be
explored with possible applications to teaching methods and
formats for public schools and churches, attempts in some of
these areas having already proved successful. I have purpose-
fully provided a general account of creative playwriting experiences, for this more specifically summarizes the work to date
and the process of accomplishment.

I have made an initial assumption that the reader has a background in theater, though I know this may not always be true.
Such an assumption is necessary, however, in order to maintain
a consistent viewpoint; emphasis is upon the creation of the
script and not upon the first production of the play. The experience of *creating* is more important than development of writing
skills or a polished production. Consequently, areas of technical
theater merit attention only as they relate to the needs for
effective play creation. The scope of this book does not allow
expansive treatment of theater production; it is the origin and
development of play ideas that remain paramount in importance.

Creative playwriting is a group experience and class divisions
reflect this. In our situation student groupings are as follows:
children eight and nine, children ten through twelve, teens in
junior high, and teens in senior high school. Classes meet weekly during a span of nine months with children meeting one and
one-half hours each week and teens meeting two hours every
session. Since the process of creative playwriting is similar for
the different ages, there is no clarification of age-group in the
text unless such identification seems necessary. This material
covers the first experiences in creative playwriting except for a
few examples from some of the advanced studies in theater.
Further playwriting activity follows a similar pattern and varies
only with the format of the class and the age and interests of
the group.

I do not intend to provide a systematic method of playwriting
to be imitated in detail, but to convey the essence of the process
as it has developed through actual experience. Through this
method of integrating play creation, writing, and production we
have simultaneously used various art forms to stimulate, inter-

penetrate and enrich one another. Each play then becomes a new experience for both the teacher and her students. Growth for one is dependent upon the other. Over the years I have watched both become more confident in their abilities and sense of personal achievement. And I have certainly experienced this myself. But I have also realized the tremendous opportunity for developing constructive thought processes and encouraging wholesome attitudes. Inner thoughts and concepts spring to the surface when students experience the freedom to create their own characters, situations, and dialogue. A teacher in creative playwriting contributes enormously to a student's thinking through the encouragement she gives and the habits or attitudes she fosters. In a classroom learning is relative to the information absorbed, but in this situation, the teacher works primarily with what the students bring to class and the extent to which they give of themselves. I am cognizant of the responsibility this places upon the teacher of creative playwriting, for I have seen the influence of many teachers on their students. Gratifications are deep if we make contact with a boy or girl. Hopefully, we have made constructive contributions to concepts and attitudes which mold character.

It is not my purpose to suggest that all children and teens should participate in creative playwriting. But making the experience possible and available has many merits, even for those who only enjoy the exercises until they reach a point of departure into another phase of dramatic activity. A student's theater experience should not end with those plays he has written himself. It is essential that he become familiar with the writing of skilled playwrights and that he see live performances of many styles and forms of drama. As the student grows in his awareness of the theater, he will become more discerning of the well-drawn character, the tightly constructed plot, the quality of a production, and the strength of ideas presented through a dramatic performance. It is possible that he may become an artist in the theater or one of its dedicated patrons. It is more important that through his own experience he will begin to develop as an independent, productive individual with a wonderfully creative imagination. Then he can contribute in any area that calls for originality and purposeful action.

It is my hope that this book will stimulate its readers to offer experiences in creative playwriting and, through their own experimentation, find new ways for encouraging children and teens to discover the strength of their own ideas and use them to write original plays.

Ruth Byers

I've learned to take just an idea
and develop it into a play.
                    Kathy Grimes

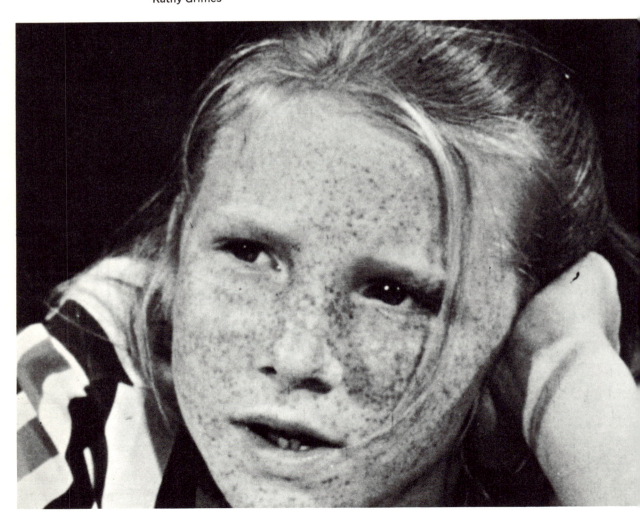

CREATIVE PLAYWRITING

Children are natural storymakers and storytellers. Their stories may originate with their toys or with their parents' clothes—an apron, a hat, a pair of highheeled shoes surreptitiously borrowed from mother's closet. From these props originates the stimulus to create and to project into a wonderful world of make-believe. A child can surround himself with a world of fantasy. At the snap of a finger he can become a tree, a rabbit, a stoplight, a raindrop, the wind, or a bird. It never seems to matter that others do not know what he is, for the observer may see a bird from only his viewpoint, while the child sees something entirely different. Undeveloped, this activity is recognized as dramatic play,[1] but as a form of creative drama it can become a tool for character development and lead to a more rewarding dramatic experience. A child needs only a little encouragement to add sound to a neon sign, movement to an old oak tree, human characteristics to a pickle or giraffe, and dialogue to the inevitable story which develops. As children develop their characters and stories in improvisation[2] they engage in yet another form of creative dramatics.[3] And under the teacher's able guidance a student's creative experience can extend even further—in first discovering and developing ideas, then creating plays, writing scripts, designing and building the production, and finally performing before an audience. This process entails the use of many forms of drama as a means to create; it also involves exploration of different art mediums in experimenting with ideas leading to the production. All of this activity contributes to *creative playwriting.*

A little girl named Skippy always comes to mind as a choice example of the many possibilities of a simple dramatic experience. One afternoon a group of six- and seven-year-olds were improvising the various movements and attitudes of character animals who live around a pond. As the children first began to

1

imitate and then develop their own interpretations of birds, insects, and four-legged creatures, Skippy crouched down in a corner of the playing space and became very still. Any observer would have thought her shy and not yet confident about what she wanted to be, but when asked who she was, Skippy replied without hesitation that she was "Mrs. Duck." "And doesn't Mrs. Duck feel well today?" her visitor asked. "Oh, yes, I feel fine, thank you," answered Skippy. "But you are so quiet and still, . . ." the visitor began. "Oh, I have to be," said Skippy, "I'm hatching eggs!"

Skippy initiated her own form of dramatic play and with further encouragement could continue in creating her make-believe character. Through improvisations Skippy's character might then contribute to plot development for a story, and then through story dramatization,[4] dialogue and action could evolve. Simultaneous activities in design and crafts might easily be used to work out various aspects of play creation, with these activities later contributing to production of the play. In this way Skippy's simple character idea of Mrs. Duck leads her to a broader experience of creating script, sets, costumes, makeup, and character portrayal for a live theater performance—all steps in completing the process of creative playwriting.

The words "creative" and "playwriting" may seem to have obvious connection, because of a general assumption that all endeavors in playwriting are the product of creative work. However, the term is used here to describe a method of writing which grows out of improvisations, spontaneous response, and exercises designed to first motivate creative thinking. The *experience* of playwriting rather than the end result is the point of emphasis. Creative playwriting then becomes a way of activating the creative process in both children and teens through encouragement and utilization of their inherent inclinations to imagine, to invent, and to pretend as points of departure for more expansive activity. The student's natural abilities enlarge in an atmosphere of freedom, experimentation, and unobtrusive but inspired guidance. Creating an original play can become more than a means of self-expression. It can provide a *creative learning experience* over an extended period of time. Depth and scope of this experience vary with each student and with each age-group from eight through eighteen.

By the time most children are eight, they are amazingly resourceful with original stories and are constantly seeking ways to act them out. This intense interest in self-expression can evolve into prolific activity in the creative arts if the child's energies are so directed. The most natural inclination of childhood is to work under a constant ebb and flow of impromptu inspiration. Channeling this energy into achievement is the purposeful process of creative playwriting. Although children under eight can and do invent stories for play-acting, it is usually the eight- or nine-year-old child who is ready to participate in playwriting exercises. He has mastered the mechanics of handwriting so that he can express his thoughts. He is conscious of characterization, conflict, and plot,[5] although he does not know these terms as they apply to playwriting. Attention span is longer, and there is interest in evaluating and improving ideas. Furthermore, the capacity to work with others is greater than at earlier ages. This is particularly important, since the nature of creative playwriting makes group activity one of its most important features.

It is practicable to design exercises which encourage and direct the creative impulse in children, stimulating each student to release his own ideas and to discover the most effective way of communicating them. His ideas will enlarge in form and content if he freely expresses them in movement, sound, design, writing, art, and acting. He may finally evolve a combination of several art forms which readily transform into a highly imaginative theater experience. It is always the *act* of expression that is most important. Scholarship becomes subordinate to the freeing of personal viewpoint and instinctive response. Handwriting is not requisite for many beginning exercises; the teacher can remember or notate ideas. In some cases a play exists only in the minds of its young creators; they never record it. This free form is natural to young children; however, it provides a specific method of learning for students ten through twelve or in junior high school, especially if the form grows out of a study of structured improvisations characteristic of specific types of comedy. By the time a child is nine or ten he is usually curious to see his words on paper or hear them read aloud. He is beginning to show ability in visualizing the structure of action and dialogue in sections and as a whole. He can sense the necessity for change, for rearrangement, or even elimination of a thought or movement. In this way he becomes aware of dramatic form, and eventually, of style. At this point he is not just a participant in playmaking. He is becoming a playwright.

Teen-agers do not have the same writing problems as younger children. Dramatic form comes easily to them, but they have lost their spontaneous response and their personal viewpoint, because their environment tends to demand the stereotyped reaction. They will generally react in ways that are expected by their peers or express opinions that reinforce their current self-images. Their world abounds with their own generation cults and the fad of the moment. Consequently, any preliminary efforts with the teen-ager aim toward freeing his preconditioned responses. He must learn to seek original or novel approaches to a problem and to place value and confidence in his own ideas and experiences without making competitive comparisons with others. He needs more specialized encouragement than the child, such as specific, positive comments about his personal abilities.

Although problems differ with each age, the basic approach is the same. Students first engage in projects or discussions designed to stimulate original thought and personal reflection. Then the student works through many expressive activities to stretch, reshape, extend, and clarify an idea. He may work in various art mediums—drawing, writing, movement, artcrafts, sound, and improvisations—but the final effort emerges in manuscript form. His ultimate tools of communication will be words. As a young playwright he must make decisions concerning ideas, characters, plot, story, dialogue, motivation, conflict, climax, and resolution. His first realization of this newfound power may come when he manipulates his characters to make the story come out the way he wants it to, regardless of characterization. Proper guidance, however, will prompt him to examine the motivations involved. He can become aware of how words and actions reveal personality, why a person has a conflict within himself and with others, the impact of outside influences upon thought and action, and the consequences involved. He begins to accept reasons for differences of opinion in other people and the wide variety of personality traits in human nature. In addition to this increased knowledge, his achievement comes from learning to organize his thoughts and feelings in a creative media.

Once the play begins to take shape, excitement and purposeful activity gain in momentum. The group visualizes action on stage. All previous creative work becomes useful to theatrical production: costumes, sets, makeup, props, sound, and lights. The play is staged. From the growth of one idea a major project has emerged, and each person has participated in a *total theater experience*. Regardless of its imperfections when finished, the play will be both exciting and satisfying because the best plays from the student's viewpoint are usually the ones he invents himself. He feels both pride and confidence when he views the results of his efforts. Each performer and participant in backstage work relate to the entire production which is their creation.

The freshness and originality of a new play depend upon several factors: the encouragement of each student to believe in himself and in his ideas, the ability to sustain an environment conducive to concentrated work, and the effectiveness of the teacher as a motivating influence. Every student is different. If his environment encourages it, he will learn to think, talk, and write in his own way. Subject, viewpoint, and expression will vary according to age, maturity, experience, interests, capabilities, imagination, and mood. The key to creative work then is in knowing how to motivate a student to conceive, develop, and express his own ideas with freedom, objectivity, and clarity.

One of the most influential factors in creative playwriting is the physical environment surrounding a class. Any attempt to inspire the student's interest and response is difficult if the physical setup is distracting. When possible the work area and its surroundings should sustain a free, relaxed, and happy atmosphere. Motivation of a student's thoughts and senses can begin the minute he enters a room or a work area outdoors. Stimulation comes through what he sees, hears, how he feels, what is said to him, and what attracts his attention. He also brings outside forces into the work area with him: his reactions to a change in the weather, the memory of an unpleasant incident, the carry-over of his greatest interest of the moment, some recent happening, and his physical and emotional state. For this reason a carefully chosen work area can be an asset to the mental, emotional, and psychological preparation of the student. The proper work area is important, but the degree to which environmental factors will affect a student ultimately depends upon the teacher. She can instill within him an attitude and a desire to do creative work which can often overcome environmental handicaps. In many instances she alone can penetrate boredom, disinterest, and unproductivity so that the student will begin to utilize his imagination and energy on a creative level.

The role of the teacher receives full attention in a later section, but it is pertinent to mention here some of the qualities and attitudes the leader of a creative playwriting group should possess. An adult can discipline herself in ways that are needed for her creative output; she can also accept limitations and make them work for instead of against her purpose. But the child or teen does not always possess this maturity and objectivity. He often needs assistance in preparing his mind and spirit for creative thinking. He needs encouragement to release ideas, to take a fresh look at an old one, or to discover new relationships and make new combinations of the ideas he has. He needs guidelines to test his ideas while directing and reshaping them. He needs to learn how to select, combine, and integrate the best of his work. He may also need the final prod to make a conclusive statement by finishing his work and then evaluating it. Each phase is valuable to him as a person actively involved in creativity. The teacher can provide encouragement and guidance so necessary during this time. She leads him to experience the total creative process.

The teacher is a direct and indirect influence upon the student. Astute comment from her can lead to the discovery of intrinsic form and the use of essential dramatic technique. Ideally the teacher should have a background in theater with experience in creative playwriting, but this is not always possible. She should, however, acquaint herself with creative writing experiences, play structures, children and teen-age literature, and the interests of her students. Her personality, knowledge, and training will always affect her students and the development of their ideas. More important, however, the teacher's concept of theater should grow out of a respect for ideas and people. She must believe in the creative potential of every young student. She must respect his world, his abilities, his viewpoint; moreover, she must be deeply interested in his creative efforts. There may be times when the student will need incentive to have a new thought, to take a thought in a different direction, or merely re-focus it for clarity or a different point of view. A friendly exchange of ideas on the subject, evaluations, and encouraging remarks by the teacher or a group of students can frequently rekindle the first inspiration and excite new energy. If the teacher shows genuine interest in the activities of her students outside of class, she often inspires a free exchange of ideas and personal thoughts. The student and teacher will discover other areas of mutual interest and experience, and this insight will be helpful to both.

The relationship of teacher to student should never become so personal that he is dependent upon her and values her approval above the integrity of his own work. To avoid this dependency the teacher must be always cognizant of the differences in each student's methods of work and in his sources of inspiration. She should never make comparisons that provoke unnecessary competition, but she should cultivate individual growth so that each student strives to attain his own maximum potential. A good teacher is a friend, a guide, a catalyst, a participant, and an observer—quick to encourage, flexible in changing her approach or total plans, if necessary, and sensitive in evaluating her students' achievements. She is aware of the tragedy which occurs when rapid, premature judgment stifles creative growth. Self-confidence and initiative spring from the student who receives sincere compliments rather than negative criticism; but the teacher must be selective in both instances. Specific comments made in an optimistic manner without vague generalizations can lead to the kind of rapport between student and teacher which makes possible essential evaluation leading to a critical analysis of ideas.

Creative playwriting requires a discussion leader, not a lecturer, one who motivates rather than directs and one who inspires self-discipline in her students. The teacher must be alert, aware, responsive, patient, and willing to listen without comment. Sometimes she serves only as a sounding board, and nothing more is necessary. She knows when and how to ask or answer questions and is equally aware of the value of silence. Such a person teaches by example and restraint as much as by words and demonstative actions. She knows when to wander from the immediate subject and when to check a rambling, unrelated discussion. Sometimes a student needs to express his thoughts, even though they may not be relevant to the specific problem. Through this brief summary of the qualities and attitudes a teacher of creative playwriting should possess, it seems obvious that the most inspiring teachers are those who regard their work as an exciting adventure and a constant challenge. A successful teacher is always looking for new methods and continues to change her personal approach without fear of trial and error. She functions on a high level of sensitivity, intuition, and insight, for she realizes that creativity cannot be taught. She can only hope to instill the attitude which may foster it.

Creative playwriting is more than a means of writing a play for students to perform on stage. It can become a gateway to imagination, dreams, feelings, and knowledge of oneself. It can also develop the aesthetic sense of each student. His growth begins with a personal involvement with an idea. By working objectively and subjectively, alone and within a group, he develops an original play from idea through performance. This can be a challenge to his mind and energies, for although he may not be consciously aware of his creative powers at work, the student will catch a glimpse of the excitement and satisfaction that comes from inspired work and will be enriched by the experience. As a result creative playwriting can make a student more aware of the worth of his own ideas and how they can be used to bring about a theater experience which is both fresh and original. Then he will have discovered that theater does not begin with a play but with an idea, for this was how he began.

---

1 *Dramatic play* is the spontaneous activity of young children who imagine themselves to be make-believe characters completely unrelated to a story and with no thought of an andience.

2 *Improvisation* refers to extemporaneous drama, where general plans are made in advance, but detailed action and dialogue are left to the players.

3 *Creative dramatics* is a term for all improvised drama created by the players, although idea, character, and plot may be either original or from a story by someone else. For a thorough discussion of the various forms of creative dramatics, see Winifred Ward, *Playmaking with Children* (New York, 1957), 9-10.

4 *Story dramatization* is the spontaneous improvisation of a story that is either original or from a known source.

5 *Plot* is the conscious arrangement, or organization, of the events in a story.

It is very interesting to develop an idea
from merely an object to a full play. And
not *just* a play, but a play you can be
proud of and will not mind working on.

Ann Armstrong

GROWING AN IDEA

An idea for a play may come from anywhere at anytime and without purposeful motivation for creative playwriting. It may grow out of an observation, a memory, an experience, a chance conversation. Discussions of self-portraits, personality characteristics, or a child's individual problems may provide ideas or insights into children's potential playwriting activity. When an idea is expressed, it often reveals characteristics unique to a particular student—how he thinks and responds, his attitudes toward his problems, his background and experience, his secret wishes, his imagination, his intelligence, and his ability to communicate. The teacher must be alert to all the sources of inspiration that influence the dynamics of playwriting.

During a discussion of self-portraits drawn by a class of children, one child's personal problem came into focus. She saw herself as someone who was always getting into trouble. When she tried to do the right thing, her problem seemed to become more complex. She explained that she could not stay out of trouble because she did not use her "thinkers." This remark brought sympathetic comments from other children in the class, and they began to add their own suggestions and experiences, forming the outline of a story. The Thinkers quickly became three in number who possessed distinct personality traits but shared one major responsibility—keeping their master, a little boy, out of trouble. Much to their distress the little boy continually resisted them by refusing to use his Thinkers. This simple plot with its imaginative characters so charmed the children that they began to improvise various scenes between the little character and his Thinkers, and soon afterwards, they wrote *The Troublemaker*. Drawing freely from their own experiences, and adding characters they knew or had created in earlier exercises, the children found it easy to invent woes and defeats for the little Troublemaker. Simultaneous chatter and movement made it apparent that the group needed quiet activity to motivate each individual toward independent thinking about the specifics of his character. Much to the delight of the children they began a new activity. On large sheets of paper with colored chalk they sketched the physical appearance of their character, where he lived, his friends, and what he liked to do most. As details fell into place, the characters came alive. Each child knew his character so well that he was able to think, talk, walk, and act like the personality he had created in his imagination. It was an intensely real experience for the children, and their natural channels of expression led them again into noisy activity. This time ideas were combined, and the group worked together to select the most appealing combinations.

WIND: See that little man there? He's a troublemaker.

SUN: He gets all his friends into trouble; even his girlfriend!

TROUBLEMAKER: Oh, what have I done?

GODDESS OF SPRING: Oh, nothing much. You've just caused the *whole world* to skip two seasons, that's all!

1st THINKER: Promise to use me in the morning?
2nd THINKER: Promise to use me in the afternoon?
3rd THINKER: Promise to use me at night?

TROUBLEMAKER: You see, little flower, I need a friend. If only you and I could be friends . . .

Some of the most imaginative ideas have come from group participation in exercises designed for purposes other than playwriting. On one occasion a plot emerged from pantomines by a class of eight- and nine-year-old children.

The class was asked to observe the movement of an animal and to imitate that movement in pantomime. The results were a complex series of actions, tending to form an entire story. Characteristic movements of each animal were then selected, such as the pecking and drinking motions of birds and the smooth lope of dogs. Simplicity through selection was the point of the exercise, while teaching the children the value of close observation. Sounds were added, stressing basic simple noises made by animals, and characters began to emerge.

An idea was presented in which all the animals were to be placed in a barnyard invaded by wolves. The situation had only one restriction; all sounds had to be animal sounds. The result was a humorous conglomeration of noise that the children loved to make and to hear. The bird sounds were selected for their clarity, and they were used to improvise the same basic situation. During the scene the little boy playing the rooster kept crowing all the time. One of the girls (who later became the bossy chicken, number 5) told him to wait; it wasn't time yet. Then the little boy had the idea of a rooster who crowed at the wrong time and woke everyone up; finally on one day he crowed just in time to warn the others of the wolves' attack. Here was the basic plot for a play.

Continuing improvisations, the children were encouraged to speak, but to keep the animal quality in the words, if they could. Everyone wanted to talk at once; in some cases spontaneous choral statements were made. The class decided they didn't want to be individual birds; they wanted to speak in chorus, directed by a farmer wearing a silk hat. In discussing what the birds would sing about, the group wanted to concentrate on eggs and feathers and began to improvise poems to nursery rhyme rhythms. This was the inception of plot, characters, and dialogue for *Cock-a-doodle-oops!*[1]

Cock-a-doodle-oops! is another example of characters and plot which developed from impromptu situations. First the characters emerged from exercises in pantomime and animal sounds.

Then several pivot characters placed in a single situation—a barnyard—aroused a central conflict through the reactions of the surrounding animals. Development seemed to come more naturally in this instance when ideas converged through improvisations rather than through "talking them out" as in *The Troublemaker.* Both plays grew out of spontaneous expression only because the teachers were alert to the opportune moment when it appeared. Each saw the direction her class was taking and encouraged the children to bring their ideas into focus, so that they became interested in developing them. Plays do not grow out of such spontaneous activity and free expression without the motivating influence of a teacher. Few children recognize the dramatic possibilities of their casual expressions. Even less will take the initiative to work out details. The teacher must see the potential in a passing idea, quickly seize it, and lead the group to explore its possibilities. Although it is a good idea, it may fail to spark the imagination of the children. A play idea must excite the group, or it will fail from lack of interest and enthusiasm.

Occasionally a child will be highly self-motivated; he writes, produces, and directs a company of neighborhood players in a magnificent bit of entertainment. He seems to thrive on his own resourcefulness. His enthusiasm and determination to express every idea on paper drive him to work hard and long until the task is finished. With such intense concentration he will automatically complete a script in one sitting. A student with this ability and initiative should not be discouraged from creating a play by himself. But in a class of students involved in creative playwriting, where group activity is important, the selection of his companions should be a thoughtful one. He requires a group congenial to his energy and stimulating to his intelligence, so that he not only recognizes a challenge but also senses his importance to and acceptance by his peers. If he is ahead of his group in resourcefulness, his inventiveness and contributions may dominate the others to such an extent that they feel it unnecessary to add anything. In such instances it is best for each student to work separately both on the creation and in the development of his idea. After the idea enlarges to its fullest potential, the exposure to each others' creations increases cooperation and diminishes the risk of domination by one person.

In creative playwriting it is not necessary to await chance inspiration. Ideas grow out of exercises planned specifically for this purpose. Exercises for beginners are more successful if designed to stimulate character ideas first. Story will then evolve more naturally and with better structure. Conflict becomes character-motivated, and the student's understanding of this dramatic device is clear. There are many other types of exercises useful to playwriting. Provocative conflict ideas, situation-dialogue, and abstract thinking can lead into specific attempts at story and character creation. These activities are creative exercises in that they inspire original work from the student, but in order to distinguish them from later exercises used to *develop* an idea, it seems appropriate to call them *Ideation Exercises*, their purpose being the production of an idea, or ideas, for a play.

IDEATION EXERCISES

An Ideation Exercise is always activated by a well-chosen stimulus, although the students' response may take the form of writing, discussion, improvisation, or brainstorming. The stimulus should be something that a student relates to—a personality, an experience, a picture, music, an object, a word. The most effective stimuli have been:

> photographs
> paintings
> music
> musical instruments
> sound instruments (pipes, piano strings, wood blocks, "canned" rocks, etc.)
> items for the Sensory Exercise
> exaggeration of a neighborhood personality
> type characters
> a personality trait or weakness
> newspaper articles
> names from the telephone directory
> self-portraits
> familiar characters or stories
> characteristics of animals, vegetables, or objects useful to character creation
> colors
> words
> emotions
> suppositions
> movement studies
> themes
> inanimate object studies
> problem-solving
> a trite subject
> studies in theater

The stimulus should prompt the student to make imaginative use of his experiences, memories, dreams, his powers of observation, association, imagination, and inventiveness. Immediate responses to a stimulus may not be in character or plot ideas. For example, the Sensory Exercise unfolds in this manner: one afternoon a group of children were brought to a table covered with various items to taste, touch, smell, examine, or to listen to. Each child selected the object of his choice and described its qualities in single words or simple sentences. One child selected a bottle of perfume and whispered, "light, airy, and sweet," while another said, "flowery and like purple." A shy little girl turned a saltine cracker over in her hands and noticed that it was "square, pale, speckled with salt and dented." The sound of a plucked piano string impressed its listener as "low, big, strong, and hard." The children voiced spontaneous, original reactions over the touch of velvet and sandpaper, or the taste of lemon, whipped cream, and ice. Each child described his sensory perceptions easily and inventively.

A few minutes later the children translated each description they had written into a physical characteristic or a personality trait. They began to outline a specific character, their imaginations supplying additional details to both physical form and verbal expression. One little boy had selected an earring made of circular seashells, centered with a rhinestone. After looking at the earring for a long time, he described it as "white, hard, curving, cold, shiny, and pointed." Thinking about his words, he created a person who was "clean, strong, swift, mischievous, and had shiny eyes." The character became an elf who wore white because he was clean. Since he was also very strong, he cleared away the fallen branches along the park sidewalks, but his shining eyes were clues to his mischievous qualities, too, so the child wrote about one of his pranks. "One day, a lady was picking flowers in the park; and when she stooped to get a daisy, the little elf slipped up behind her and pinched her!" Once visualized the little elf became alive and full of action. A situation developed, an incident occurred, and the child rapidly produced ideas which could be useful in playwriting. Creativity began and took impetus from the object he selected, but his teacher had first provided an experience in abstract thinking, another way to approach character creation.

The character created does not have to be a person. It might be an animal, an inanimate object, or an abstract shape with human characteristics. For example, the character developed from a bottle of perfume was a perfume king who allowed only sweet smells in his castle. Old Man Dill (shaped like a pickle) was always bumpy and grumpy because of his *sour* attitude. A saltine cracker became a little girl who cried all the time because of the acne on her face. Still another cracker became a character named Crunchy who had pimples and stuttered. In an exercise with teen-agers, characters grew out of a study of colors and took the form of abstract shapes known as Dr. Plasmic Red, Mayor Plumed White, Miss Petty Pink, and Mrs. Powdered Poosh. Regardless of the physical form, the character has a definite personality, and it is with the character's inner spirit that the student identifies. Once on the inside of a personality, the student should continue to explore the character; the more deeply he can understand the inner personality of his creation, the easier it will be for him to understand and utilize motivation as an integral part of playwriting technique.

In order to extend the child's thinking, the teacher might invite him to clap his character's rhythm pattern or express his personality through line, color, shape, and texture in a design or movement exercise.[2] He might discover a relationship to an abstract painting, a musical composition, a poem, or piece of sculpture. On the other hand, this particular child might perceive his character more quickly in terms of movement and sound. He might interpret it in pantomime or dancing. Many media can aid a child in developing his character image, but the choice is usually the one most appropriate or most appealing. The more numerous the creative media a child elects to involve himself in, the more his final concept will reflect depth of emotion and insight.

Whatever the stimulus may be, it should never allow the stereotyped, hackneyed response. Instead, it should serve as a springboard for original work, so the unfamiliar usually becomes the desired prerequisite. For example, the student may rely upon an earlier impression of familiar music or art and be unable to go beyond it. Adult subjects in a painting or a poem will often tempt him to write only what he has seen or heard on the subject if it is beyond his actual experience. Sometimes a painting or poem is so forceful in content or emotion that the student cannot extend his interpretation. If such a stimulus is too strong to allow his imagination free range, the student will again revert to preconceived ideas and even direct copywork.

Sometimes a familiar stimulus can be effective if it is approached from a new perspective. A class may confront a subject with which they are almost too familiar and still derive an original plot outline. This result is particularly evident in working with teen-agers, especially if they see the possibilities in *treatment* of the material. They are intrigued with action, complicated situations, development of unusual problems, and the mental exercise of arriving at a unique solution. A novel approach can make them objective toward a subject, so that they concentrate upon playwriting as a craft and not as a summation

GINGER: Where are they?
HAZEL: Inside with Hecate.
AMY: It's awfully quiet.
WANDA: Are they really as bad as Ginger says?
GINGER: If we can remodel *those* [girls] without the use of magic . . .
WITCHES: Sssssssh! That word!

of knowledge on a topic. On one occasion senior high students gave the usual trite, stock replies when asked their ideas on witches, but after the teacher had called their attention to character witches in literature and various depictions by cartoon artists and television script-writers, the students began to discern a new frame of reference. Original thinking began to operate in the group as each student considered the eccentricities of various kinds of witches and the problems inherent in their craft.

The tremendous enthusiasm of these students for developing their ideas, coupled with the excellent guidance of two teachers——one a young playwright himself——led to the writing and production of a musical comedy. *Bewitched* was called a "magical musical," with book, music, and lyrics by the student performers. The plot deals with a group of witches who try to live normal lives, but their good intentions always fail them. Each witch possesses unique talents which are sources of power when she practices magic, but they also provide her with a vocation in the natural world. After suffering banishment from every historical age, the group arrives in the twentieth century and agrees to relinquish all witchcraft and become normal people. A charm school for young ladies seems to be a method whereby each witch can devote herself to using her natural talents. The first students to enroll in the school are six girls; awkward, ugly, and eccentric. After all else fails, the witches turn in desperation to their special crafts for help. Their tricks become treatments; of course, the results are overwhelmingly successful.

Another approach to playwriting, using the familiar as a stimulus, is to write a spoof on familiar characters and conventional story conception. This is a difficult undertaking but it has tremendous appeal for junior high students. One class wanted to do takeoffs on all the things they were outgrowing, though they did not recognize this as a conscious motivation. They were an exciting group, independent, fun-loving, outspoken, mentally and physically aggressive, and overdramatic. And they wanted to comment on fairy tales, stock characters, scary supernatural animals, melodramatic actors, radio programs, and television commercials. Each student selected characters which appealed most to his imagination, listed supernatural elements in order of their emotional excitement, and discussed the plots and locales which were unusually intriguing. After numerous sessions of brainstorming, improvisations, and both individual and group writing, they completed a thirty-minute play. Total coordination in writing the play made it possible to cast and stage it extemporaneously as the scenes developed through improvisations. Writing and producing *The Purple Tiger Who Liked Pancakes* became an integrated process. The students' approach to the project gave the play its unique structure and delightful characters.

A chorus alternating from narrators and sound-effect artists to village characters and supernatural animals provided an especially original effect. The transition was written into the play itself so that the cast did not leave the stage once the play began. Thus the use of a chorus and its commentary was a natural structure, growing out of the viewpoint of the material and its creators. An experience like this provides the teacher with a unique opportunity to discuss how the concept of an idea can determine the ultimate creative form. This discussion and evaluation can take place at a later date when the class undertakes a critical analysis of the play.

It is important to recognize that the originality of this play did not depend upon the subject but on the viewpoint. Far more important than the stimulus is the *design of the exercise,* for this will affect the subject of the play and often provide a direction for story treatment. For example, in the Sensory Exercise the objects used as stimuli—a bottle of perfume, a saltine cracker, a plucked piano string—could have supplied props for impromptu pantomimes or sources for imaginative interpretations of their owners or of suggested personality-types. Although any of these reactions could have led to a play, a more imaginative, intuitive, fresh approach was desirable. Original thinking took precedence over functional ideas for playmaking. Perception of abstract relationships was the game, but personal viewpoint determined the answers. The design of the exercise determined the power and extent of inspiration and experimentation. The motivating power of the stimulus was not in the objects selected but in the methods of using them. This made the difference in the play which resulted.

If music or sound effects comprise the stimulus, it is wise to remember that tonal qualities and rhythm are so vast in their relation to artistic themes that the mind and imagination will dart in many directions unless focused toward a specific motif. The listener can be free to imagine anything inspired by the music, but specific suggestions sometimes elicit visualization of a character, locale, or event which the music evokes. A rhythm study, for example, might come from a record of drum beats used to suggest character rhythm or movement studies; melody singled out by one instrument could inspire a mood, locale, or story idea; realistic sounds such as a train whistle in the night, sounds of the sea, or carnival noises can stir memories or provoke associations with people, places, and occasions. Usually the music selection itself offers sufficient direction to stimulate imaginative ideas. The teacher should avoid selections already a part of the student's experience, unless a reaction influenced by a previous criticism is desirable and useful to the playwriting exercise.

An abstract painting will stimulate a variety of responses in students, who usually find extraordinary freedom for imagination and interpretation in this medium. Reactions incline to be subjective and impulsive. Paintings by Paul Klee and Jean Miro have proved to be exciting to all ages. As one little girl put it, ''You can see anything you want to.'' This nine-year-old was particularly elated over Paul Klee's Oriental Sweet. The design of this exercise was as follows: after a class discussion on the words *simple* and *complicated* as related to line, shape, color, ryhthm, movement, and texture, each child classified prints in these terms from his own point of view. The teacher then encouraged a verbal description of what the student saw in his picture. To this little girl Paul Klee's painting suggested sky people. She told how the people had become bored with blue and white clouds day after day, how they wanted a ''happy'' sky, and how they painted the sky to look like a patchwork quilt— suggested, she thought, by the painting itself. One problem arose, however, when the sky people failed to anticipate what the reaction on earth would be to their happy sky. As the play developed, each child rambled on and on in dialogue so that the script became very talky. Nevertheless, colorful characters and highly imaginative language contributed to a twenty-five minute production of *The Patchwork Sky*. Using the painting by Klee as an inspiration for set and costume designs, the children also incorporated their earlier ideas from the ''simple and complicated discussion'' by consciously using texture, line, shape, and color in a more effective way.

When another class received instructions to select a print and to write a poem, song, story, scene, or character sketch from the ideas and emotions inspired by the picture, a fourteen-year-old girl selected another Klee painting, Woman in Native Costume, as a basis for a poem:

He walks the dark, dark streets at night
Filling all the children with fright.
He's made of iron and shining steel
And walks with a little kind of squeal.
All parents bring their children in,
But really he is only a friend.
He decided he would paint his steel
And oil his hinges and stop the squeal.
He painted his face so ghastly pale
That now the children they all wail.
He's a guy so very sad
For people think he's oh so bad.
No one has really tried to meet him;
They don't know the joy he might bring them.
It only proves what they say in books
That on first sight you are judged by looks,
So keep yourself neat and clean wherever you go
And don't be like poor old armor-clad Joe.[3]

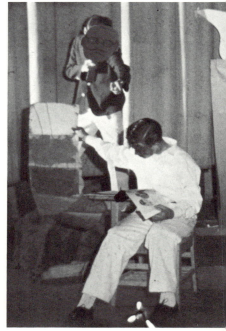

After each student responded individually the class selected ideas which seemed to have the most dramatic interest. Note the lack of emphasis upon the quality of writing produced; attention focused on the most appealing idea. Selecting this poem, the class divided into groups which discussed the poem, using it as a springboard for several story ideas.

Numerous group sessions of sharing ideas and directing the dramatic conflict resulted in a final version which features a tin man who is an outcast from society because he is painted chartreuse. The play begins with his entrance into a town of pure colors and his subsequent discovery that the citizens have never seen a mixed color before; hence he frightens them. They fear his possibly harming their children or spreading strange and dangerous ideas. They forbid their youngsters to play with him and shut their doors in his face. The children, upset by this restriction, go on strike, picketing the town with signs, and reprimanding their parents for their intolerance. Townsfolk include Miss Petty Pink, the town gossip; Mrs. Powered Poosh, the "aristocrat" who allows no one to forget her eminent social position; Mayor Plumed White, who is running for re-election on his (plumed-white) pure record; Dr. Plasmic Red, who goes "bloop-bloop-bloop" in time with the heartbeats of his patients as he makes his rounds giving physical checkups to the children; Whisper Blue, a shy child; Pixie Purple, a bright and mischievous

Original characters in *The Tin Man and the Painted Town* (photos left to right): ATOMIC GREEN, the TIN MAN, the PAINTER, BRUSHES the DOG, MR. FIZZLE, BOY in study hall, DR. PLASMIC RED, MRS. POW-DERED POOSH, MISS PETTY PINK, and MAYOR PLUMED WHITE.

imp; and Atomic Green, the neighborhood bully. Although costumed and made up to represent fanciful people, the characters confront authentic problems such as teen-age curiosity, parental authority, individual rebellion, prejudice, hypocrisy, and the desire to be different. The group may not have been aware of the total impact of these implications, but *The Tin Man and the Painted Town* is an excellent example of the vigor and insight of youthful ideas. Creative playwriting amazingly reveals the questions and attitudes young people wish to express; it offers them a constructive way to articulate their thoughts and conflicts.

Ideas for playwriting, the product of individual minds working alone or in group creative thinking sessions, often come from what *appears* to be spontaneous inspiration, but there is usually some preparation or prior motivation which stimulates and prepares for creativity. Offering a class a single stimulus or a multiplicity of stimuli is only the beginning. There must be some selectivity and direction in the motivation, and this comes through the design of the exercise. Even then, response from one class does not guarantee success with another group. Sometimes it is necessary to try several different types of stimuli before an idea with dramatic potential will crystallize. At other times the same stimuli proves effective if the design of the exercise specifically accommodates the needs and personalities in the class. Observing the personality of each class can provide clues to the most successful stimulus, but response also varies at different age levels.

MOTIVATION BY AGE-GROUPS

A young playwright's age usually determines the general subject matter of a play as well as the type of characters he will create. Eight- and nine-year-old children habitually create talking animals, fairytale characters, make-believe people they have heard about, magical adventurers, and children their own age in a fantasy environment. Fantasy, which is almost synonymous with childhood, satisfies several important needs of children: the need for escape when normal environment imposes strain; the need for experience unrestricted by real-life controls, making it possible to solve problems by testing action which neither causes harm nor solicits punishment normally accompanying such action; the need for wish-fulfillment through expression of those impulses usually inhibited in real life; and the need for vicarious satisfactions when real ones are lacking.[4]

Creative playwriting and playacting have served all of these purposes for most children. For example, the child who felt that

Captain Underwear and his Pirates sight their good luck charm in *Polwackit, the Magic Cat* written by 8- and 9-year-olds.

she shared the dilemmas of *The Troublemaker* seemed to identify with her problem as it was solved in the play. She was overjoyed each time the character in the play began to use his Thinkers. Her parents later confirmed the fact that the experience had helped their child face her own problem and try to solve it.

Exercises built upon spontaneous activity more adequately suit the eight- and nine-year-old child, for these children have vivid responses, but they do not always like to work out details unless curiosity and genuine involvement are part of their working scheme. Their best work usually comes from improvisations followed by discussions. Similar exercises are also successful with ages ten through twelve, and there is a greater capacity for concentrated effort in these older children than in the younger group. Children ten, eleven, and twelve are more interested in detail, complexity of plot, and realistic people in a fantasy situation, or conversely, in make-believe characters with realistic problems, for they are becoming more interested in life about them. They enjoy biographies, adventure stories, mysteries, slapstick comedy, domestic humor, and stories of war, science, and space fiction. Expansion of the child's interests, experiences, and capabilities occurs naturally as a corollary to growth. And a child's abilities in playwriting reflect his personal growth. Plays by older children will have more variety in subject matter, greater depth of character, a more inventive plot, character-motivated dialogue, more meticulous use of writing techniques, and explicit descriptions of action, sets, and props. Older children will also be more interested in writing dialogue, consequently, the script will be longer.

MOCKINGBIRD: Numbskull! After all the trouble I go through to write this speech for you, you ask questions! Now repeat, I the Bear . . .

BEAR: I da Bear . . .

MOCKINGBIRD: Go on.

BEAR: I da Bear . . . but my name ain't Ida!

MOCKINGBIRD: What this modest, fearless, honest, intelligent, leader-type soul wishes to say is that he challenges the unworthy Lion to an election for King of the Forest.

JUDGE OWL: As Supreme Court Judge, I'll preside. I suggest you have a series of contests after which everyone may vote.

CYNTHIA MONKEY: The Bear was going to bash me in but the Lion stopped him.

MRS. RABBIT: He told the Bear to leave her alone or he'd have bear meat for supper!

UNCLE MONK: I say give the crown to the Lion. Who says he can't rule the forest?

An excellent example of an original script by ten- through twelve-year-olds is *Don't Cross That Lion*, which centers around the election in the animal kingdom of a new King-of-the-forest. The antagonist is the Mockingbird, who is hungry for power and recognition. Discovering a perfect dupe in the lazy and stupid Bear, he persuades him to challenge the Lion to a contest. He then proceeds to convince the Bear that he would make a better king than the Lion, and to cleverly entice him with all the rewards accompanying the title of King. It is obvious that the Bear is a pawn incapable of making any decisions, and that the Mockingbird would be the actual ruler. This depth of motivation in each character plus the complication of plot give evidence that these children delve deeper into their material than do the younger groups. Although fantasy characters implement the plot, the play is more than an ingenious story about animals. It is a commentary on human affairs, attitudes, and actions as seen through the eyes of children. Written during a national election year, which may account for the development of serious interests in an election contest, the play reveals the student's awareness of politics on the national and local levels.

MRS. ABBOT: It's all decided then. To put a stop to this marathon poetry recitation, we're going to have a contest.

There is greater distinction between individual students on the junior high school level than in any other age-group. To assure more successful attempts at creative playwriting, it often becomes necessary to subdivide a class of junior students according to physical size and general maturity. Failure to adjust the class in this manner often causes strained relations between students who are younger and need more individual attention and those who are older or more aggressive and feel no challenge in working with a younger person. In most instances, the best stimuli for junior students are those which motivate a broad, humorous expression of theater. These students tend to write comedies, fantasies, melodramas, and even light satire. The plot usually projects a romantic interest among some of the characters, but the emotions expressed are straight forward, and scenes are generally short. *Zanadon't You Dare* is one of the few plays by junior high students based entirely upon a romantic story. In this play romantic attachments are numerous, for the conflict derives from the "romantic" lead, a young boy in an ancient village who can only speak in poetic phrases when in the presence of girls. Naturally such an unusual circumstance has innumerable repercussions, two of which are the constant swoons of the girls who chase the poor boy, and the competition in poetry writing he unknowingly agitates among the other boys. Few plays have given junior high students a greater opportunity to create out of their own aspirations and curiosities than did this one. There was little difficulty in developing it into a full three-act play.

ARIANNE: Oh, Peter, please recite some poetry for us.
ANGELICA: He couldn't recite poetry if he had it written
    down in front of him.
PETER: (*Taking the borrowed poem from his pocket*)
    ''Come live with me and be my love
     And we will all the pleasures prove
     That valleys, groves, hills and fields,
     Woods or steepy mountain yields.''
    (*Angelica swoons*)
    That will do, ladies. Thank you very much.

Senior high school students write about their own world and problems in a constantly increasing range of interests and knowledge. Representative plays include those about a fake seance, a teen-ager's search for trust and acceptance in a correction home, a trip to Mexico taken by a group of students from a finishing school, young college students with bitter backgrounds of broken homes and personal tragedies, and the struggle between a small town and the federal government over building a freeway which would destroy historical buildings and monuments in the town square. One group of students wrote a musical comedy using an imaginary situation to provide material for both farce and satire on current fads and attitudes. The play, aptly titled *When Gabriel Blows His Horn*, is the story of young Gabe who must learn how to play his trumpet before he can blow it; he then plays it too soon. Scrambling to catch all the notes before they fall to earth, he loses notes "A" and "E". Subsequently *Agnes* and *Ethel* appear in heaven and literally turn the clouds inside out in attempting to redesign the gowns of the heavenly hosts. Writing a musical comedy is demanding and requires such specific techniques and talents that it should develop only as a natural evolvement from the work of students

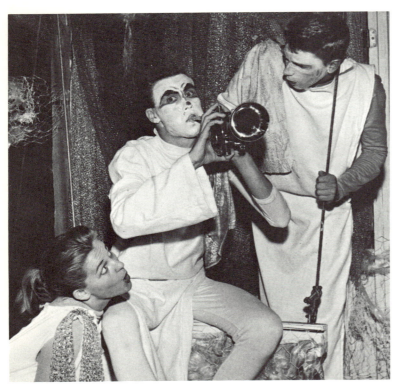

WHERE OH WHERE ARE THE
A AND THE *E*?
(original song)

Oh, gee, oh, gee, where're the A and the E?

We've got the B C D and the F and the G

But where, oh, where are the A and the E?

A? E? A? E?

B-C-D-F-G

B-C-D-F-G

Oh, my, oh, me, where're the A and the E?

They're lost on earth and it's too far to see.

Oh, where, oh, where are the A and the E?

A? E? A? E?

We've caught all the notes in eternity

But we can't find the two beneath the galaxy.

It's a fact but it sounds like a fantasy

That we can't find the A and we can't find the E.

Where, oh, where are the A and the E?

FLOWER SELLER: Fiddlesticks! You make friends easily enough. You talked to me, a perfect stranger. You can't go on living in your dream world.

SECRETARY: Dream world? Yes, I guess I have always dreamed. First it was Eddie Fisher . . . then the captain of the high school football team . . . and now it's Mr. Johnson my boss. All of them impossible.

FLOWER SELLER: Dreaming itself isn't so bad . . . a little of it's necessary. But you're old enough that your dreams ought to be ones you can take and use . . . practical dreams.

in a class. Even then, it should not represent their first attempt at playwriting unless the class is an unusually talented one. Students should write about those things they have experienced or know something about. Only disaster results if they are inadequate in approaching their subject—a fact often difficult for them to understand. When a senior high class began to investigate the word "love," they discovered that there were many definitions, shades of meaning, and implications. They realized that the subject had to be narrowed to a specific viewpoint, one they were capable of writing about, so they wrote short vignettes of love's growth and change from childhood to old age. *Lufu: Definition Please* is an unusually interesting production, clearly revealing the students' sensitivity and insight into meanings and feelings of love as they change with each age. The most believable scenes are those written about people their age or younger, yet their viewpoints and expressions are recognizable and meaningful within each age-group.

One of the major differences between junior and senior high school playwrights lies in their approach to the material. Interestingly, it is easier for the junior high student to avoid conventional story ideas and writing structure. Perhaps it is because he is yet unfamiliar with a great variety of plays in English literature; and as a rule, has had no wide experience in school productions. He is daring and experimental with material if so encouraged. He is curious, quick, and willing to try almost anything, because in most cases he has not acquired a set standard which might inhibit his writing form. If a junior and a senior student confront similar real-life situations common to their experiences, two patterns of work emerge. The junior student will not stress character motivation as much as the older student, but he will arrive at a complicated, fast-moving plot. Dialogue will be quick and simple; action, abundant; and the probable result, a light comedy or fantasy. The senior student will inquire into motivation, consider character reactions and consequences, and tend to present a strong, moral viewpoint or a provocative idea. Whether or not the play develops into a comedy or a serious drama—and it is usually dependent upon the personalities of both class and teacher—the dramatic work will project well-rounded characterizations and clear motivations. Naturally, there are exceptions, and a general trend never indicates an inevitable pattern of development. But distinct characteristics which differentiate the two groups can provide guidelines for those working with either of them.

Almost all stimuli discussed thus far are adaptable to every age-group, but the design of an exercise will vary according to the age and personalities in the class. Teen-agers, particularly, should learn to recognize their trite subjects, borrowed ideas, or obvious copywork, because these devices are effective only if they are a part of the student's *conscious* writing technique. They then become an integral part of the playwriting exercise.

STUDIES IN THEATER

A study in theater offers extraordinary motivation for creative playwriting, especially when the study concentrates on a style representative of a specific period in theater history. A continuous, progressive study of the development of drama and art gives the individual, as well as the class, greater knowledge and increased sensitivity to other people, countries, and cultures. Through this approach, creative playwriting becomes an extensive and intensive learning experience for the student. An original play can assimilate details learned about a particular period; the production will then reflect the style and content of classic drama.

An Egyptian Romance written as a
pantomime with narration by
8- and 9-year-olds.

In a format of study which emphasizes styles of theater and art, Primitive and Egyptian periods can provide material for one year's concentration followed by a full year each for Greek, Roman, Medieval, Elizabethan, and other succeeding periods selected according to the age and the interests of the class. The child's understanding comes from a personal involvement with concepts of the period, concepts that have formulated a spirit and style, making it distinguishable from other periods because of its unique characteristics.

Communication with children does not begin with the historical approach to theater but with a basic vocabulary of expression—common to all art expression—consisting of space, movement, line, shape, texture, color, light, sound, and rhythm. Each expression can make a significant statement about any period of history, a statement also reflected in art forms representative of the period. The style resulting from any combination of expressions can then consciously direct the student's creation in art, writing, design, acting, movement, light, or sound. Through the personal involvement that such activity generates in a child, he encounters a series of mental, emotional, and physical patterns which formulate his perception of the spirit and style of a period. From an intensive focus on all aspects of a period, the student derives his personal viewpoint and interpretation of a style of drama. The teacher's task is to design exercises which provide this experience.

Possibly the first activity in the study of the Greek period is to discover the Greek concept and use of space by leading the student through a similar experience. As a beginning exercise the child attempts to become as big as he can, then shrink in size, to extend and then contract, to be strong and then weak, to be loud then soft, to move quickly, to move slowly. Working in contrasts, the student becomes aware of degrees of intensity. He is then ready to explore space in its levels and planes, and to move freely in a variety of rhythms and directions. He encounters the idea of cutting space with movement and penetrating silence with sound.[5] He begins to make comparisons between space as a tool for the actor's body, silence as a tool for the actor's voice, and a blank sheet of paper as the tool for the artist's pen or brush. Sound, movement, and design then integrate into one expression. Once the student comprehends the relationship of these three expressions, he can coordinate action with dialogue (movement with sound) in a manner reflecting the style of Greek drama. First, the student begins to work for size, extension, and continuity, words whose meaning he became aware of during preliminary exercises. He learns to project his voice with maximum volume, energy, and emotional discipline; at the same time his gestures are large, but controlled and graceful in extended movement. A way of accomplishing this result is by asking the child to pretend he is in a football stadium, standing in the center of the field. He is to speak and move so that everyone in the stands can see and hear him. This not only motivates correct action, but it leads to better understanding of the reason for the Greek actor's style of performance in the amphitheater.

Another provocative and effective exercise involves suggesting to the class emotional words to inspire movement, sound,

Camea, a Greek tragedy written by
10- through 12-year-olds.

33

The Greek chorus in *Persephone* (top),
Camea (left), and *Hilorsity* (right),
original plays by 10- through
12-year-olds.

design in color, and finally some form of writing. Love, hate, fear, joy, and grief are emotions which are strong motivating forces in Greek drama. The teacher might ask a child to describe his feelings when his best friend moves away, when he is lonely, or when someone close to him dies. Answers often contain words such as *unhappy, sad, full, tight, hurt*. Another approach requires the student to draw how he feels, demonstrate his emotions in movement, or clap the rhythm of his feelings. Thus, definitions and shades of meaning receive clarification when each child shares his own responses and attitudes with others, and the class begins to understand the diversity possible in emotional expression. Indirectly, all of these exercises prepare the child for later efforts at playwriting, but the teacher should avoid reference to creation of a play at this time. Finally, in order to apply this new understanding to actual performance of Greek drama, the child should again visualize a football stadium as he attempts to enlarge an expression of emotion, sustain it, and work toward progression in both insight and expression. This is one way the child can become familiar with motivation as a technique and conscious of its purpose in character portrayal.

A child should learn to experiment with sound as expressed in volume, level or pitch, rhythm, line, and texture or timbre. He can then apply his knowledge to choral speech, monologues, and various mechanical and vocal sound effects; such application will suggest numerous activities such as dramatizing prose, poetry, factual information from newspapers, catalogs, or advertising sheets. Even for older children nursery rhymes have appeal as a "sound" project. Each project clarifies ideas and leads the student to another experiment, while at the same time broadening the initial experience with sound. Eventual application of knowledge gained from various sound exercises manifests itself in the speaking chorus in Greek drama.

Each exercise motivates the child to explore and experiment with freedom of ideas and expression. Design and content of an exercise will determine the general direction followed in such experimentation. However, the ideal creative experience is a cumulative one. For example, a specific study of the masks of the gods in Greek drama will easily inspire mask-making with papier-mache. Ideas for making the masks may come from a character created by the child in another exercise. Conversely, exposure to pictures of authentic Greek masks can influence the style of expression in character interpretation. The exercise is never an end in itself; it reflects previous activities, and it anticipates the ultimate goal, the writing and staging of a play. In this instance mask-making is both an exercise in expression and a preliminary step toward actual play production. The students are aware that the chorus will wear the masks in performance;

they therefore emphasize utility as well as creativity. As a result, the chorus should be able to wear the masks with ease and to use them in movement, both in speaking individually or in unison. Additional exercises can provide insight into architecture and theater design, music and dance, clothes and accessories leading to makeup and costumes, and dialogue and play structure of Greek drama. Interaction between one art form and another leads to gradual integration of ideas and expressions. These usually become the creative force for origination and development of characters and story into a play for performance. A few classes, however, may prefer to adapt a story or myth. This was the choice of a class of eight- and nine-year-olds who adapted the myth "Orpheus and Eurydice" into a play. Many class sessions preceded selection of this myth as a subject for playwriting exercises, since the teacher wanted to eliminate any preconceived notions about the story. She also wanted to introduce the class to central ideas and temperament of the period and of the myth so that they would have a fresh response to the story and a more personal approach to classic drama. *The Tragedy of Orpheus and Eurydice* became the students' own interpretation and expression of Greek drama. It is never apparent to the teacher at the beginning whether an original play will emerge or whether the final result will be an adaptation of a myth or even a Greek play such as *Prometheus Bound*. She is certain, however, that the play will represent the period under study, and consequently no exercise on style or content of Greek drama will be without value.

There are several reasons why concentration upon the Greek period is appropriate and valuable to children of this age, especially if it has been preceded by the study of Primitive and Egyptian periods. This is a period which reflects strength, dignity, intelligence, grace, and beauty. The drama of its people portrays the tumultuous interaction motivated by love, hate, joy, pride, revenge, and grief. Students learn to understand the drama of this period through vicarious exposure to the forces of its culture as reflected in Greek life and art. Awareness must be more than superficial in the general areas of geography, climate, religion, government, social structure and customs, motivations, dreams, and goals of a people. Even more important than this awareness and knowledge, when the studies and exercises result in actual performance of a play, is the student's ability to assume the Greek attitude and pattern of thinking. He must understand and identify with Greek characteristics. Then, imaginatively, he can project himself into the environment and events of ancient Greece. That world becomes his; he relates and communicates from a new vantage point.

There is a valid reason for encouraging a period of saturation in the framework of time, lives, and attitudes, as well as in the art forms. Intuitive thinking proceeds from broad knowledge of a subject; increased awareness of general patterns then heightens sensitivity to basic structure. Constant saturation creates a rhythm, a mood, an emotional climate that the child senses and can eventually reproduce. Elusive as this process is, it supplies a gestation period for all the child's future ideas concerning actual playwriting. As the child responds to this period of saturation, he develops a mental, emotional, and physical relationship with the period and culture he is studying. The vocabulary of expression now becomes the means by which *he* articulates it. But a new kind of discipline in expression emerges; at least it is new to the child. From roots in the Greek period a recognizable style now emanates into the child's work. At this point he should be thoroughly familiar with the Greek viewpoint through participation in creative exercises; either Greek art forms have supplied a motivating stimulus or concepts of the Greek way have inspired expression in various art forms. Now the student begins to assimilate his experience; he makes it work for him in creating his own expression which, because of the nature of the exercises, results in some form of drama. Children are capable of writing, designing, and producing plays in a specific period of theater and in a style which combines contemporary and traditional techniques of classic drama. They learn to use ''what they know'' as a point of departure. At the end of a year's study of the Greek period, it is possible to see significant growth in the student's ability to project and to control his voice and body, to compel attention, to unify thought and emotion in progression toward a climax, and to communicate clearly and effectively to a large group of people. There may be intensified interest in various aspects of the period—literature, art, architecture, music, sculpture, and drama—but this is secondary to the student's heightening personal interests and insights. Nine- and ten-year-old students seem to possess an emotional and intellectual affinity for the Greek style and spirit. The extent to which this accelerates the child's ability to relate to the period is unknown. That some children do achieve a remarkable identification with and assimilation of Greek principles is clearly evident, as the following examples demonstrate.

Bill was a third-year student in the theater study program and had studied the Primitive, Egyptian, and Greek periods of art and drama. He was cast in a contemporary adult drama to be produced professionally. During a rehearsal one afternoon, the director could not make Bill understand that he was to increase the volume of his speech, at the same time retaining the emotional tension of the scene. Finally, the director turned to one of Bill's teachers, asking that she try to help the boy understand what was demanded of him dramatically. After a brief whisper from the teacher, Bill not only projected but managed as well to intensify his emotional interpretation. Later the director asked the teacher what she had told Bill to prompt his abrupt technique change. The teacher replied casually, "Oh, I just said 'Think Greek, Bill. Think Greek'."

Another example of the extensive understanding of the Greek period attained by numerous students is the experience of Martha Ann, a nine-year-old who had studied Greek theater for a year. During the summer she attended an outdoor performance of the Biblical drama, *The Book of Job*, staged in a style reflective of ancient Greek theater. After the performance Martha Ann went backstage to talk with the actor who portrayed Job. Slightly baffled by the youngster's question as to why the Biblical drama had been staged in the Greek manner, the actor asked Martha Ann to explain her question. She began to expound on the style of the production and performance and its relationship to Greek theater as she knew it. The actor was impressed by the authenticity of the child's viewpoint and her comparison of the production to Greek drama.

The study of Roman drama proves equally exciting and challenging to children ten through twelve. As does Greek drama, it includes both comedy and tragedy, but the comic element is more appealing and has more to offer this age-group. A review of the eleven-year-old's character traits quickly reveals those qualities which might prompt a spontaneous interest in comedy. Subsequent comparison of these same qualities to the general characteristics of Roman comedy suggests reasons for the heightened appeal such drama has at this period in a child's development.

The eleven-year-old is remarkably different from the ten-year-old, for this is the beginning of adolescence. The once complaisant ten now begins to show signs of self-assertion. He is curious and likes to explore; he is talkative and likes to argue, but it is impossible to argue with him. He is restless and eager to be on the move, to see things, and have new experiences. He does not like to be by himself. He is inquisitive about adults and has all sorts of schemes for exploring interpersonal relationships with his parents and peers. He often mimics them. He is subject to contrasting outbreaks of laughter, anger, yelling, quietness, and his moods change with the hour of the day. He is sensitive, proud, selfish, competitive, and often uncooperative. Yet he can be the opposite among grownups away from his family. The eleven-year-old is a free-wheeler in conversation, politely factual, detailed, earnest, sincere, and friendly. But he cannot stay still for long. He moves about, he twists, and squirms. He likes to exaggerate and dramatize expressions. He is a good punner and enjoys corny jokes and limericks. Slapstick humor has great appeal for him, especially when things are so impossible as to be ridiculous. He can easily make quips about serious things and is quick to catch the point. His expressions can change quickly from uproarious laughter to a deadpan look. He has a growing interest in people and can always give an endless recital of entire plot and action when a story or experience is involved.[6]

Compare this description of some of the more prominent eleven-year-old character traits with the account of an early Roman comedy by Plautus.

> He made the action more lively and boisterous. He introduced roguery and imposture, beatings, scolding matches, gross depictions of eating, drinking, and lovemaking. Through these physical incidents and through verbal means he created a rollicking and obvious humor. Disputations, loud retorts, puns, and coarse jests were his frequent devices to provoke laughter. All in all, it was a comedy of simple robust wit and constant movement, one perfectly adapted to the average Roman audience.[7]

With the exception of a few ideas, the above description of a Roman comedy could easily be a general formula of physical and verbal expression designed to provide outlets for the eleven-year-old's needs. Many of the emotions, attitudes, and physical attributes associated with this age level are almost identical to traits of stock characters in early Roman comedy. Slapstick and farce have always had great appeal for children, because they enjoy the energetic and offensive dynamics of these dramatic forms. In broad comedy, the child is free to participate in aggressiveness, because in the context of this particular dramatic medium his attitude is both understandable and desirable. Even encouragement is in order if accompanied by purposeful motivation. The child learns to achieve his desired effect—to be funny and thereby get attention—through intelligent selection of material, technique (timing and expression), and the discipline of performance. At the same time he understands *how* he is achieving the humorous effect.

This is a wonderful time for a child to take a good look at himself through the eyes of others. His audience—any audience—becomes a mirror by which he gauges what is successful and what is a flop. He is his own tool of expression; there may be props and all sorts of costumes or set gimmicks to help him, but it is in relation to him that the audience sees the humor of each trick. Through this study in comedy a child can learn to

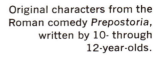

Original characters from the Roman comedy *Prepostoria*, written by 10- through 12-year-olds.

accept, even exaggerate and make fun of his own flaws and mistakes. He makes use of an extra large nose or a severe contrast in height. Roman comedy draws out of the child that unique quality that is his alone and makes him glad he has it. More than any other period studied in theater, this period allows the distinct personality of each child to emerge, stimulating a merry outlook on people and on life. For the most part, Roman comedy provides a means of introducing children to stock characters, broad and exaggerated movement, timing, inventive business, commentary, and direct communication. Discovery of what makes a line, movement, sound, or gesture funny fascinates children. And seeing how this relates to their own world of jokes, puns, tricks, and humorous writings promotes a more objective attitude toward movies, television, stage plays, comedians, comic strips, and humor in general.

Since Roman comedy is a distinctly visual performance, relying heavily upon audience response and the actor's intuitive timing and interpretation, a script is never an adequate record; yet many plays have come out of the study of this period. One of the funniest Roman comedies created by a class was never recorded. *The Curious Komedi* grew out of many improvisations evolving from the story idea in ''The Stone in the Road.'' The students created various characters and situations to present contrasting attitudes and actions toward the indescribable object in the middle of the road. Any attempt to describe the intangible qualities of the performance is completely futile. It was a rare demonstration of complete self-awareness being used as a tool for comedy.

The most popular script used for adaptation is the authentic Roman comedy, *Pot of Gold*, by Plautus.

It contains all the characteristics of his farce-comedy: (1) a rapidly developed situation with an even more rapid *denouement* by a faithful and clever slave, Strobilus; (2) type characters, like the old female servant, Staphyla, and the wealthy middle-aged bachelor, Megadorus; (3) humor of physical action, such as the beatings of Staphyla and Congrio by Euclio; (4) broad wit from the talk of servants—Anthrax, Congrio, and Strobilus, all of whom play on words and utter with surprising ease the most apt, though occasionally suggestive, comparisons; (5) colorful passages of satire on contemporary living, similar to Megadorus' long speech on spendthrift wives and modern luxury.[8]

The prologue by the Household God which relates the circumstances leading up to the play; the plot intrigue; the physical comedy techniques such as chases, tricks, masquerades, pratfalls, and verbal wit employing the artificial and crude contrivances that characterize Roman comedy—all of this seems to be quite compelling to the interests and energy of eleven-year-olds. It becomes even more meaningful if the student has a background in Greek drama. The fact that Roman comedy allows comment on present-day society can be a great inducement for young playwrights to include current expressions, fads, local jokes, inventive poetic passages, and detailed business which could go on and on unless carefully selected and edited. Because the complete script of *Pot of Gold* is lengthy and too adult for children, the class used only the general story line with its basic characters as material for improvisations, and from this exercise *Where is My Gold?* emerged.

Creative exercises in art, sound, writing, and movement; improvisations for pantomime, stage business, and dialogue; and an introduction to basic elements and techniques of physical and verbal comic situations give the student a thorough saturation in this period of classic theater. The original play, or the resulting adaptation, will reflect an imaginative interpretation of the spirit and style of Roman comedy.

During all of these exercises in a theater study, each student is acquiring a special discipline in thought and action. For the child the essential difference between each period lies in the practice of this discipline. And, when analyzed in terms of the vocabulary of expression, this discipline supports a specific style, an attitude of being, and a method of expression. Once it is experienced the child will recognize it in total, or in part,

Cathleen Ni Houlihan, an Irish folk drama by W. B. Yeats.

Pierre Patelin, a medieval farce, anonymous play of the 15th Century.

The Magical World of Mime created by the players.

wherever it appears. He will notice relationships and similarities between periods, artists, ideas, and expressions. Some children are amazed to discover kinship to a period or an artist because of a parallel between their own ideas and those expressed in the general tenor of the period or in the specific artist's work. An individual artist's personal viewpoint or style of expression may seem similar to those of the children, thereby increasing the awareness of kinship. Depth of perception in regard to any style will automatically expand a student's awareness. His eye sharpens to distinctive style in art, business, fashion, advertisement, entertainment, individual dialogue, and human personalities. At times this new vision cultivates in the child an entirely different perspective toward life and art.

Op art inspires a production of *The Italian Straw Hat*
by Eugene Labiche and Marc-Michel.

Much Ado About Nothing
by William Shakespeare.

This brief description of methods used in studying the Greek and Roman periods of theater is equally applicable to the Primitive, Egyptian, Medieval, and Elizabethan periods as well as to contemporary styles of theater. As students advance from early historical periods to more formalized drama, their performance scripts will be scenes or complete plays by noted playwrights of the period. There is little difference in the approach to teaching different styles of theater, though specific areas of emphasis do vary. For example, understanding and speaking the language become points of more detailed emphasis in the study of plays by Shakespeare or anonymous writers from the Medieval period. As students advance through the periods they are also growing older; methods of work differ with each age in relation to the period under study and according to the personalities of individual classes. Progressively, the approach to each theater study becomes more specialized.

1 Synopsis of report on creative playwriting by Sally Netzel in the graduate school teaching program of Teen-Children's Theater, Dallas Theater Center, 1964.
2 A more complete discussion of creative exercises designed around this basic vocabulary of expression is found in Jearnine Wagner and Kitty Baker, *A Place for Ideas: Our Theater* (San Antonio, 1965).
3 Poem by Kay Dennard, student in Teen-Theater at the Baylor Theater, 1956.
4 Eleanor E. Maccoby, "Why Do Children Watch Television?" *Public Opinion Quarterly*, XVIII (1954), 239f.
5 This concept of space and the artist's relationship to it is more completely discussed in Wagner, Baker, *A Place for Ideas: Our Theater*, 37.
6 Arnold Gesell, Frances L. Ilg, and Louise Bates, *Youth: The Years from Ten to Sixteen* (New York, 1956), 66-71, 87, 336, 440.
7 William Smith Clark, *Chief Patterns of World Drama* (Cambridge, 1946), 135.
8 *Ibid.* 135-136.

Writing has always interested me, but in working on
our play it was the first time I had collaborated
with anyone, much less a whole class. This was very
stimulating because when writing I tend to prefer
my own ideas and in this case mine were mixed in with
many, many others in order to select a plot and fill
it with characters and dialogue.

Tanda Lu Dykes

PLANNING THE CLASS

Only the teacher can decide how much preparation she needs before designing exercises for creative playwriting or for studies in theater. She must first know and understand her material. Preparation should instill confidence in her approach and in her method of presentation so that she feels competent to handle class response and discussion. Because it is impossible to know the mental attitude of the student before he arrives for class or to predict the responses he will make to an exercise, the teacher who thinks through each stage of her plans in advance is better equipped for a session in motivating students to produce creative work. The problem is seldom one of knowing too much about a subject, but of taking a flexible attitude toward the material. Although she may have immediately available an enormous fund of information and plans, she should always be ready to take directives from creative sparks that appear when ideas are in action.

It is not only advantageous but almost always necessary to place students in a class where all members have similar backgrounds in creative playwriting. Still, a teacher might ask herself certain relevant questions in preparation for the class. How many students have already participated in this type of activity—writing, movement, design? What have they produced in these areas? If one student interprets everything literally, what problems will he have with a subjective or an abstract stimulus? How can he be encouraged to try something different? What materials are available? Under what limitations will he be working as to space, time element, interruptions, physical surroundings, number of students, contrasting personalities within the group? And, most important, what should an exercise accomplish at this particular point? It is also necessary to consider the teaching format for the group. If a program uses theater studies as a basis for teaching, the planning of a specific ideation Exercise may not be necessary, for a play idea may come from one of many exercises or as a by-product of a phase of the period studied. Nevertheless, a certain amount of preparation is essential in planning creative exercises whether for a theater study, for initial ideation, or for development of distinctive aspects of playwriting after a story has been written.

In envisioning exercises for creative playwriting the teacher should keep in mind the following conditions: the age of the students participating; the type of stimulus most appropriate, or the material to be covered in a theater study; and the design of the exercise. The teacher should outline every exercise in detail. An exercise should have motivating power, progress at a pace which accommodates both thought and work from each student, and challenges creative energies. It should stimulate progression in thought and discipline, but also retain sufficient flexibility for new interpretations, diverse opinions, and varied approaches.

The following exercise was designed for children eight and nine, who were studying the Primitive period. Specifically a creative exercise in a theater study, its purpose was to introduce early art to the child through personal encounter with the ideas behind it. It also stimulated interest in line as a means of expression and encouraged the child to use this term in his own vocabulary.

> The teacher provides large sheets of newsprint paper and a nylon cord approximately 12 to 18 inches long. Each child is to drop the cord while standing or kneeling in an upright position until the cord falls on the paper in a way that is pleasing to him. He then traces the cord and examines the line drawn. The child now turns the paper around until, in his imagination, he sees the shape of an animal or figure which could be completed with a few more extensions of the original line. The completed drawing usually represents an animal of some kind, but there are students who will see only people, and a few will be completely unique in their interpretations.

> The children now repeat the exercise, but this time after completing the drawing, they add colors to shade the figures. The crayolas used are brown, black, red, and yellow.

> Now the class looks at the drawings. The teacher emphasizes inventiveness in the use of original lines, clarity in representation of animals or figures, and effectiveness of communicating with a continuous line. She then compares results of the exercise to drawings by early man, noting his use of surface and

materials, including colors. A discussion should follow concerning the earliest records of art expression and the meaning behind them.

It is also practicable to suggest relationships to single ideas which may be applicable to contemporary art, such as the use of line as a means of communication. Works of modern artists could provide examples.

Materials needed: newsprint, charcoal, thick nylon cord, crayolas, pictures of cave art similar to the portfolio *Cave Paintings of the Great Hunters* by Walter A. Fairservis, Jr., (Marlboro Books, 1955). Prints of selected works in contemporary art which illustrate the use of line in art expression.

This particular exercise can serve an additional purpose for the observant teacher. It gives her insight into the way a student thinks. Most children draw a snake, a bird, or some animal that requires little effort in interpretation. Others force the line to become what they enjoy drawing most such as a cat or a clown. Then there are a few who not only allow their cords to form complicated lines but then interpret their drawings so imaginatively that the thought processes used are revealing to the teacher. One girl took advantage of such a line and drew another child skating in a unique position of balance while in motion and under stress. The intricacy of this drawing provided insight into the mental capabilities of this nine-year-old. The teacher later discovered that the child was in an advanced class in school and that she showed exceptional aptitude for math and science. There appeared to be a correlation between the thinking processes displayed by the child in the art exercise and her abilities in a more exact discipline. When a child draws something this complicated and original, it may not relate directly to what the teacher is trying to accomplish, but it is a significant example of ability to communicate visually with a single line drawing.

Sometimes the teacher will improvise a completely new exercise—at least, it is unique to her experience. The impetus may come through reading about creative endeavors in other fields. The capacity to recognize relationships in art forms and activities and to use them demonstrates resourcefulness on her part, but it may prove helpful to test these ideas first in conference with a colleague so that she can objectively evaluate their effectiveness, particularly when applied to her own class situation. When designing Ideation Exercises, however, most teachers use exercises they have found successful during their own experience in creative playwriting courses or in school assignments which encouraged inventive expression. Two of the more popular exercises are the Inanimate Object Exercise and the Design Exercise originated by Paul Baker and developed extensively in his beginning drama course, *Integration of Abilities*. Variations of these exercises are recognizable in the Sensory Exercise mentioned earlier, and in the following application of the Nature Object Exercise employed by one teacher. This teacher was working with teens, and the results obtained led to the writing of an original script.

> *Who is Cassandra?* is a one-act play which grew from a study of nature objects by senior high students at the Dallas Theater Center in 1965. Students brought natural objects to class. The object was to be directly from nature, unaltered by man. Some of the items were sea shells, branches, leaves, flowers, stones, berries, and petrified wood. At the teacher's request the students drew the object realistically on a large sheet of paper. They then selected the lines which interested them most and drew several line drawings in black and white. Walking out the pattern of these lines on the floor they changed the rhythm and energy of movement as this was felt in relation to the movement of the line. Participants notated adjectives to describe their feelings while walking out the line; they then recorded adjectives describing the object itself. These descriptions and the initial line movement stimulated abstract movement studies, complemented by subsequent addition of abstract sound. A discussion followed pointing out the emotional qualities of the exercises. Designs emerged through inspiration from the initial line drawings and the emotional qualities of the line movement. Students then translated the adjectives, lines, designs, sound and movement studies into a personality. When each student had fully developed a character from his work, the group presented the characters, combined for improvisations, and then exchanged for other combinations. From this activity the germinal idea for the play emerged. Production occurred several months later.[1]

This exercise with natural objects is one of the most exciting and comprehensive exercises available to teens; it is especially successful with senior high students. It is evident that the exercise requires the talents and insights of a mature teacher, preferably one who has participated in the exercise herself.

INDIVIDUAL: Who . . . is . . .
    Cassandra?
ALL VOICES: We are.
CONFORMIST: I am!
REBEL: No! I am!
INDIVIDUAL: Nobody is . . . yet.
GIRL: I wonder which one . . . I won-
    der which one I am.
INDIVIDUAL: Funny how a person
    isn't just *one* on the inside, but
    many. Many faces, many voices
    all trying to be heard . . . trying
    to be seen . . . trying to take
    over . . .

REBEL: It's one of those coffee
    houses.
CONFORMIST: Look how dirty it is.
REBEL: So what? Haven't you ever
    seen dirt before? It's still suave.
    Listen to that folk singer.
INDIVIDUAL: I've never been any-
    where like this before.
REBEL: Really going to like this
    place. Great music. Wild people.
CONFORMIST: People with no future.
INDIVIDUAL: Maybe they're looking
    for their future.
GIRL: Like me . . .

A theater study with strong motivating power for senior high students is the Growth Study[2] which includes a series of exercises on the stages of growth explained as follows:

Concept of the Levels of Growth.
What is growth?

There are several different levels of growth. These levels take different tensions.

These tensions have various ideas or drives which set them in motion.

Each level of growth has its vocabulary, word, movement, form, color.

1. To some, growth is almost all memory and recollection: names, facts, happenings renamed; the latest slang, movies, athletic and social gab; the continuous enumeration of where, when, what, without selection; what to wear, to eat, to buy.
2. To some, growth is learning how gadgets work—how to put motors together, how to attach pipes, mix formulas, solve problems—never with the idea of developing a new way but of becoming extremely adept at redoing, becoming faster, quicker than the next, contemplative, telling others how to improve the (formula)—the robot materialist.
3. To some, growth is the extension of ready-made faith which sets an individual apart, making him superior to the common herd. He does not grow through faith; he applies well-worn formulas, recollects, memorizes, improves standards and talents, develops a cult, builds systems to estimate how far below his standards others may fall. He joins, dictates, slaps backs, smokes cigars in back rooms in important committees; becomes a pseudo artist, musician, actor, prophet, teacher, politician, a name dropper; surrounds himself with position, societies, club sponsors, members.
4. To some few, growth is the discovery of a dynamic power of the mind—there is a long period of intense study, criticism, and discovery. Directions do not quickly reveal themselves; words do not come easily; growth is of little immediate interest to anyone else. The stimulus to growth comes from within the person and is fed by ideas and sensations from nature, books, works of real

faith, bodily movement. The growth is precious and very private. It serves neither for display nor for immediate use. It does not deal in the mass or grow in a gang. It has no formula. It has faith, love, steel guts, impatience with mediocrity. It demands utmost extension of the body it inhabits. It works and slaves. It engulfs whole ideas, absorbs, performs surgical operations on pat formulas, laughs heartily at mediocrity and opens new worlds of insight. This mind is at home in any period, any place where genius has produced lasting works.[3]

The Growth Study gives each student a point of view from which he can look at his own generation's environment objectively. This study begins with an unrestrained discussion of the levels of growth. The innumerable activities possible include collecting dialogue from actual situations in public places—a drug store, a party, or a girl's dormitory; even field trips for the purpose of observing the dynamics of behavior as a reflection of attitudes and needs identifiable with specific levels of growth. To begin with, however, there may be assignments for individual work within the class:

List adjectives and phrases which describe each group. Find examples. Look for the most obvious forms. See the good and bad sides, the comic and the tragic elements. Comment on the attitudes most prevalent.

Select one level of growth. Make drawings to show the movement, tension, color, texture, and rhythm pattern underlying this level.
Present a movement study of this level.
Collect materials which best depict qualities dominant in a level of growth and make a collage. Bring pictures, objects, happenings in books, magazines, or newspapers which capture the flavor of a level of growth.

Write a poem, a story, or a theme paper.
Create a composition in sounds or sound effects.
Relate to people, places, things, ideas, events.

The class may now divide into groups of those who have been studying the same level of growth. They prepare a scene growing out of their work. After presentation of the scene before the class, the performing group leads in a discussion of the exercise and how they arrived at their presentation.

GROUP 1 is represented in the play by Nancy, the daughter in college, her state of mind and the girls in her dormitory.

GROUP 2 is represented by Father and Nelda the science-minded daughter.

GROUP 3 is represented by Mother. Her ideal state of mind is most productive at a political meeting.

GROUP 4 is not represented in the play for it is an ideal level of human existence reached more rarely than any other level.

After students have viewed and commented on all the scenes, the teacher asks the class to relate their discoveries to their own lives and habits—where and how they spend their time.

Unlimited time may be spent on this one study with all of its various exercises and assignments. The Growth Study is not a single ideation exercise but a study in theater which easily covers a year of weekly sessions in class, especially when the study produces ideas used in playwriting. One teacher used it as a format for her class, and they later presented a play containing a composite of ideas about these different levels of growth. They were written into the personalities of individual members of a family in an original script called *Breakthrough*. Since behavior patterns of each character had to be "blown up" in order to effectively present the idea of the play, the story became a space fantasy; the family's fantastic adventures occur on the way to their annual interplanetary picnic.

One of the crucial turning points for a teacher occurs in attempting to recognize the *best* idea for a play when it appears. Obviously in most theater studies or ideation exercises there will be many ideas and many directions to consider. How does one know when the "right" idea presents itself? For every teacher it becomes largely a question of experience with ideas and with playwriting; and then she may not be completely certain of the validity of an idea until it finally emerges as a story. It is much easier to evaluate a story than it is to judge all the ideas which may contribute to its final plot. Eventually the teacher becomes skillful in recognizing ideas which have greatest potential for creating a play, but in the beginning she must train herself to visualize and anticipate potential characters and plots which will offer conflicts suitable for play construction. Conflicts should be strong enough to carry the play, involve other characters, sustain the interest of students who will do the writing and, above all, provide a story within the understanding and capability of the young playwrights.

No subject offers greater difficulty in writing than that of the handicapped individual, but one class of teen-agers chose to write a play about a deaf girl. The plot evolved from incidents relating to the girl's deafness. To write such a play the students needed to understand some of the problems and characteristics of deafness. They participated in various exercises in silent communication, exploring difficulties and limitations imposed by lack of hearing. One exercise emphasized individual reactions to the absence of sound. First presenting a pantomime about the deaf girl, the students then re-created it to reveal her personal interpretation of what had happened. Discussion centered on specific facets such as the difficulties of manual and oral speech, adjustment problems, and physical limitations. During their field trip to a school for the deaf, a teacher from the school spoke to the group. This was an unusual class in creative playwriting in that the subject was not new to their interests and experiences, nor was it new to the teacher. Yet there was a great need for teacher and class preparation. *The Glass Tunnel* is more than the product of an exercise in playwriting; it is a study of crucial moments in a life of deafness. There was good reason to question the ability of the students to write about this subject. However, interest in the idea was strong, and the conflict well-motivated. Exercises, a field trip, and related discussions represented an attempt on the part of the teacher to assist them in carrying out their ideas. The class completed and produced the play, although they were never completely satisfied with the script. As was evident to the students, the script does have weaknesses. Yet in any final evaluation of the success of creative playwriting, it is the *act* itself which remains paramount.

Sometimes the teacher, because of her age and experience, will find that her interests in the conflict of a story and those of her students proceed from widely different viewpoints. She must not allow her own ideas to control the viewpoint of the students. For example, *Don't Cross That Lion* could have been an interesting vehicle for adult commentary on politics, but class activity truly molded the story, even though mature insight motivated characters and situations. It was still *their* play. The teacher can become aware of those things which influence a student's thinking if she is knowledgeable about current television shows, popular movies, plays, and musicals. If she is not alert to these areas of entertainment, she may discover that her students will in a pinch oftentimes knowingly ''borrow'' from plots which are useful to them. *Xanadon't You Dare!* was an original three-act play written by junior high students, but the frame of the story was almost identical to the beginning and ending of *Brigadoon*. Within the frame the story was original with the class, but the basic idea was not their own. This technique is certainly not unusual in theater, for it has been used by many well-known playwrights. It is important, though, that the students be aware of what they are doing so that they will not resort entirely to plagiarism. A teacher underestimates the resourcefulness of her students if she allows this to happen.

When a teacher sincerely works at encouraging students to use their own resources in playwriting, she discovers that the resulting play will develop a style and viewpoint reflecting the class personality and possibly employing the class talent. Students will often write scenes to include a pianist, guitarist, dancer, or singer in production of the play. *Bewitched* was written as a musical to employ such talents, as was *Who is Cassandra?*, which included a folk singer and a guitarist. This resembles the practice prevalent in earlier days when playwrights wrote for specific actors and occasions, but again, this form of writing is most advantageous when incorporated into the script with integrity and because of a genuine need for its theatrical contribution.

Potential action in the story should be another consideration in selecting the best idea for a play. It is not advisable to choose a play idea which will lead to excessive dialogue and restricted movement; there should always be visual action in the plot, especially in plays to be presented by children. It is equally wise to select a plot which requires minimal scene changes. On several occasions a play has demanded too many different locales in proportion to its length. This requirement retards the story progression and the climactic build because it results in excessive time lapses between scene shifts or complete scene changes. *Thunder N' Blue Blazes* is an original script by junior high students which requires a number of scene changes, but the play contains some genuinely imaginative characters and subplots, partially because of these many different episodes. If presentation had not been in a theater where several stages permitted the necessary scene changes to run smoothly, and had sets and props not been minimal, it would have been almost impossible to present the play effectively without rewriting. Basically the plot concerns Don Mosquito, a bumbling sheriff patterned after Don Quixote, and his sidekick, Chigger, who roam the world looking for the famous Lady Bandit known as Lady Bug. The audience can always recognize Lady Bug by the gold tooth in the center of her mouth. But she is able to disguise herself (and the tooth) in masterful ways, as she flees picturesque countries through amazing subplots, always managing to escape Don Mosquito in the nick of time and avoiding discovery. Each scene is a well-written vignette within itself and poses a production problem only when all scenes are combined, thereby requiring immediate set changes in order to maintain the proper pace of the play.

Finally, in selecting the best play ideas, the teacher should look for potential in each character which can be interestingly individualized so that he will contribute to the central plot and can be easily cast from among the students performing. Frequently a teacher with a group of first-year teens in creative playwriting will type-cast the play in order to use the talents of the entire class. As soon as she learns the capabilities and needs of each student, however, she should cast them in parts which will challenge and expand their talents and abilities, helping them to realize undiscovered assets. Sometimes this is impossible until the second year of theater. This was the case with Allen, a young teen-ager who was immediately classified as a comedian when he began theater classes. His humor was seldom forced, for he was in all honesty a very funny person. Obviously it seemed wise to use his natural talent in the first original script he helped to write. But in his second year of theater he received a more serious part, and eventually when his class presented one of the classic Greek tragedies, he was able to portray the leading role. Although this boy functioned spontaneously in the role of a comic and enjoyed ample occasion to develop this type of part, he found the opportunity to "try" tragedy an invaluable new experience. He had a chance to test his abilities in other acting roles which not only gave him deeper insight into character portrayal but also provided a vital growth experience for him.

Plays which offer the best opportunities for teen-agers to grow as performers may not be original scripts but possibly scripts representing a specific style of theater or playwright.

A theater study may originate from a published play selected for production, providing still another opportunity for growth. Many of the exercises used in creative playwriting for developing character, plot, and story can help the student understand a published script and the character he is to portray; consequently, techniques for developing original theater also function in producing published plays. Past experiences in creative playwriting can then contribute to both student and director producing a published script.

As the teacher considers the play ideas which appear and the potentialities of her students as they emerge in creative playwriting, she will soon discern instinctively those ideas which have potential from all vantage points and those which are not so impressive. In many cases she may want to try several ideas or combine different characters to experiment further with characters and plot before she is certain just what will work. Details of this process and exercises for story development receive extensive treatment in the following section.

After the teacher has completed the outline for an exercise and envisioned all possibilities that may appear, she should continue to assess available "raw materials" which the students bring with them. Contact with students before class enables her to ascertain what they have been doing, what they are interested in at the moment, what they have been thinking about, whether they are physically tired or "keyed-up" (in which case physical activity may be a good starting point), and whether their casual conversations between one another can suggest an appropriate introductory class exercise for that day. Because creative playwriting deals with ideas and experiences which are alive and growing, the sources of inspiration for both teacher and student will change constantly. Once the teacher can train herself to be instinctively aware of what her students bring to class that can be useful, she will find it easier to arouse their interest and to involve them immediately in activity along some line she has planned.

A teacher can begin motivating the thoughts of her students when they arrive for class. Books, pictures, music, art objects, props, or various items of special interest can ignite the spark of curiosity or discussion which will establish a sound base for an exercise to build on. This can serve as an introduction to the exercise. For example, one teacher requested a class of senior high students to view an exhibit of caricatures in the theater lobby before class began. As the students began to discuss what they saw, the teacher encouraged them to select the caricatures which appealed to them most and to analyze why they thought their choices were good. She then asked what an artist must look for in a person that he intends to caricature. This activity and discussion prepared the class for concentrated work on the day's exercise. Each student selected someone in his neighborhood whom he knew rather well and wrote a verbal caricature of him. Analyzation of the person selected was to highlight his most distinguishing personality traits, habits, and attributes. The students selected those which could be imaginatively exaggerated to form a personality profile and soon assembled a gallery of verbal portraits on "unusual people." A more detailed character analysis was written. Then each student portrayed his character in improvisations involving comic, melodramatic, and satirical situations—forms of drama which could use the caricature-type portrayal. From these presentations and the constant regrouping of characters to create more improvisations, several situations developed which were stimulating ideas for playwriting.

One Ideation Exercise which usually requires some form of introduction is the Sensory Exercise. The design of this exercise is quite different from the customary "What does apple pie smell like? What does it make you think of?" routine. The problem posed is to describe one's sensory perceptions of the item in a way that the adjectives may translate into personality traits and qualities. Selecting one object as a demonstration and showing the class how observant they can be in descriptions will insure a better response from each student, especially if the students are children. Since the teens who wrote *The Tin Man and the Painted Town* had participated in previous creative exercises and playwriting activities, they needed no introduction to the abstract painting employed as a stimulus. Had this group not used a painting earlier for another activity, they might have profited from initial activity to make them more receptive to the exercise. It is impossible to stress flexibility too much, because in every class possibilities and reactions will vary. Once the teacher decides that an introduction is necessary she should plan it in a way that will serve to anticipate what follows as well as to stimulate thought in a definite direction or pattern of movement. Success in motivating students to thought which in turn produces action will usually depend upon verbalization used by the teacher. Her presentation is the first step in channeling a student's thought in terms of playwriting.

Sometimes an activity like the Sensory Exercise or the Nature Object Exercise allows division into several parts. The student selects an object, describes it verbally, and then takes inspiration from the word descriptions. These activities lead to character analysis, scenes, pantomimes, designs, and other forms of expression. Although the teacher is aware of steps taken in the exercise, she should not initially reveal a set pattern to the student. If he is not conscious of ways the exercise might unfold, he will take more time with his work and be more thorough in his efforts.

All exercises are more effective if presented as a fun project. No announcement of procedure or purpose should precede the activity, because this dictate will inhibit the spirit of spontaneity and freedom. Nevertheless, the teacher is always alert to the way an exercise is progressing, the ideation success of each student, and how ideas, comments, and attitudes are directing or pacing the work. Although the teacher plans the progression of an exercise, she should never enforce these directions if others are indicated. She may find that she can follow each step as outlined, that she must skip one or two steps, or that the exercise takes a completely new direction of its own accord. There is only one effort more important than thought and preparation by the teacher before her class begins, and that is intuitive encouragement and inventive teaching while class is in progress.

It would be erroneous to suggest that the teacher's personality does not enter into construction of an original script. It is always interesting to see a play when one knows both teacher and students. The teacher's guidance and influence in various directions of work will give her classes distinctive characteristics. She must watch that her influence is not overbearing, but merely a reflection of her teaching style.

1 Synopsis of report on creative playwriting by Claudette Gardner in the graduate school teaching program of Teen-Children's Theater, Dallas Theater Center, 1966.

2 A study of growth developed by Paul Baker and used as a major exercise in the drama course *Advanced Integration of Abilities*.

3 An unpublished paper given to students enrolled in *Advanced Integration of Abilities* taught by Mary Sue Fridge Jones. This course is an extension of Paul Baker's drama course, *Integration of Abilities*.

I've learned to express my own ideas and to make something of them.

Mary Phelan

A PATTERN FOR THEATER

A child's work is more original if he is unaware he is working on a play; he knows no pressure, no definite procedure, and no set goal. His joy exists in the immediate act of self-expression, but with encouragement, his concentration increases and his ideas expand. While the student may not recognize his total involvement, his teacher will. She has planned it that way. She knows that if a child is conscious at the beginning that he is writing a play, his work will be artificial, or he may announce abruptly that he cannot write, and the project will end. He may also become so concerned with the end result that his ideas become superficial and rely on gimmicks. He may even use plots, dialogue, and tricks he has seen before and thought highly successful at the time. Often if a child knows he is going to write a play, he immediately begins to compete with others in the class; convinced his own ideas are best, he tries to sell them to the rest of the group. A child may never become a playwright in the adult sense of the word, but he is always a playwright in the creative sense. He is constantly conjuring up characters and situations. As he matures, his ideas become more complicated and his work better organized. The older the child, the sooner he will realize that he is involved in playwriting. Yet even teens can become deeply involved with an idea for a play before they have an inkling that they are working on play material, especially if they are beginners at the craft. Any student who has previously participated in creative playwriting knows that eventually he is going to write a play, but by this time he should realize that ideas come from everywhere. His greatest task is to sort out ideas as well as to recognize their validity when they appear. Eventually an idea acquires its own dynamics, and the student becomes more interested in developing his present concept than in continuing explorations. The perception is his; he is curious about its potential and excited about its growth. The fact that it may lead to a script for a play is of secondary importance to him. Once an idea develops into a story, or plot outline with characters, the class can consider it as a play possibility. They then begin to make decisions concerning action and dialogue which apply more directly to theater and dramatic technique. It is far more important that work be original, however, than that it be immediately applicable to playwriting. The experience of *creating* theater is more valuable than attaining professional standards of writing and production, since creative playwriting is a process more than a technique. It becomes difficult to divide into topics such as *casting* or *rehearsals,* because writing and producing are an integral process. There is no set formula for arriving at an original play, but a distinct pattern emerges through repetition of the process. This pattern is outlined in an orderly progression to help the teacher understand the process and therefore adequately fulfill her role in motivating students through these phases:

Preparing the student
Ideation
Experimental Playmaking
Writing the Script
Integrating the Production
First Performance
The Final Draft

Strict adherence to this outline has never been a didactic procedure but, in general, it has been followed with satisfactory results. The purpose of describing it is twofold; an indication of a way for the teacher, and as a definitive restatement of the structure which has emerged thus far.

PREPARING THE STUDENT

Students require some form of mental preparation if they are to participate successfully in Ideation Exercises or if they are to create a play in a specific style of period theater. Initial exercises in self-expression usually prepare a child for ideation, and accomplishment is possible in one or two creative episodes. With theater studies, however, the needs are different; creative exercises build upon one another and demand a certain amount of background information and understanding for full participation, thus requiring many *preparatory exercises* before playwriting actually begins. These exercises serve two purposes: they engage the child in specific patterns or viewpoints of thinking that stimulate his interest and provide vital information while simultaneously encouraging creative expression to increase learning. For the student in a theater study, all exercises prior to creative playwriting provide a period of gestation—a time for collecting information and gaining the insight requisite to writing a play in a style of classic drama. Exercises designed to nurture this growth are progressive in concept, relationships, and expressive activities. In study of the Primitive period the child is introduced to line, rhythm, movement, sound, shape, color, and texture (the vocabulary of expression). He learns to recognize this vocabulary in nature and in the man-made world about him, and he learns to apply it to his own expressive activities. These exercises are a natural outgrowth of any study of the Primitive period since the earliest forms of art originated in this period of history; in addition, the style of art found in the period closely relates to the child's own artistic efforts. Themes and subject matter for various activities may derive directly from the life of Primitive man or may relate to it through artistic resemblance. For example, one might ascribe to man's earliest expressions the descriptions *free, simple, honest, basic, natural,* and *subjective.* Studies in the Primitive period explore interpretation of early man and his art in terms of the vocabulary of expression as these terms apply to movement, sound, art, writing, and pantomime. In movement the child may work toward a personal emotional release; in sound he strives for simplicity and clarity in realistic imitations and abstract impressions through sound pictures; in graphic art he learns to communicate individually and integrally with every element of design; in writing his goal is to be subjective, simple, and direct; and in pantomime he seeks simplicity and brevity of ideas and their expressions. The essence of the concept lies in beginning with the elemental approach to each art form; because of the simplicity of this viewpoint, it is easy for the child to comprehend and reflect a similar outlook. His response is an unconscious one; he must therefore become aware of these elements as tools of expression before he can consciously use the approach in his own work.

Mental preparation provided by these exercises in the Primitive period brings the child to a point of readiness where he will free his ideas and proceed to develop them in ways leading to an elementary theater experience. Although a play may result from study of this period, it will not be a period drama in the sense that it reflects any classic form of theater. Unlike results obtained through other studies in theater, a play from the Primitive period gains its inspiration in other ways, usually through an Ideation Exercise. But the exercise can still grow out of a concept of the Primitive period. For example, in the Sensory Exercise, each child used the basic vocabulary of expression to describe his sensory perceptions of an object; then he expressed his character concept in diverse medias, learning to relate the vocabulary of expression to multiple artistic efforts and then integrating them all into a single dramatic statement. This is the evolving process learned in study of the Primitive period.

Preparation must always begin with the mind of the student —his attitude, awareness, and thought processes—not his acquisition of technical knowledge. Students in a theater study are more conscious of the skills of drama, for their classes generally meet in a theater environment where they receive constant exposure to acting, directing, and technical theater. An acquaintance with techniques in these areas acquired prior to the experience of creative involvement in any one of them can often have a detrimental effect on the student's total concept of dramatic creativity. If he first develops an individual viewpoint toward his work and then masters dramatic techniques as a means of communicating it, the student can more imaginatively use theater as an exciting media for personal expression. To summarize, studies in theater are not always the teaching format, but in using them preparatory exercises should prime the student for creative playwriting while he is learning and working simultaneously in other expressive activities. For the single Ideation Exercise, preparation is not always necessary unless the student needs some form of introduction to the exercise or some initial experience in ideation and creative work. With the single Ideation Exercise, the necessary gestation period for studying the nature of the idea and for letting it grow to the evaluation stage comes during the period of ideation and during the next developmental step, Experimental Playmaking.

IDEATION

Ideation is the process of forming ideas or images; the Ideation Exercise encourages this activity. The exercise builds around a stimulus for motivating original thinking. Exercises for children are usually more effective when the first motivation is on an individual basis as in the Sensory Exercise, but with teens, group ideation is highly successful, as when a discussion of witches led to the writing of *Bewitched*. Ideation usually occurs during total concentration and involvement with the stimulus. It requires a maximum degree of saturation. Once the Ideation Exercise is in motion, the student (or group) should be free to work alone. When a mental block occurs the teacher should provide impetus to consider the stimulus from a new angle. The student examines its characteristics, explores its possibilities, and then tests it in many directions until an

I felt awkward writing our play at first, like I was getting nowhere. Pretty soon it became interesting and things just started popping into my head.

Debra Pinney

independent, dynamic idea emerges. During this period the teacher should avoid inhibiting the student through observation, haste, judgement, forced production, or comparison of his work to that of others. This is the opportune time for unrestrained creative thought without pressure. If the student is following a completely different line of thought—one that is new, imaginative, and, above all, stimulating to him—he has reached the pinnacle of creative thinking; the teacher should be cautious in disrupting this spontaneous flow of ideas. A private brainstorming session is in process, producing as many ideas as possible. The student at this point, however, must refrain from making a final selection of one specific idea. He oscillates between close involvement with details of the stimulus and a detached view of it. If the stimulus is an object from the Sensory Exercise, a student's response to what he sees, smells, hears, feels, or tastes may be fairly quick, and his transferral of adjectives to personal characteristics should be immediate. However, as soon as the character begins to take form, work can extend in many directions while thinking focalizes. Character expression may be in line, color, shape, rhythm, texture, sound, movement, pantomime, improvisation, or words. The student can make a collage study of his character, a physical sketch, or a personality design in tempera or chalk. He may write a character analysis. He may set dialogue to music and create a dance. He may visualize the character in clay or wire sculpture. He may answer or demonstrate specific problems: What is his character's personality rhythm? How much space does he use when he is moving? How does he walk? What patterns would he make, moving across an empty space? Would he make quick, punchy movements, or would his stage presence demand soft, floating movements? Perhaps now is the time to ask the student to draw the type of house the character lives in or the neighborhood where he resides. If a teen is developing a characterization, there are several ways to extend his perception. He may bring a record which captures in music the personality and movement of his character; he may select a poem, story, picture, or painting which reflects a similar personality, style, mood, locale, or period detail. An excellent way to let him apply his own talents is through choosing his own character interpretation, as did one girl who sketched a series of costume designs showing her character in different moods on different occasions. It is possible to express character analyses in diverse ways: through writing, visualization, or interpretation in different media. Variety depends entirely on the imagination and ingenuity of student and teacher. If the stimulus is music, the student will not respond as instantaneously as in the Sensory Exercise. This is because in listening, one perceives only fragmentary portions of the stimulus at a time; in viewing a painting, one can perceive the entire stimulus at a single instant. In either case there must be free time to absorb the stimulus, to become impregnated with its many images, emotions, associations, memories, and fantasy reactions. The student may concentrate on sound quality, rhythm, or melodic line of the music. He should not feel that he must tie every scene or reaction to an exact change in the music. But he is free to do this, or disregard it, as the musical pattern moves him.

Of course, the *way* a student saturates himself depends upon the stimulus and design of the exercise. The more freedom in the design of an exercise, the easier it is to relate spontaneously to the proposed stimulus. If students listen to two records, expecting one to stimulate a character idea and the other a story idea, they operate under unnecessary restriction. Ideas have more room for growth if the teacher directs the student's attention toward specifics such as melody or rhythm, rather than toward achievement of a specific result or reaction. Some successful Ideation Exercises have required specific results, yet allowed freedom in the treatment of those results. For example, junior high students confronted a series of words designed to stimulate ideas for a story. The words were: gold, townspeople,

LUCY: Here, little flowers. You can have a drink, too.
MISS AGATHA: . . . gold! I saw it with my own eyes! A whole chest full of gold teardrops!

VILLAINS: We've got to get that gold.
VILLAIN 1: A chance in a lifetime.
VILLAIN 2: A real treasure right under our noses. And in a little town like this.
VILLAIN 3: It'll be just like taking candy from a baby.

VILLAIN 1: Are you the lady of the house?
MAID: No, I'm the maid. Can I help you?
VILLAIN 1: Yes, Ma'm. I have a product here that will revolutionize the drudgery of opening cans; it carries with it a lifetime guarantee . . .

daisies, villains, teardrops, gossip, and fortune-telling. The exercise led to creative thinking by forcing relationships between words to outline a story. Group ideation produced the best result. Both fantasy and melodrama were integral ingredients of the final story. The plot concerns a young girl who lives alone in a field of ten-foot daisies. She tells fortunes with teardrops, and afterwards, the tears turn into gold. When the townspeople hear about the girl's strange powers, they gossip, but only the word "gold" reaches three eavesdropping villains. They begin to plot how to steal the money. The townspeople, the girl, and the villains are in for a surprise upon discovery that the golden teardrops possess a most peculiar characteristic which changes the outcome of events for everyone. The play is appropriately titled *The Golden Teardrops.*

In this exercise the words selected gave a degree of direction to plot and to style of the story (villains, teardrops, gold, daisies). The chain of responses within the group also supplied direction. Awareness of early trends in ideas is helpful if it produces additional thought in a particular channel; however, a premature decision on direction can also provide a crutch forcing any additional ideas into its mold. In this case the student or group accepts the first direction, when later ones could be more exciting and provocative. Preventing early judgment, although difficult, is important bcause of the ultimate results obtained.

If an Ideation Exercise is to generate a full-grown idea, it is advisable to write it into a character sketch, plot outline, or detailed story so that its potential can be evaluated. Ideation is complete only when an idea has developed to the point of independent existence. Then it will live and communicate on its own merit. Ideation includes many different types of activities, but the eventual outcome should be character, plot, or story suggestion. Although some judgment occurs in the process, decisive action is imminent. The task now is to select one or more of these ideas and develop it into a script for a play.

EXPERIMENTAL PLAYMAKING

Experimental Playmaking is the most important part of creative playwriting for it is this period, even more than the actual writing phase, which determines structure and style. This is a period for experimenting with the ingredients that make a play—a time for testing, combining, and creating additional ideas which lead to a detailed story. Dialogue generally begins during this phase, since it is almost impossible to separate the integral development of character, conflict, story, and dialogue. At this point, however, the objective is to determine all characters and conflict leading to a plot with one or more subplots, and then to complete the detailed story for the play. An atmosphere of fun yet prevails for spontaneity directs much of the action—in the form of improvisations, discussions, and brainstorming sessions. Still, the project of creating a play is always in the back of the teacher's mind and she offers the group opportunities to solve problems of playwriting—through trial and error. The goal of all activity is group participation, since from this point on the most effective way to develop the play is through *group playwriting.*

Writing a play with a group of students at any age level may seem initially to be an enormous task. But the values and reasons are numerous. Seldom will a child or teen adequately discipline himself to write a play individually. But when he works with a group, it seems easy and fun to engage in playwriting. The experience and enjoyment of group interaction can function as a sizeable learning experience as well as a delightful opportunity for self-expression. In the minds of the group by this time the play is the goal, but the teacher should make sure that each student absorbs skills enabling him to function with reasonable success; through this positive action he thereby discovers his own assets. Technique is secondary to involvement, but it acts as a tool to involve the student on the highest level possible.

To insure the success of this method students must learn to work together. For some individuals this is a giant achievement, as is clear in Joann's summary of her first experience in creative playwriting with other teens:

> As I think back over the long months of writing and rehearsals I wonder how such a mixed group of people could have been able to work together as we did. One girl in the group is domineering, demanding, and a loud-mouth. Another girl is quiet and waited until the very last minute to learn her lines. Our social, religious, and ethical backgrounds are also very different.
>
> We all had to compromise in writing the play and while some of us could not be friends we had to tolerate each other to get the job done. Very gradually we developed a group spirit and became determined to give a good play and a good performance. There were many times when we felt like screaming at each other and we did a few times. It would have been easier to write the play if the group would have been less varied in personalities. Just because it would have been easier, though, does not mean it would have been as good. We could not have presented as many different ideas, ideas which gave the play variety and originality. Our job is done now, and I think that what was once only tolerance has grown to become more like friendship and respect. We are all still very different. None of us have really changed except in the way we have learned to work together.[1]

One of the greatest assets to group playwriting is the extraordinary energy and enthusiasm created by batting around ideas and eventually joining forces to expand one "special" idea. As the idea grows, simultaneously the creative energy grows. Through give and take the students express, adopt, sometimes reject various viewpoints. Each student is capable of contributing by seeing the value of an idea, questioning the idea, visualizing its development, or merely giving support to ideas already flying thick and fast. Individual assets come to the fore: some students are better at character inspiration; others prefer to outline a plot and write the story; some concentrate on motivation and logic; and there are always one or two who readily provide critiques for everything. Each student must find his place within the workings of the group so that he can function with confidence and with reasonable success. He begins to identify with a group, feel a group spirit, yet he must retain his own individuality. The feedback received from this group activity helps a student understand his self-image as seen by others. Eventually a diverse group develops cohesiveness through a common goal, mutual interests and concerns, and a group personality emerges. But the evolution of group cohesiveness still allows for contrasts in energy, rhythm patterns, attitudes, and expressions of the individual. Working together and discovering methods of work most appropriate to them, the students add depth and personal style to their original play. Corporate energy and blending of ideas expand the group's capacity far beyond that of a single individual.

Group interaction has great value in its ability to encourage individual growth, especially when there is common ground for exchange and acceptance of ideas. This environmental attitude doesn't just happen through a miracle of class enrollment! It is a cultivated thing which must begin with each individual. One of the most severe tests for the student is the first presentation of his ideas to the class for their comments. Prior to this he has been subjective in his work; now the time has come for objectivity. He must "let go" and see how his idea stands by itself. This can be a very painful moment to anyone. In one class of eight- and nine-year-old children, the teacher asked each child to present his character idea to the class, and to tell how he created it. Upon examining a large pink velvet powder-puff, Teri had envisioned a lovely, gracious, pink lady who was soft, spoke agreeably to everyone, and "did not have any strong ideas about anything." And she loved the color pink. (No doubt this was Teri's favorite color, too.) During Teri's presentation, the children had begun to visualize the pink lady also. In subsequent discussion the students began adding their own impressions, describing *their* imaginary character with "pink hair, pink lipstick, pink dress, pink fingernails . . . " when suddenly Teri broke into tears and began crying, "No, no, no!" Teri felt that her character was no longer uniquely her own; she reacted as a child does when something she created and loves is suddenly possessed by someone else.

It is easy for a child to accept words of approval about his work, but he is often overly sensitive to suggestions for another approach or to adverse comments. Recognizing this as a vital

I've learned to listen to people better.

Bill Maguire

part of the playwriting process, it is also important to distinguish between a group which tries to possess and abruptly change a person's idea, and the group which offers constructive, positive comments. The teacher and the group are at this time working toward impersonal and impartial evaluation of another person's work and toward helping him accept honest criticism. This is an important avenue of learning if he wishes to improve an idea and become a more discerning and skilled artist. Encouraging children to discuss their work in detail allows them to assess its value, as well as to assimilate thoughts and expressions with clarity and conviction. As they hear each child comment as he chooses, the children learn to listen to one another, and at the same time to respect opposite viewpoints. The child whose work is discussed learns to view his creation objectively through the eyes of others. Although he may become defensive at first, in the right environment he will realize that he does not necessarily have to change his work or accept another's statement as valid. It is an opportunity to check his flexibility in communicating ideas and listening for suggestions which can make him more articulate. He can select or reject these comments. This is his personal prerogative; the final decision is his alone.

After each student has presented his ideas, he has another lesson to learn. Once his idea develops to its fullest potential and group activity involving decision-making begins, he must be willing to give up his idea if another student presents a more plausible one. It is often difficult for a student to change his ideas, or to accept another one as better than his own, but as he adjusts to group playwriting he discovers that this is the only way to advance the play. The teacher can soothe his hurt by convincing him that elimination of an idea does not mean it is worthless, but merely that in this particular situation another is more suitable. Reassuring him of the value of his work and his ideas is imperative. Perhaps the greatest disadvantage to creative playwriting is the impossibility of using every student's original ideas; however, there will be other opportunities to contribute successfully. Democratic operation must exist in the group so that each student can function individually and on an equal basis as far as his capabilities or desires lead him to contribute. The task now is to fuse the best ideas into a plot, using all, or as many of the characters and story ideas as possible from each student. First the conflict and characters must be agreed upon, then the plot determined, and dialogue written. With employment of this constructive organization, the class should soon complete the first draft of an original script, the product of imaginative minds working both independently and as a group to create a play.

Conflict

The most essential ingredient for a good play is a strong conflict. Until an interesting conflict develops, the story for a play remains static. Consequently the search for a conflict is prominent in the mind of a budding playwright. Students in creative playwriting will usually find their most promising conflicts in characters developed during ideation, but sometimes a specific story offers the best conflict. Conflict large enough to motivate a play may come from a single character, a single story, a combination of characters, or a combination of stories. A well-developed character like the Troublemaker or the Rooster in *Cock-a-doodle-oops!* may provide an inherent conflict in his personality. However, such conflicts may not even be apparent until characters relate to a situation or to another character. This usually happens during *improvisations, brainstorming, and discussions.* For example, the real conflict in the story of *The Tin Man and the Painted Town* did not appear until the characters of the story began to interact in improvisations. It was then that the presence of the chartreuse tin man in the town of pure colors stirred up a conflict. The reactions of the sky people to their blue and white clouds did not emerge until the class began to discuss the story idea leading to *A Patchwork Sky.* Conversely, in the character of the little elf, there were not enough complications developed for building a larger conflict. In addition the story revolved around only a few characters—too few to involve the whole class. Any other group might have had great fun with the mischievous little elf, but for some reason this group reacted negatively toward the entire character idea. Usually at least one character will have a personality trait that can be enlarged upon to promote a search for other characters. Unlike the elf, the passive Lion in *Don't Cross That Lion* did not create conflicts, but he had his own problems; he was unable to function as the protective king-of-all-beasts. A more aggressive character (created by a more aggressive child) emerged in the Mockingbird who had all the potential of an antagonist.[2] His portrayal was an intelligent, power politician; thus conflict arose quickly when the Lion and the Mockingbird confronted each other in an improvisation. The Mockingbird continually maneuvered events to usurp the Lion's title and power, and it became obvious that the Lion was a false image of a king. An interesting side conflict arose in this improvisation. Because there were other children in the exercise, a third child portrayed a Bear who was lazy and stupid. In order to include him in the improvisation, the Mockingbird used him as a buffer for the variety of strategies employed to trick and disgrace the Lion. Because of the interaction of these three characters, the class realized the need for a supporting cast, and soon a story was in the making.

In contrast to the Lion, the Tin Man could easily have developed as the antagonist, but he assumed some of the qualities of the protagonist.[3] The original poem described him as "one who walked the dark, dark streets at night filling all the children with fright." But with the lapse of time between creation of the poem and its adaptation into story form the Tin Man's purpose became entirely different. He did not create conflict; it resulted from his presence in the town and from the effect this had upon the townspeople. In each instance the initial idea for a conflict acquired the movement of a boomerang, continually thrown out until it either succeeded or failed to motivate action for a plot. Experimenting with various conflict ideas in order to trigger reactions and thereby discover relationships between characters is the key to story development in a group. The methods employed in determining conflict are the same as those directed toward story development, as the two in most instances crystalize simultaneously.

Characters and Story

After Ideation the class may function as one large group, or divide into smaller groups of four to six people. If several smaller groups are all working on the same problem, the result will be a greater variety of play possibilities, but each subgroup must be willing to work together. Activity need not take the form of group writing, since discussion and improvisation are more essential. The general procedure is to form a plan, discuss it, improvise scenes, and present the resulting ideas to the class for commentary and approval. This continues with variations until the class agrees on a story.

All direction for the play comes from ideas stimulated by Ideation Exercises. If individual or group ideation produces only character ideas, then the group must proceed to select or combine characters, develop a conflict, and create a story. On the contrary, if story ideas do develop, the students can select one or more plots for testing or combination to form a larger story; then character development must occur, often accompanied by a written analysis. The story may take its form from one of several methods:

1. After each student has presented his story or character idea, the class includes all characters in one story, or enlarges one story to include all plots. Variation is possible through rewriting the primary story to contain one or more subplots. In this way it is practical to try almost all ideas, eliminating only a few.
2. It is feasible to use selections and combinations of plots and characters. This has proved to be most effective if the group can generate new ideas based upon those already conceived. Then it judiciously selects the most appropriate plot and characters. This method requires a certain sophistication and knowledge about playwriting.
3. If the class has developed only story ideas, it can select one or combine and develop several plots into one story.
4. When only character ideas have developed, the class may present them in a single story or include a few of these characters and create new ones.
5. A playwriting committee may assemble; its function is to eliminate all the unusable suggestions and eventually settle on one idea or a combination of ideas as worthy of concentration for play production. This method is effective in large classes of teens, but there is a marked disadvantage. It limits the number of students who can participate unless the class is divided into several playwriting committees, resulting in the writing of more than one play. This is not a satisfactory solution for the students; they generally prefer to work together on the same project and would rather have smaller parts than write two plays. On several occasions, however, this method has been the most convenient way to work.

The teacher can vary her techniques in playwriting, but she is the only one who can decide the most effective methods for accommodating the personalities of the group and their needs of

Characters have to be introduced
in a way that the audience
will be able to believe the play.

Helen Waldorf

76

the moment. After a story is in outline form, its presentation in class can emerge as a slightly rehearsed improvisation or as a full, written story. If there are subgroups reporting on the same story idea, a second elimination process is then necessary. The students then select the most appealing plot, possibly combining it with others so that it will merge into the master plan for a play.

If additional work is still necessary to polish characters or plot, rewriting should continue until the class is satisfied with the material. The teacher continues to work within the group or groups, helping with character motivation, progression of action, and continuity. She functions in this capacity until the story for the play is complete.

Of paramount importance now is the specific writing process. The amount of handwriting a student will do depends upon how old he is and how well he can communicate in writing. Children can often write selected portions of the play, and thereafter work out blending of ideas through discussions and improvisations. The teacher can expedite story development with younger groups by remembering the action and recording it after class. In this way she can refresh the child's memory at the next session by bringing his work up-to-date and then letting him build from this. Another way is to record ideas by notation in class. Children are then left free to think and compose in response to the exercises, questions, and discussions. The teacher may take notes as they dictate, or she may jot down pertinent details and complete notes later. In either case she should never be obvious in her notation. Children ten through twelve and junior high students can write their own stories and usually prefer to do so. However, they often elect a secretary from among their group to take notes, too. The basic problem is not one of handwriting skill but of time, since their enthusiasm dictates a need for rapid notation. At this age students seem to find it easier to remember their story and may not write it down until it is complete in their own minds. But then *they* want to write it! Senior high students demonstrate greater interest in the written word and usually prefer to spend less time on improvisations and physical activity. They want to come immediately to grips with conflict and plot ideas. Until composition of a story, actual writing procedure should pose no insoluble problem as long as some means of recording it is available. It is in the next phase, writing of the script, that the method of writing becomes important.

WRITING THE SCRIPT

At this point it is advisable to make specific references to playwriting terminology: antagonist,[2] protagonist,[3] pointer,[4] plant,[5] subplot,[6] and any other information helpful to the process of playwriting. Students take great pride in learning vocabulary peculiar to a skill; they are even more pleased upon discovery that they have used a technique without realizing it. But technical dramatic terms should receive attention only when students are ready, interested, and can make use of them. Otherwise, they will become too concerned with structure and device. Acquisition of these formal terms leads to a primarily intellectual approach to playwriting, neglecting the importance of emotional and other creative resources. If problems arise in plot or dialogue, solutions should come from the students whenever possible. Forced interference from an adult hinders the learning experience and may even destroy the playwright's original idea. If the teacher interferes too frequently, the creation ceases to belong to the students. The wisest course seems to be the subtle one; the teacher might employ technical terms in describing an accomplished action, or she may demonstrate how to handle a weakness in script through reference to a standard dramatic technique.

With children it is sufficient initially to know that a story or play must have a beginning, a middle, and an ending. With teens there is increasing absorption in the plot and in techniques of playwriting. But until they have experienced the vitality of an idea so that they are more loyal to it than to structure, techniques serve only to clarify what has been done, or what is needed to create a dramatic experience. With teen-agers, particularly as the story is developed into a script, structure may be outlined by letters forming the word *PASTO.*

> *Preparation:* introducing who, what, where and when.
>
> *Attack:* the protagonist and the antagonist are revealed, and the conflict is defined.
>
> *Struggle:* the longest portion of the play when the question of the victor hangs in the balance.
>
> *Turning Point:* the climax of the play when events change and conflict is resolved.
>
> *Outcome:* the results of all action are known and the consequences revealed.[7]

The story can now break down into a synopsis of scenes, divided according to changes in subject matter or the entrance or exit of a major character. With children the teacher specifies only general divisions in the story—suggested by the word *PASTO* or more simply the *beginning, middle,* and *ending* portions of the play. A discussion of what to include in each scene might follow. Sometimes this attention to structure comes after development of dialogue in a children's class; thus they sense no restrictions in their improvisations and creative playmaking. With teens, however, this breakdown of scenes might be helpful at the beginning.

Dialogue

Initiation of dialogue occurs through *improvisations, story dramatization, discussions, individual and group writing.* In *The Tragedy of Orpheus and Eurydice,* students discussed a scene, improvised it, and each wrote dialogue as he felt it. They then read the dialogues and, under the teacher's supervision, rewrote the scene using the best ideas and speeches from individual writings. On the other hand, the children dictated dialogue for *The Troublemaker.* This use of dictation accounts for some of the stiffness inherent in the play. Additional improvisations with the teacher taking notes could have freed the children's expressiveness and the natural flow of dialogue. Improvisations are vital to developing dialogue with children, both before and after the writing of speeches. The freshness of the student's interpretation improves through repetition, and if there is no pressure to remember each word as written, characterization and expression are spontaneous. Next to improvisations and group writing, individual writings by the students are the most successful source for dialogue. Any method is acceptable if it helps the student think in terms of dialogue as a means of natural expression. He can analyze how it sounds later.

In working with children, if creative exercises given in the beginning of each writing session re-create the mood and emotion of the play when the group last left it, then concentration and energetic productivity will double. Creative powers will become active again. Sooner or later playwriting poses an intellectual challenge to the teens, but in working with children of younger ages, creation of a play should always remain on the intuitive, fanciful level; they must continually "feel" in order to visualize and compose. The creative spark in a child is an intangible thing. It may radiate for one minute, and then subside for hours before there is another spark with equal fire and intensity. This is the reason that some plays by children have scenes which seem to shimmer; then the next scene is lost. The ideal goal would be to maintain this "shimmering" level of creativity once it is reached.

In addition to individual and group writing, teens may want to use a tape recorder, but this involves a risk of producing self-consciousness because any attempt to record usually inhibits natural expression. The recording of an entire class session might possibly contain usable dialogue, but such an undertaking demands excessive time from both teacher and students. The chances of obtaining stage-worthy material by this method are sparse.

Once concentration focuses on actual writing of dialogue, there may be some students who lose interest. They cannot adhere to the discipline that writing demands; moreover, they may not be able to keep up with the writing pace. It is more profitable for the student to continue working on the play and see it through, but a few never achieve the complete experience in playwriting. When this occurs, or when the class is too large to concentrate upon further playwriting, work can continue within a small playwriting committee. The rest of the class then proceeds to work on various projects connected with production such as scenery, costumes, and props. Each group keeps abreast with the progress of others through class reports and summations. There are numerous advantages to this type of class organization with teens, particularly if the group is a large one. They will want to write a three-act play, an ambitious undertaking at the outset. They will be willing to meet extra hours in addition to scheduled class time in order to work toward a polished script. Sometimes the assigned period does not provide the group enough time to function in any other way if the class is to fulfill the total idea of creative playwriting. In this setup much depends on the speed and dedication of the playwriting committee.

Writing or thinking of an idea is not writing a play. There must be action, dialogue, scenes that connect and have purpose.

Barbara Kamholz

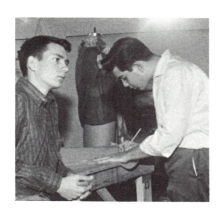

Playwriting, I have learned, is completely different from any other form of literature because all must be said instead of written.

Charles Wells

A playwriting committee writes either as a group or as individuals, functioning similarly to the way any class writes its play. In one committee they divided a story into French Scene Outlines,[8] with each student assigned one scene to be completed with dialogue by the following week. This assignment required outside work on the part of each person, but the committee in this instance consisted of exceptionally capable, responsible, interested students who were extremely serious about their work. It is obvious that a written play emerges rather quickly this way, but the result can also have weak scenes alternating with strong ones, a wide variety of style, and a lack of central unity in the finished work. One of the plays written in this manner was *Thunder 'N Blue Blazes*, but this play did not suffer because the major characters—Don Mosquito, Lady Bug, and Chigger—received consistent treatment in each episode despite the variety of writing styles in different scenes.

In one class another version of this writing method proved more successful——all the students undertook to write the same scene. At each session they read scenes and pooled ideas, writing the play in a stairstep progression. The group used a tape recorder to transcribe discussions and decisions. After each session the teacher took the written scenes and decisions and brought the master script up-to-date for the next session. Efficiency achieved with this group was a rewarding experience for all participants, but the teacher's work load doubled. Another group met with the teacher around a typewriter and wrote scenes session by session. A script develops twice as fast this way, but it does not always produce desired results. The teacher usually discovers that she is entirely too much in the forefront of the project; consequently the result frequently is inattention to individual concepts of character and their styles of expression.

Regardless of the methods used in writing dialogue, the teacher is final coordinator of the script and is responsible for pulling it together. She is the one who deletes superfluous dialogue, checks for a conclusion to subplots, and generally becomes the master secretary—sometimes even the master writer. She often assumes this latter responsibility because of the tight schedule that prevails. Time flies by all too rapidly as there are production assignments to complete and a performance deadline to meet. The extent to which the teacher contributes her talents is somewhat dependent upon the students. She must never do the work for the group, regardless of her own enthusiasm, unless it is mandatory to completion of the script by a set date. She must judge the maximum required of her, and if she does a major portion of the writing, editing, and assimilation of material, the students should not receive full credit for the script. They must earn the credit given them, for integrity in playwriting is a practice as well as a precept.

Casting

Original versions of plot and characters may be subject to change as dialogue is written, inasmuch as the group often will visualize a particular student in a part and write the dialogue with him in mind. The subject of casting comes up very early in writing sessions, and discussions of possible casting inevitably influence writing of dialogue for a character, even though there are constant reminders to be consistent with original interpretation. Of course the most interesting parts are not always the largest or the leading roles. One of the advantages of an original script is that development of his character is left to the student. He can often determine size and importance of his part by the way he develops it. It soon becomes apparent that casting an original play does not present the same problems as casting a published script. There are enough parts for the entire class; each part projects interesting development; the parts accommodate the exact number of boys and girls in the class; and the play is within the capabilities of the group performing it.

In most creative playwriting sessions there are more girls than boys. It is usually possible to solve this predicament coincidentally with development of the story and determination of characters. But when it appears that the magnitude of the problem requires consideration before story creation, the group can utilize its ingenuity in conceiving of the situation as a directive, stimulus, and problem to be solved. One class consisted of a large number of girls and only two boys. Obviously the Ideation Exercise centered on the problem of writing a play to include this group. Every student in the class had spent several summers at camp, and they soon discovered that a majority of the girls had attended the same camp. Location of the girls' camp directly across the lake from a boys' camp of the same name provided the stimulus for a plot. After some discussion the question arose as to whether or not a boy might have a girl's name. The conflicts incipient in such a situation are numerous; every character could be a prize part! With such a rollicking plot outline, the task lay in deciding what to include and what to delete. *Make Room for Francis* became a three-act play which warranted several sequels had there been more time.

With children, play casting is inherent in creation of characters. When a student has invented a character used in the play, he will expect to portray that character. For this reason it is almost impossible to separate the child from the character he has invented. And as the play develops through creative dramatic techniques and discussions, the child is simultaneously working on memorization, interpretation, and character portrayal. In a way rehearsals have already begun.

I learned how to go about criticizing a play.

Tony Abdo

The First Draft

After the first draft of a play is complete, it is advisable to read it to the entire class. At first there may be so much pleasure over completion of the script, that there seems to be little room for improvement. A playwriting committee, if it uses its material skillfully, will find the class a strong sounding board for its writing efforts. Some of the most productive work can come as a result of class criticism. The students should hear and discuss every comment so that reasons are clear on both sides. Sharing ideas and decisions promotes group cohesiveness and responsibility; it also provides those who have not served on the writing committee the opportunity to experience direct involvement with playwriting problems. Another advantage of this session is that the play undergoes objective evaluation. The listeners are attentive to the way lines read and the sound of dialogue. There are two inescapable and important functions of dialogue: it must advance the plot, or it must reveal characterization. This analysis demands intelligent, impersonal criticism. The student again must learn to let his work stand alone on its own integrity, but he must be willing to accept necessary changes.

After evaluation of the first draft, need for another draft will be evident. Each new draft improves the play, but usually time allows no more than three drafts: the first draft, a second working draft, and the final draft completed after performance of the play.

The Working Draft

Even though production is well underway when the working draft is complete, there are always opportunities to change the script if change will improve the overall concept of the play and its content. At this point, attention might focus on the freedom allowed student playwrights, in comparison with license taken with a published play. The students should know of responsibilities assumed by anyone granted production rights in addition to the protective features and rights allowed a playwright through copyrights and royalties. This is one of many ways to reinforce respect for another author's work. For the immediate playwrights, it may be necessary to release the second draft to a select group in the class in order that the others may begin work on the production itself.

INTEGRATING THE PRODUCTION

A play is written to be performed, but in creative playwriting there is not always a clear distinction between the processes of writing and producing. As character and story ideas were developing, sketches, designs, and a few props emerged which now become useful to design or completion of costumes, sets, and properties. Story and dialogue developed through improvisations and story dramatization, so in a way the play has been sketchily rehearsed. The task now is to assemble and integrate all of this activity and material for use in preparing the play for performance.

Design Ideas

Historical and technical data are readily available in costume, makeup, and scenery books. Of greater importance is the realization that there are many sources for design ideas. Inspiration can come from a painter's style, painting techniques, a mask, a tapestry, sculpture, figures on a vase, a frieze, another art form, and unlimited experimentation. The student should be equally as resourceful in design as he was in writing the play. If the play reflects a spirit and style more easily expressed in a particular art medium, this concept can provide inspiration for new design ideas. A particular artist's use of space, color, line, texture, light, and composition may excite a designer to absorb these influences into his own ideas of costume, makeup, props, sets, or lights. However, a student designer should realize that the greatest influence upon him is the play itself—its style and viewpoint. Structure and treatment will influence a design, just

The standard rigid form of structure is not solely to be strived for. A desirable effect may be achieved by changing scenery or sets while the play is in progress.

Marc Lang

84

as locale, season, and period of the play are important considerations. When a play is experimental in form, there is more freedom for design ideas than in a conventional drama.

Design concepts can be so imaginatively stimulating that they
suggest new approaches to directing, and the entire play may
change its visual form because of the force of design. Varied
performing areas offered students, ranging from a small,
irregular-shaped room to a conventional proscenium arch stage,
can create inspiration for the designer, director, actor, and playwright. Using this new and different frame of reference demands
greater ingenuity and imagination. Theater space also affects
the actor-audience relationship, a discovery which is both stimulating and challenging to inventive minds in theater. Limitations often imposed upon a producing group can stimulate far
more exciting inventiveness than the granting of every wish,
provided the group is aware of these limitations in advance and
uses them as a directive-stimulus. Much depends upon the
attitude and flexibility of the teacher.

Costumes and Makeup

When children begin to design costumes, they should have maximum freedom. Size and shape are important to them, and imaginative sculptural design may be more meaningful than conventional costume silhouette. First, in consideration of designs, originality and interpretation of character and play should take precedence over practicality. Character drawings and personality collages made earlier by the student can now expand into makeup and costume ideas. Selections of fabric in relation to requisites of color, texture, pattern, and weight are practical considerations. Even drawings of the character's physical appearance might suggest ways and means of evolving costumes.

If the class is producing a play from a theater study, they should know the important features of costumes from the period under study. Students working on Greek drama, for example, must observe and heed the significance of costume draping and its various effects. Consideration of fabrics, colors, borders, belting, jewelry, shoes, hair styles, hand props, and period silhouettes is requisite. One of the most important details to remember is that the children who will perform the play need adequate practice in wearing their costumes, moving in them, and learning to use them.

Teens discover that even a contemporary play requires a certain amount of study. Sources for modern references may be found in magazines, posters, books, photographs, movies, art, and by observing clothing, expressions, and habits of people. If time provides, the student will profit from fundamental pointers on basic costume and makeup design, including figure drawing, pencil sketches, watercolors, and other artistic work incorporating fabrics. Makeup should integrate with costume so that the character's appearance reflects a unified concept. Designs may originate on paper, but eventually they must be applied to the face for adjustment.

Sets and Props

Only as a last resort should the teacher obtain costumes, sets, and props needed for a production rather than supervise a class in the actual construction of them. She may have to rely on some available ready-made items, but whenever possible the student should experience building from his own designs. Then he learns the reason for detailed production notes, completely intelligible descriptions, and accurate dimensions. He will also understand why he should think practically and economically in relation to added scenes in his play involving set changes, and the complication of elaborate sets. Simplicity of production is

Everyone does his part, no matter how large or small, hard or easy. This teamwork gives them pride in the finished product, the play.

Eugenia Born

a desirable and often a necessary quality. After all, the primary emphasis of creative playwriting is on creation of script, not on perfection of production. Performance enables a class to evaluate the script and to understand its interpretation by other creative artists in the theater.

When production is in a well-equipped theater, it is difficult to refrain from utilizing expensive equipment readily available. This does not mean that the teacher should not explain to her students the technical possibilities of set changes, lighting, and special effects, but that in working with children, it is wiser to keep all effects simple so that the class can both create and control them. This is the constructive way to encourage student resourcefulness.

After the children have sketched sets for their play, they must adapt these plans to the space available. A student's experience with set production should consist of more than design exercises. He should learn manual skills useful to set construction within his own capabilities. If examples are available of ground-plans, elevation drawings, color sketches, working drawings, and models from other plays, the teacher is justified in departing from the immediate project to discuss the step-by-step process of set design. She might also suggest pointers on fundamental stage design, research, technical layouts, and scenery types and styles. Age and experience of the students will determine the extent of material presented, although with beginning students a brief introduction can include pictures from books, authentic designs, and photographs. Then if a student is interested in this phase of theater, he will have some conception of how and where to begin.

Lighting

Lighting is one of the most fascinating aspects of technical theater. Students are always intensely interested in and intrigued by the magic of the panel board, types of lighting equipment, and special effect machines. They not only want to see "how lights work," but they want to manipulate the dimmers themselves. There can be great excitement in discovering what dimmers do, the effects of colored gelatin, the way to connect lights, and the procedure for lighting a specific show. Detail and amount of information covered will depend upon the experience of the teacher, interests and ages of the students, facilities available, and the time allowed for this phase of theater production.

Sound

Sound effects, both live and recorded, often evolve from an earlier exercise. If the students used music for a movement exercise in character or story ideation, this same composition could now serve as mood music for the play, if it is suitable. A teacher can delegate complete responsibility for sound effects to a teen-ager, because he is usually willing to spend many hours finding just the right sound for a show; however, he may need specific instruction along with this responsibility. If the class constructs original instruments or sound effects in an early exercise, these might be useful throughout the show. Total effect is more unusual when the children make all their own sounds, but sometimes there is no substitute for appropriate recorded music. Musical sound should never be larger than the play itself, a frequent risk when children's plays use recorded music.

Publicity

Publicity and promotion are vital to the life of a play, but a creative playwriting class rarely has time to explore this area. Sometimes a class may design posters and a program for their play. Teens may even find time to work on advertising schemes. Students should receive a glimpse into methods for creating an image of a play in the minds of prospective ticket holders, an image which not only sells the play but also arouses interest in the entire production.

Stage Management and Backstage Crews

Few students are aware of the sizable responsibility and scope of activities of the stage manager and his crews. The ideal way to learn these duties is for one class to work backstage for another class in production, and then reverse the process. Often this is not feasible, and the solution is to give students who have shorter roles in the current play major responsibilities backstage during performance. The greater responsibility given students in ''running a show,'' the more mature their attitudes will be toward the total work involved in theatrical production.

Rehearsals and Crew Calls

Conducting rehearsals and production laboratory work at the same time can be a formidable challenge to the teacher as well as the students. The easiest method is to be well advanced in rehearsals before production crews begin to function on a routine schedule. It is simple to arrange crew work according to production needs. If the play contains scenes which do not require all students on stage simultaneously those students not in rehearsal can participate in crew work. There will always be days when either crew work or rehearsal consumes all available times; otherwise, appropriate assignments can involve the entire class working at a fairly even pace.

In teen classes, while a playwriting committee is at work, the rest of the class can begin production lab activities immediately. Students who do not have major writing assignments might assume greater responsibilities on the production staff. A teacher must work out a pattern of equilization in status of playwriting, production staff, and play casting, in order to satisfactorily distribute work load and credits.

Dialogue memorization is not as difficult with original scripts as with a published play. Students find it easier to commit to memory their own dialogue than to learn the unfamiliar lines of another author. They have created the ideas; the emotion of the scene and character motivation are theirs alone. The stickler for memorization is the eight-, nine-, or ten-year-old who becomes glued to the script in his hand. To prevent this, rehearsals of scenes using creative dramatics techniques will help the child relate to ideas and emotions behind his words. The teacher can also return to earlier exercises which developed the same emotion in movement, pantomime, or sound.

One cast used movement studies to create physical attitudes for character movement when they worked out character portrayals. The exercise was so effective that it was easy to refer to it again during preliminary exercises before rehearsals. The teacher gave each student the action word most applicable to his character: *punch, press, float, dab, flick, glide, slash,* and *wring.* These are terms developed by Rudolph von Laban in *The Mastery of Movement,*[9] but simplified presentations are possible for children. They motivate a response which reveals itself through character movement and in outward physical expression. The student easily comprehends the meaning of these action words and does not hesitate in using them to obtain a character portrayal. Since children instinctively respond to any activity in movement, this is a particularly effective exercise for reminding the class of their characterizations before rehearsals begin.

The Tragedy of Orpheus and Eurydice developed essentially through improvisation, story dramatization, and individual writing. The children did not receive the script until they had almost completely memorized it; thus there were no mental blocks concerning perfect memorization. All of this evolved as a natural consequence through repetition of rehearsals. The children came to know their play so well through their writings and playmaking that dialogue came easily. Movement exercises appropriate for the Greek character and attitudes were nearly always a part of the beginning rehearsals. As a result eventual performance maintained a high level of sensitivity throughout.

A playwright-actor has a head start over the performer of a published script. Inasmuch as he has absorbed background knowledge of character and plot while writing the play, he does not need to read and research the script from a totally unfamiliar background. While he creates the play, lines become so familiar that he often commits them to memory long before rehearsals begin. Not only does he know his own lines, but he has memorized the lines and actions of other characters leading to early establishment of cues.

Directing

Since directing is primarily the teacher's role she will benefit greatly from the activities which have preceded rehearsals. Both she and her students already understand the play and motivation of its characters so that it should be easy to give and take direction. If time allows students may even block some of the scenes themselves—in fact they probably did this in original dramatizations, but final authority on all blocking belongs to the teacher-director.

The first difficulty she may face lies in helping the cast realize the difference between clarity in their own minds and clarity of presentation to an audience. Character portrayal requires concentration, and players cannot enjoy the same freedom as in earlier improvisations. Character rhythm must be clear and consistent; action must show motivation and timing; cues must come at the right second they are needed. Once set up and decided upon interpretation must not change. Transitions between scenes must have motivation, and the play must build to a series of peaks and to one definite climax. Thus, and only through these attributes, the play becomes a *living* experience.

It is common knowledge and common experience that a delightful play can completely fail in production if the director and cast miss the inherent style of performance indicated in the script. Some of the magic is lost as well as the meaning. This does not often happen, however, when the teacher is alert to the personalities of her students, for the style of the play is a reflection of their viewpoints and personalities. Occasionally a teacher may not be able to discern the individual styles of her students, and so she misses the potential viewpoint of their characterizations. Most frequently the reason for this is that the teacher herself does not have adequate experience in acting or directing styles. In one such situation the problem lay in the fact that the teacher had visualized in her own mind what the character should be rather than relating the character to the student himself. As a result she had no concept of the root of her problem and needed an immediate objective evaluation. A few teachers have difficulty learning how to develop conglomerate personalities into a single, integrated viewpoint which will result in a unified, consistent style of performance. It is not an easy task.

It's a lot easier to act out your part if you've been writing the script for 80 billion years! You know your character so much better than if someone came up, handed you a script, and said, "Go to it!"

Janett Massey

Another error occurs in concentrating too much on the style of the set and costumes, almost forgetting to focus on acting style. This oversight may seem unthinkable, but it is easy to understand when one realizes that a teacher may have several classes in creative playwriting and her own focus becomes distorted with production details. The pressure of time remaining to prepare the play for performance may lead the teacher to believe that she has no chance to develop the indicated style. One of the great advantages to working on theater studies as a format for creative playwriting is that it is often possible to eliminate this time pressure. Creative exercises utilized to prepare the student for playwriting also develop a sense of period style. Although plays which come from a theater study are not as lengthy as those developed through single, independent Ideation Exercises, the more important accomplishments are the deeper awareness of style and a conscious use of it.

An excellent example of a play that loses some if its charm with the absence of proper style is *The Golden Teardrops*. Although this play is not a melodrama, it does possess stock characters. An exaggerated style of performance with precise timing would portray a more honest concept of the play than presentation as a fantasy. On several occasions when this has been the case, the play has lost much of its humor and the production been less interesting. The teacher enters a different phase when rehearsals begin, just as the students are no longer playwrights but actors. The teacher becomes the director who studies the viewpoint of the script and the personalities of her students in a new light and concentrates upon blending them into a style of performance. In order to achieve the best production possible, the director must condition her cast to the discipline of acting and the concepts of the play as indicated, uniting them for ensemble playing in a consistent and imaginative interpretation of characters and script. Accomplishment of this goal usually entails more than the average number of rehearsals. But by this time students should have established a standard for themselves and for the play. Achieving this standard is a readily accepted goal notwithstanding the amount of work involved. They realize that the quality of their production depends upon hard work as well as cooperation between cast, crews, and director. In the final analysis, it is the director who pulls everything together in a coordinated, smooth performance.

FIRST PERFORMANCE

Nothing quite equals the thrill of a first performance. There is a feeling of anticipation in the audience and a sense of challenge behind the curtain before the play begins. The performance is the students' way of seeking approval and of gaining reward. Some of the least impressive scripts have resulted in such enthusiastic productions that the actors' joyful presentation completely obscured the play's weaknesses. Audience applause is like a gold star of approbation. It matters little if the play is not the best production in the world or if the performance of the actors is far from perfect. Recognition gives each student a sense of contributing, commending him on his efforts, enabling him to grow because of new belief in himself and in his abilities. The student gains immeasurably in self-confidence and fulfillment. To extend this experience, there should be at least two presentations of an original script; additional performances increase the student's awareness of variations in audience response and in his own performances. The teacher should take notes on each performance and distribute them to the cast at the end of every show. Then at the next class session, the cast can make an evaluation of successful and non-successful aspects of the entire production.

THE FINAL DRAFT

Each student enjoys a personal triumph in performance of his play, but he must realize that this is only the beginning of his knowledge of drama and all that creates the experience. All the virtues and faults will now become apparent, and the playwrights must return to work and complete their final draft. Last minute production changes which proved successful become a part of the script, along with additional changes needed in the play. The final draft should include production notes and ground-plans if possible. Finally, the script is complete with the addition of the names of the original cast and the teacher-director, and with notation of the place and date of the premiere performance.

1 Portion of a paper on learning experiences from writing an original play in Teen Theater, written by Joann Schaible, Dallas Theater Center, 1966.

2 An *antagonist* is the adversary of the hero or the one who creates conflict.

3 A *protagonist* is the leading or central character in a play.

4 A *pointer* is an idea in dialogue or action which indicates future direction of the play.

5 A *plant* is a subtle form of preparation that justifies and enhances the emotional effect of later action.

6 A *subplot* is a story of secondary importance to the primary story of a play but is a part of the total plot.

7 Structure of a play as outlined by Gene McKinney, playwright-in-residence at Trinity University, San Antonio, Texas.

8 *French Scene Outline* is a method of outlining a play by dividing the story into scenes according to subject matter or the entrance or exit of a major character.

9 Rudolph von Laban, *The Mastery of Movement* (London, 1960).

Our play has shown me that behind what the
audience sees there goes a lot of work and
understanding. Our play may have a collection of
thoughts but it contained viewpoints, beliefs,
and ideas as well.

Sherry Wigley

LEARNING EXPERIENCES

Creative Playwriting contributes in innumerable ways to the growth and learning experiences of a student. It begins by freeing his imagination, enlarging his vision, and stimulating his powers of observation. He learns to make practical use of his knowledge and past experiences. He comes to believe in himself by discovering that he is capable of producing ideas which are both imaginative and useful. In this way he becomes aware of his creative talents.

In group activity he learns to work with others and he becomes more tolerant, yet more discerning. He also learns to listen. Language and ideas heard may sharply contrast with his own background or training, but listening with respect and an open mind often broadens his viewpoints. He begins to recognize value in new and different thoughts, and the importance of contributions from many sources. He realizes also that his ideas are not always the best, but that he is capable of selecting the most appropriate ones even if it means rejecting his own.

While creating his play, the student becomes aware of personality traits, character motivation, and the consequences of words and actions. As he develops character, plot, and dialogue, he cannot help but bring his own ideas, feelings, and experiences into focus. This provides an emotional outlet, at the same time bringing him to a point where he can analyze a thought or act objectively. He eventually arrives at a critical evaluation of his own work, an evaluation which reflects some degree of accuracy. Through all of this he is learning to organize his own thoughts and concepts in a creative media. And he is discovering the value of working in different mediums of expression while continually experimenting with different ways to communicate. He knows, too, the satisfaction of completing a project. From this total experience he begins to develop a viewpoint toward theater as both an art and a craft. He recognizes the work that goes into playwriting and is more aware of the power of words and ideas. His cognizance of all artistic areas in theater stimulates appreciation for the value of individual contributions. Every effort gains respect.

In a more personal way he is learning the importance of self-discipline, concentration, and flexibility of thought. But he is also learning the value of postponing judgment so that an idea has a chance to grow and develop. In varying degrees he develops confidence and initiative as he begins to exercise independent thought. Perhaps more important, he begins to demonstrate faith in himself. When this happens a new energy bursts forth, a new self-image emerges. The creative center of the student has become active, deepening his sense of worth. His future efforts may be highly different from his original ones, for his motivation directed him toward a very personal kind of creative achievement.

If a student works within the total experience of creative playwriting he can begin to attain many of these creative accomplishments. Growth and learning are dependent upon both him and his teacher. They result from the efforts of both. At the same time inner growth is not confined to the student. In some ways the teacher's learning is even greater. She not only learns from her students, but she is growing from her own experiences. A teacher's capacity to learn from a student about ideas and individual expression increases with the ability to draw out potential in that student and then recognize what she has helped to release. Then she must often motivate a desire within the student to put his creative powers to work. Learning gleaned from this process is immeasurable. Excitement over every achievement and discovery is contagious. It immediately affects the efforts of her students, for they depend upon one another for inspiration and encouragement.

Through the meeting of minds in creative action, a teacher ceases to be "the teacher." She is a joint participant in a learning experience that provides untold discoveries for each person about himself and about those around him. Each encounter reenforces her own sensitivity to the inner growth of her students and to the nature of ideas—their abilities to grow and flower. Sometimes her energies support directive action and at other times quiet reflection. During this period she learns the value of waiting—a time when her subconscious mind works for her. Through experience she discovers valuable truths concerning the nature of the creative process.

One of the sure signs of her mature growth is in allowing what seems to be chaos while students work out their ideas. She learns to distinguish between incoherent, haphazard activity and the free form of experimental probing necessary to creative discovery. This perhaps is one of the most important lessons any teacher can learn. Yet acquiring the courage to apply what she knows is still another achievement.

Growth and learning of both teacher and student are relative to prior creative action and their sensitivities to future experiences. They have no limitations. One thing is certain: creative playwriting can provide an exciting involvement with original ideas and with the process of creating theater.

Not only did I learn a tremendous amount
about acting and the other phases
of theater, but I also learned
to be open and receptive to
new ideas in theater, and to be
adventurous, creative, and
courageous in trying new ideas—in
experimenting and striving to use
my imagination to the fullest.

Honey Hobson

NINE ORIGINAL PLAYS

written and produced by children
and teens ages 6 through 18

THE TROUBLEMAKER

a play in one act

from a story idea by Sallie Baker

written by 6- through 9-year-old children

supervised by Ruth Byers

The Troublemaker was written and produced by Baylor Children's Theater, Waco, Texas, in the spring of 1956. The student playwrights were also the original cast.

The Troublemaker	SALLIE BAKER
The Wind	LINDA MARTINSEN
The Sun	LESLIE SEGAL
1st Thinker	MARY JANE WEST
2nd Thinker	LYNN CARROLL
3rd Thinker	SUSAN RHODES
Spring Goddess	SARA SMITH
Rose Pink, her assistant	LINDA LUTZ
Juno	JANIS FARROW
The lamb	PAM BAILEY
First Statue	SKIPPY WHITCRAFT
Second Statue	ANNE LITTLE
Third Statue	NANCY RHODES
Fourth Statue	MARCIA GOODWIN
Uncle Dill Pickle	W. A. LITTLE
Peppermint Kid	DOUGLAS HUGHES
Crunchy Cracker	PATRICIA BROWN
Cinnamon Fairy	SARAH SEGREST
Perfume King	ALLEN SMITH
Dog (Jupiter)	PAT BURCH
Cat (Venus, Goddess of Love)	MARY SUSAN BIRD
Cow (God of the Seasons)	ANNE RUSSELL
Troublemaker's Girlfriend	PAM BAILEY

PLACE: In the land of Trouble

TIME: Almost all the time

The set is designed to represent four locales: a hill, the forest, a temple, and a store in town. Downstage left is a grassy hill with a puppet flower growing on top. Several steps to the right and upstage is a rock for sitting. Above, at center left, there are six cut-out trees whose branches are like a two-page calendar. By turning the calendar branches, the seasons change. Three trees can be winter or spring and three can be winter or fall. At present they are all winter and should never be included in the lighting area of the hill. If necessary changes are made, however, they can be spring trees all at once and then serve as a background for the first scene.

In center stage there is a platform with steps which is the floor of a Greek temple. A simple, square altar is in the center of the temple.

At center right there is a stylized counter and shelf which is part of the food market. Later, the food people will sit on the shelf and have to jump off the counter to the floor. Since the play progresses from one locale to another, both area lighting and a follow spot can be effective in each scene though they are not imperative.

When the play begins, there is a sound of running feet and the Troublemaker, tired and out of breath, throws himself on the soft grass of the little hill. For a minute he just lies there and rests. Then he raises his head and comes face to face with the puppet flower, who, being a little shy, begins to back away.

TROUBLEMAKER. You aren't afraid of me, are you little flower? If you aren't, you're the only one who isn't. Everybody runs away from me. (*Begins to sob*) I just can't understand it. (*The Little flower moves closer with concern*) I don't mean . . . I really don't mean to . . . I just try to be helpful. (*He gets on his knees and moves closer to talk to the little flower who listens attentively*) You see, little flower, I need a friend. If only you and I could be friends . . .

(*Suddenly the wind blows in*)

WIND. (*To the audience*) See that little man there? He's a troublemaker.

(*The Troublemaker and flower continue to talk in pantomime for they do not hear the wind or see the sun as she comes out on the other side of the Troublemaker*)

SUN. He gets all his friends into trouble; even his girlfriend!

WIND. (*To flower*) Watch out, little flower. Stay away from him. He's a troublemaker.

(*The little flower takes the warning and disappears*)

TROUBLEMAKER. See here, now. What are you trying to do? Take all my friends away from me? I didn't do anything to you.

WIND. No, you haven't done anything to me, but you have to nearly everyone else. Do you realize, little man, that there are only a few more people left in the world?

SUN. And there won't be that many if you don't stop getting people into trouble.

TROUBLEMAKER. But I can't help myself. I try to help them when they need me and the only thing I do is get them into more trouble and get myself in trouble, too.

WIND. Just name us one time when you've tried to help someone.

TROUBLEMAKER. Well, I guess it all started with my girlfriend. I had to get a job to make some money to buy her a gold tooth.

SUN. A gold tooth?

TROUBLEMAKER. Yes, you see, one day she had an awful bad toothache and the dentist's office was closed so I tried to help her pull the tooth out. I put a string around this one (*Points to front tooth*) and pulled it out.

WIND. Well?

TROUBLEMAKER. Later, I found out she had meant another one back here, see? (*Points to jaw tooth in back of mouth*)

100

SUN. (*Curious to see and hear more*) Uh-huh!

WIND. (*Bored*) I'm not surprised.

TROUBLEMAKER. (*To the sun*) I pulled the wrong one out, that's all. (*To the wind*) And now she has a hole in the front of her mouth . . . a big black one. (*Shakes his head sadly*)

SUN. (*Reflecting his sadness*) Oh. So you had to work to get your girlfriend a gold tooth. What did you do?

TROUBLEMAKER. (*Beginning to feel a little important*) Well, I got a job as kitchen boy in the king's palace. I had been there only two days when the king had a birthday. Everyone was to make the king a birthday cake and the prettiest one would be sent to his table, and carried in by the cook who baked it.

SUN. (*Excited*) Yes! Go on!

WIND. (*Interested but skeptical*) Well?

TROUBLEMAKER. I wanted to make the king the biggest cake in the kitchen, so I gathered up all the yeast I could find and baked a cake. But you know, an amazing thing happened.

SUN. Yesssssssss!

TROUBLEMAKER. As soon as the cake began to bake, it grew larger and larger and larger and larger and larger until it filled the whole kitchen.

SUN. Oh!

TROUBLEMAKER. And it still kept growing until it came through the windows and out through the chimney and into the ballroom and out into the first street, the second street and soon it was as big as the palace.

SUN. What happened?

TROUBLEMAKER. The King was awfully mad.

SUN. He was?

TROUBLEMAKER. He was furious.

SUN. And what did he do?

TROUBLEMAKER. He locked up the whole town.

SUN. Everybody?

TROUBLEMAKER. Everyone but the people who lived outside the city limits.

SUN. Well, how did you get away?

TROUBLEMAKER. (*Growing more excited and going into even more detail*) When the cake began to swell, it made funny noises. It puffed and spewed and crackled and made such a fuss that the chief cook got mad and ran me out of the kitchen. And so (*Meekly*) here I am.

SUN. (*Breathlessly*) Yes, we see.

WIND. (*Disgustedly*) We see all too well.

TROUBLEMAKER. (*To wind*) You aren't mad with me, are you?

WIND. No, but we are going to try to keep what's left of the world out of trouble. (*Beginning to blow away*) All the flowers and leaves of the forest will stay out of the way for I am going to blow them to safety. I'll even blow the sun out of the way, for we can't do without youuuuuuuuuuuu (*Blows the sun offstage*). Goodbye, little man. And remember, stay out of trouble. (*Blows offstage*)

(*The little troublemaker looks around and sees he is all alone again. He looks down where the little flower was and even she has not returned. He falls down on the ground and begins to cry again*)

TROUBLEMAKER. Oh me, I do wish I wouldn't be so much trouble. (*He cries harder*)

(*Suddenly the three thinkers pop up from behind him*)

1ST THINKER. You wouldn't get anyone into trouble if you used us, your thinkers, every once in a while. We don't think you like us.

TROUBLEMAKER. (*Surprised, but he knows who they are*) Oh, but I do. I do!

2ND THINKER. Then why don't you use us?

3RD THINKER. We'll try to help you if you'll only use us.

TROUBLEMAKER. I will. I will. From now on, I will.

1ST THINKER. (*Holding arm straight out to the right side*) Promise to use me in the morning?

(*The little troublemaker now stands up to face them and as he repeats the words and gestures after each one, his hands suggest the movement of the hands of a clock*)

TROUBLEMAKER. (*Repeating gesture*) I promise.

2ND THINKER. (*Pointing right hand straight up*) Promise to use me in the afternoon?

TROUBLEMAKER. (*Repeating gesture*) I promise.

3RD THINKER. (*Holding arm straight out to left side*) Promise to use me at night?

TROUBLEMAKER: (*Repeating gesture*) I promise.

THINKERS. (*Together*) Then remember, you promised . . . (*They disappear*)

(*The little troublemaker now feels much better. He turns around, yawns, and stretches*)

TROUBLEMAKER. Ho-hum. I'm so tired of being alone. I think I'll just find someone to talk to.

(*He begins to walk; he picks up a rock and throws it at a tree. He skips and whistles. Then he sees the Goddess of Spring busily painting the tree leaves green. She has just begun and most of the trees are still bare from winter*)

GODDESS OF SPRING. (*Singing as she paints*) Tum-te-te-tum tum-da tum. There! La-la-la-la! (*She continues to hum*)

(*The little troublemaker watches her for a few minutes then decides to speak*)

TROUBLEMAKER. (*Softly*) Hi.

(*Silence*)

Hi!

(*The Goddess still does not hear*)

Hello!

(*When she still does not hear him, he moves closer and tugs her sleeve*)

Hi!

GODDESS. Oh, hello. (*She continues painting*)

TROUBLEMAKER. What are you doing?

GODDESS. I'm painting.

TROUBLEMAKER. What are you painting?

GODDESS. I'm painting the leaves green.

TROUBLEMAKER. Are you causing spring?

GODDESS. Would you like that?

TROUBLEMAKER. Oh, yes, 'cause everyone is happy in the springtime.

GODDESS. Well, I try to make people happy.

(*Silence as troublemaker thinks a moment*)

TROUBLEMAKER. Could——could I try to make people happy, too?

GODDESS. Why? Don't you make people happy?

TROUBLEMAKER. Well . . . sometimes.

GODDESS. (*Turning to look at the eager face of the little troublemaker*) Well——alright, here. Try it.

TROUBLEMAKER. (*Beginning to paint*) Oh, this is fun! Can I have some more paint?

(*The little troublemaker turns to ask her again when she doesn't answer and he realizes she has disappeared. So he begins to look around to see if he can find some for himself. Under one of the trees he finds several buckets of paint and he runs over to them*)

TROUBLEMAKER. Oh, here is the paint. (*Looking at all the cans*) Let's see. (*Spelling*) G-R-E-E-N. Does that spell green or red? Ummmmmmmm must spell red. (*He puts it aside and turns to the next can and spells*) R-E-D . . . that's green! (*He grabs the bucket of paint and returns to the trees yet to be painted*) Well, here goes. I think I'll just close my eyes and paint everything!

(*He begins to paint furiously and since he has his eyes closed, he does not realize that he is not painting the trees for spring but for fall! The Goddess of Spring returns with Rose Pink, her assistant, and they both stand shocked at what they see*)

GODDESS. Oh, What have you done? Rose Pink, look!

ROSE PINK. He's ruined it!

(*When the troublemaker hears them, he opens his eyes and turns to look at the trees*)

TROUBLEMAKER. Ooooooooooh! That doesn't look like spring.

GODDESS. (*Trying to hold her temper*) Noooooooooooo.

ROSE PINK. It certainly does not!

TROUBLEMAKER. That——looks——like——fall!

GODDESS. (*Sharply*) YES!

TROUBLEMAKER. Oh, what have I done?

GODDESS. (*Thoroughly disgusted*) Oh, nothing much. You've just caused the whole world to skip two seasons, that's all!

TROUBLEMAKER. Oh, now I've gotten the whole world into trouble. (*He goes away crying*)

ROSE PINK. And spring is the most beautiful season of all! (*She begins to help the spring Goddess collect her paints and they exit off stage left*)

(*As the little troublemaker walks by the temple, he hears a sheep bleating*)

TROUBLEMAKER. What's that? Someone's crying louder than I am.

(*He looks up at the temple and sees that the roof is held up by four statues of Greek Goddesses. He walks up the steps and looks in*)

Why, here's a temple and there's a sheep tied up by the altar. Now who would want to hurt a little sheep like that? I'll go see if I can free him.

(*The sheep continues to bleat until he releases it. It runs off and the Goddess Juno enters*)

JUNO. Thank you, little man. (*Troublemaker draws back in fear*) Don't be afraid. I'm Juno, Queen of the Gods. You have released my favorite lamb from the altar of my enemy, Goddess Diana. Now it will not be killed and I must reward you for your good deed.

TROUBLEMAKER. You mean I did something good?

JUNO. Yes, you did, and I have a present for you. (*She gives him a wand*) With this wand you have the power to make three wishes come true. Choose them well; then cast the spell. (*She disappears*)

TROUBLEMAKER. (*Hardly believing what has happened to him*) A wand . . . three . . . wishes. (*He walks a few minutes as he thinks*) I wonder . . . I wonder if I could get everybody out of trouble again? Suppose it doesn't work? Let's see. How can I test it? Hmmmmmm.

(*He looks at the temple for a minute and then gets an idea*)

These statues holding up the temple look so tired! I bet they wouldn't want to hold up a roof if they were really alive.

(*He looks at his wand, holds it out toward the statues and closes his eyes while taking a deep breath*)

I wish that these statues would come alive!

(*Very slowly he opens his eyes to see what is happening. The statues begin to move: They turn their heads, open and shut their eyes. They begin to discover themselves*)

STATUE 1. My goodness. I feel different today.

STATUE 2. I feel warmer today.

STATUE 3. Somehow I don't remember feeling before.

STATUE 4. I feel like something is pressing on my head.

STATUE 1. Now that you mention it, I do too.

STATUE 2. Me, too.

STATUE 3. Me, too.

STATUE 4. Me, too.

STATUE 1. You know, I feel like walking.

STATUE 2. And I feel like jumping and running.

STATUE 3. I feel like shouting.

STATUE 4. And I feel like hopping. Why don't we?

STATUE 1. Okay.

STATUE 2. Okay.

STATUE 3. Okay.

STATUE 4. Okay. Let's!

(*Boom! They all step out from the temple and the roof falls down*)

ALL. (*Together in mock surprise*) We must have been holding up the roof.

STATUE 1. Oh dear.

STATUE 2. Oh me.

STATUE 3. Oh my.

STATUE 4. Uh-oh.

104

STATUE 1. It was too heavy anyway. Now we can do all the things we've been wanting to do.

(*They make a circle and dance while walking, jumping, running, shouting, and hopping, and finally exit off left. The little troublemaker has been standing by in shocked silence. He can hardly believe his eyes. Slowly he turns, shakes his head in disbelief and begins to walk away*)

TROUBLEMAKER. I just couldn't have really done all that.

(*The angry wind blows in and is constantly moving, blowing and puffing he is so mad*)

WIND. Now, see what you've done? You've made the statues come alive and Diana is going to be angry. She may even get all the strong people left in the world to hold up the roof to the Temple. And the strong people are getting weaker since you changed the seasons. There was no spring for planting seed to grow food!

(*The wind angrily blows out as the troublemaker calls*)

TROUBLEMAKER. But I didn't mean to.

(*Suddenly the little thinkers appear*)

1ST THINKER. No, you never mean to do what you do, but you do it anyway.

2ND THINKER. You'd better watch out. There are very few people left now.

3RD THINKER. Better think of US!

TROUBLEMAKER. Oh, I will. I will. I promise I will.

1ST THINKER. (*With appropriate gesture*) That's right. Use us in the morning.

2ND THINKER. (*With gesture*) Use us in the afternoon.

3RD THINKER. (*With gesture*) And use us at night.

TROUBLEMAKER. I'm going to do it. (*Begins to think*) Well, now I know what to do. (*As He thinks out loud, he sees the market shelf of food*) I'll just change all that food in the market into people. They can hold the Temple roof up! Oh, boy . . . then the Goddess Diana won't take all the strong people left in the world.

1ST THINKER. (*Running after him*) No, no! That's not right. That will only get you into more trouble.

TROUBLEMAKER. That's what I'll do alright.

2ND THINKER. You aren't using us . . . and you said you would.

TROUBLEMAKER. Here I go . . .

3RD THINKER. He's not listening. Oohhhhhhhhh, watch out World!

TROUBLEMAKER. (*Holding wand toward shelf*) I wish, I wish, I wish *everything on this shelf would turn into big strong people!*

(*Slowly the shelf people come alive; the little thinkers have covered their heads and are stooping ostrich-like; and the troublemaker is so excited he can hardly contain himself as he watches*)

SOUR PICKLE. What's going on here anyway? Who took me out of my bottle? I'll dry up out here.

PEPPERMINT KID. (*In Western drawl*) Don't fuss so much, Uncle Dill. Why, I haven't felt this good since they first made me at the candy factory. Boy, I feel peppy and rarin' to go. Ride 'em Cowboy! (*He pantomimes riding and shoots his guns*)

CRUNCHY CRACKER. (*Stuttering*) S-s-s-s-s-s-s-ufficating in that box. What's going on anyway? How did I get out?

CINNAMON FAIRY. We're all people now. Look at my wings. I must be a fairy. (She looks herself over) I was a cinnamon drop and now I'm a cinnamon fairy. (She whirls around) I've always wanted to be a fairy.

PEPPERMINT KID. And to think I was a peppermint stick. Whoa, there, horsey!

CRUNCHY CRACKER. And I was a saltine cracker. And you were a pickle, Uncle Dill.

UNCLE DILL. And a lot happier I was, too.

(A muffled cry is heard from a bottle on the shelf)

PEPPERMINT KID. Quiet! Did you hear a noise?

UNCLE DILL. What noise? I didn't hear any noise.

FAIRY. Shhhhhhhh. (Muffled cry again) I hear it. I hear it.

CRACKER. I do believe I hear it.

FAIRY. It's here. It's here. (Runs over to the bottle. Everyone else draws back afraid)

KID. (Trying to be brave) Stand back. I'll open it.

(He opens the bottle and the perfume king comes out. There is silence as all fall under the spell of his fragrance)

FAIRY. (Dizzy) Oh, what a divine fragrance!

UNCLE DILL. Humph! And just who are you, young man?

PERFUME KING. I'm the powerful perfume king. (So proud and confident of his looks and his fragrance, he moves among the group)

FAIRY. He's affecting me. (She swoons)

CRUNCHY CRACKER. M-m-me, to-to-too! (She swoons)

PEPPERMINT KID. I believe he's affecting me. (Staggers)

TROUBLEMAKER. (To audience) He's affecting me, too. I'd better tell them why I turned them into real people before they all faint.

(He turns to the group and tries to get their attention)

Quiet. Quiet. Hush up. I want your attention, please. I have something to tell you.

(They all turn and look at him. Those on the floor sit up and listen)

I was the one who turned you into real people. But I did it for a reason.

UNCLE DILL. (Looking more closely at the troublemaker and trying to figure him out) Oh?

TROUBLEMAKER. You see, I need you strong people to hold up the roof of the Temple. (Silence) It's over there. (He points. They look. Silence) Would you please go over and hold it up?

PEPPERMINT KID. What?

KING. What?

ALL. (Very angry) What? (They all begin to speak at once and the little troublemaker backs away as they go into a huddle to discuss the problem. The thinkers have been watching the scene and now as the troublemaker walks near them, they have only one thing to say:)

THINKERS. (Together) We told you so!

(The troublemaker hangs his head. Then the group breaks and the perfume king comes forward as the speaker for the group)

PERFUME KING. No. We have decided that we do not want to hold your roof up. We're too sleepy. (He extends his arms and as though casting a spell, everyone gets dizzy again) Instead, we've decided to dance and have fun. (All cheer) Won't you join us?

ALL. Yes, please come dance with us.

TROUBLEMAKER. (*Shaking his head sadly*) No, thank you. You have to be happy to sing and dance. And I'm afraid I'll never be happy again.

PERFUME KING. Then, goodbye, little friend. And thank you.

(*The king lifts his robes and leads the group off stage right, singing and dancing as they go. The troublemaker runs after them to call them back and unknowingly drops his wand. The little troublemaker now turns and walks slowly downstage to the little hill*)

TROUBLEMAKER. I just knew I was doing the right thing this time. But now it can't get any worse. There wasn't much food left after we skipped a season. Now there isn't any at all for I turned them all into people. (*He sits on the rock and begins to cry*)

(*The sun comes out*)

SUN. Time passes.

(*The winds blows in*)

WIND. One year, two years, three years.

SUN. And the poor little Troublemaker cried all the time because he hadn't used his thinkers.

(*Slowly the Troublemaker dries his tears and looks around. He seems to remember something*)

TROUBLEMAKER. (*Calling*) Thinkers? Thinkers? Where are you? Please help me.

(*The three thinkers suddenly appear*)

1ST THINKER. It's about time you called us.

ALL. (*Together*) Here we are.

TROUBLEMAKER. (*Running to them*) I'm so glad to see you.

2ND THINKER. We'll try to help you.

3RD THINKER. Yes, we will.

1ST THINKER. (*Sitting on the floor*) I'll think all morning.

2ND THINKER. (*Kneeling on the floor*) I'll think all afternoon.

3RD THINKER.(*Sitting on the floor*) And I'll think . . . (*Sees troublemaker watching him*) No, let's all think together. (*All four sit in various positions thinking*)

ALL. Think——think——think——think . . .

SUN. Until the sun went down (*Disappears*)

WIND. And the wind blew cold. (*Blows offstage*)

TROUBLEMAKER. Well, this is my last piece of bread, and about the only bread in the world, I guess. (*Begins to munch on the bread*) If there were only some way I could get everyone out of trouble.

(*In the distance there is the sound of a dog, a cat, and a cow*)

What's that?

1ST THINKER. I didn't hear anything.

2ND THINKER. Don't bother me. I'm thinking.

3RD THINKER. I'm getting tired of thinking.

TROUBLEMAKER. Oh, no, little Thinkers. Please, please don't stop thinking. You're the only hope I have.

(The animals are heard again)

There. I told you I heard a sound.

(Jumps up and goes down right to look offstage)

Who's there?

(A cat enters)

1ST THINKER. A cat!

(Dog enters)

2ND THINKER. A dog!

(Cow enters)

3RD THINKER. A cow!

(The animals are sad and hungry. They begin to nuzzle up to the troublemaker)

THINKERS: They look hungry.

TROUBLEMAKER. They do, don't they? *(Pause)* I wish I could help them.

THINKERS. *(Excited and pleased)* You do?

1ST THINKER. Why don't you share your bread with them?

TROUBLEMAKER. But this is the only bread I have.

2ND THINKER. That's the only way you can really help them.

3RD THINKER. The best way is not always the easiest, you know.

TROUBLEMAKER. But—

1ST THINKER. —the only way.

TROUBLEMAKER. *(Determined)* Then I'll do it!

THINKERS. *(Together)* That's using your thinkers. *(They laugh)*

(The troublemaker now gives a bite of bread to each of the animals. When the cow takes the last piece, the three animals shed their costumes and are revealed as Greek Gods)

DOG. *(Now a God)* Hello, little Troublemaker. I am Jupiter, King of the Gods.

CAT. *(Now a Goddess)* I am Venus, Goddess of Love.

COW. *(Now a God)* I am the God of all seasons.

TROUBLEMAKER. *(Not trusting himself)* What have I done now?

(The wind blows in rapidly as the Gods and Goddess go over to reassure the little troublemaker)

WIND. That's the first right thing you've ever done.

(The sun comes up)

SUN. I knew he would do it all the time.

TROUBLEMAKER. Have I really done something good?

JUPITER. Indeed, you have. You shared with us.

VENUS. We know it wasn't easy.

SEASONS. But it was the last piece of bread on earth.

JUPITER. And now we have something for you.

108

SEASONS. We found something.

VENUS. Something you lost. Your magic wand. (*Gives it to him*)

TROUBLEMAKER. Oh, thank you! I was so sad that I forgot about it.

JUPITER. Now you have one more wish to make. What will it be?

(*The little troublemaker turns front, holds the wand tight, and begins to think real hard*)

1ST THINKER. This time use it wisely.

2ND THINKER. Think, oh please think.

3RD THINKER. Think hard.

TROUBLEMAKER. I wish—I wish—I WISH . . .

1ST THINKER. Don't forget us.

2ND THINKER. Please.

TROUBLEMAKER. I wish that everyone I have gotten into trouble would be out of trouble again!

3RD THINKER Hurrah! You did it!

(*The three thinkers begin to dance around the troublemaker. The sun smiles. The wind looks pleased. The Gods and Goddess laugh together. And suddenly all the people who were in trouble begin to come onstage cheering the little troublemaker. His girlfriend reaches him first*)

TROUBLEMAKER. Princess! (*Takes his girlfriend's hand and pulls her on the rock beside him*) Stay with me, my little Thinkers, (*They stand around him*) and I'll never forget to use you . . . forever and ever. I'll use you always!

(*All the happy people begin to encircle the troublemaker, princess, and the little thinkers, as they cheer and shout*)

WIND. (*To the audience*) And you know what?

SUN. (*To the audience*) He did! (*Winks*)

CURTAIN

COCK-A-DOODLE-OOPS!

a play in one act

written by 8-and 9-year-old-children

supervised by Sally Netzel

Cock-a-Doodle-Oops! was written and produced by the Dallas Theater Center Children's Theater in the spring of 1964. The student playwrights were also the original cast.

Chicken 1	CARLA COSTELLO
Chicken 2	SUSAN ROSENFIELD
Chicken 3	BECKY JONES
Chicken 4	DENISE CAMPISI
Chicken 5	ANN KING
Chicken 6	MARY DeBOLT
Turkey 1	DEBBIE WILSON
Turkey 2	MERRILY BROWN
Pigeon 1	JAN TAPLEY
Pigeon 2	MITZI LYNN
Rooster	DAVID TURNER
Farmer	WILSON NEELY
Wolf 1	CARTER MONTGOMERY
Wolf 2	DARREN DAVISON

PLACE: The Barnyard of a Bird Farm

TIME: The Present

SCENE. *The barnyard of a bird farm. There is roosting space for a chorus of six chickens, a separate roost for three turkeys, and another for three pigeons. The rooster's roost should be near but not a part of the chicken roost.*

AT RISE. *Rooster is asleep on his roost. The birds each in their own group, move and make the respective bird noises. Farmer enters carrying a music stand, a sheet of music, and a baton. He also has a feed bag with grain, which he places on the ground.*

FARMER. Attention! Attention all birds! To your posts!

(*The birds rush to their roosts. Farmer places his stand and music, and prepares to conduct*)

The first number this evening will be *Egg Opus* No. 2. Chickens, are you ready? Sing out now. Make this good and you'll get an extra ration of grain. (*Tapping foot*) And-a-one—and-a-two . . .

CHICKENS. (*In speaking chorus rather than singing*)
   Fried, scrambled, poached,
   or sunny-side up,
   Eggs will be eggs will be eggs.

PIGEONS. Eggs so small and eggs so sweet
   For a dietary supplement
   Cannot be beat.

TURKEYS. You can egg people on
   Or be an egg-head
   Be the last one in
   And therefore called rotten

CHICKENS. And so to thee, oh egg . . .

(*The rooster snores loudly, stopping the chorus. They stare at him in disgust and shock*)

FARMER. Dad-gum it! And it was going so well. Some birds have no feeling for the finer things. Wake up, you stupid foul!

ROOSTER. (*Waking*) What? What's going on? Who called? Is it time to crow? (*Crowing*) Cock-a-doodle-doo! Cock-a . . .

CHICKENS. No! No! Stop! Not now!

TURKEYS. It never fails.

PIGEONS. Coo-coo, that's what he is.

FARMER. Dad-gum it! Not only does my rooster have no appreciation for music he has no sense of time!

CHICKEN 1. Our crazy rooster

CHICKEN 2. wakes at midnight

CHICKEN 3. and sleeps at dawn

CHICKEN 4. only not always,

CHICKEN 5. just sometimes

CHICKEN 6. or occasionally

CHICKEN 5. (*to 6*) Don't be repetitious!

ROOSTER. (*Still half asleep*) What's going on?

FARMER. We have just finished the 1st verse of the second *Egg Opus*, and you missed it!

ROOSTER. I don't really like that song anyway.

FARMER. That settles it! Half rations for everybody. You can all just eat rock.

(*Farmer throws a fast fist-full of grain and exits*)

TURKEY 1. Half rations again!

TURKEY 2. It's really no gobbling matter.

TURKEY 3. A bird could starve to death.

PIGEON 1. Frankly, I think the *Egg Opus* is pretty awful myself.

PIGEON 2. Farmer is unfair to birds.

PIGEON 3. Shhh! Just be quiet and eat.

CHICKEN 1. (*To rooster*) Well, now you've done it!

CHICKEN 2. You—sleepy creep!

CHICKEN 3. You lazy daisy!

CHICKEN 4. You dragging dope!

CHICKEN 5. You dizzy drip!

CHICKEN 6. You—demoniac insomniac!

CHICKEN 5. Demoniac . . . what?

CHICKEN 6. I just heard that one someplace.

CHICKEN 1. See what you've done? Half rations again.

ROOSTER. Gee, I'm sorry. I just can't seem to help it. If I get tired I have to sleep—and it just never seems to be the time everybody else sleeps.

CHICKEN 2. And you crow at the wrong time!

ROOSTER. I know it. I don't mean to, but it just comes out sometimes. I just open my beak—and out it comes . . . at the wrong time.

CHICKEN 3. But you're a rooster.

CHICKEN 4. Roosters always know the time.

CHICKEN 5. They crow at dawn, always.

TURKEYS. Except for him.

PIGEONS. Except for him.

ROOSTER. Except for me.

CHICKEN 6. But you do crow well.

CHICKEN 5. When you do crow.

ROOSTER. Thanks—that's some comfort.

PIGEON 1. We overslept three days this week.

PIGEON 2. When I over-sleep.

PIGEON 3. It just ruins my whole day.

TURKEY 1. How can we help over-sleeping?

TURKEY 3. He crows all night long.

TURKEY 4. Well, at least four or five times.

ROOSTER. The moon is so bright at night, and sometimes it's dark at dawn.

PIGEONS. Hopeless, hopeless . . .

112

TURKEYS. If we were only one dope-less.

ROOSTER. (*Sadly*) Woe is me.

(*Far away the howls of wolves are heard*)

CHICKEN 1. Listen!

CHICKEN 2. What was that?

CHICKEN 3. It wasn't a bird . . .

CHICKEN 4. Or a farmer . . .

CHICKEN 5. Or a cow, horse, or pig.

CHICKEN 6. You don't suppose.

CHICKENS. That it's a wolf??

TURKEYS. Or two wolves??

PIGEONS. Or three!

ALL THE BIRDS. Or four? Or twenty? Or seventy-two? Or a hundred trillion million?

(*Farmer enters amid the clatter and taps his baton*)

FARMER. Quiet! Quiet down! (*The noise stops*) If there's one thing I can't stand it's disorganized noise. Come now——in rhythm——we'll sing the evening song and go to bed.

ROOSTER. But I'm not tired.

CHICKEN 5. And what about . . .

ALL. The wolves!

FARMER. Oh yes, that off-key howling. Don't worry. It's been a good season for wolves. They aren't hungry enough to try to come down here.

PIGEON 1. Isn't it nice

PIGEON 2. to have a protector

PIGEON 3. (*Saluting*) an inspector,

TURKEY 1. A director,

TURKEY 2. A pal

TURKEY 3. A pal?

TURKEY 2. I ran out of rhymes.

ROOSTER. That's all very nice, but why should we conform to human time?

FARMER. YOU don't! I conform to YOUR time. Do you think I like getting up at four in the morning? That's when the cow must be milked and the eggs are layed . . . and it's when *most* roosters crow!

ROOSTER. But . . .

FARMER. I'm tired of arguing with you, Rooster . . . Let's sing the FEATHER LULLABY. Here's the pitch. (*Hums*) Hmmmmmmmm. (*Begins to conduct*) And-a-one, and-a-two . . .

PIGEON 1. (*Beginning the speaking chorus*) Fold your feet under . . .

PIGEON 2. Tuck your head down . . .

PIGEON 3. Hope for no thunder . . .

PIGEONS. To bang us around.

TURKEY 1. No time for a fling . . .

TURKEY 2. So gobble your last . . .

TURKEY 3. Stretch out your wings . . .

TURKEYS. And snuggle up fast.

CHICKENS 1 AND 2. It's night-time again.

CHICKENS 3 AND 4. Get off of your legs,

CHICKENS 5 AND 6. It soon will be time . . .

ALL CHICKENS. To start hatching eggs

ALL BIRDS. Roost, roost, to the roost
        We greet night with a sigh
        And in our dreams, we'll sing all night
        The Feather Lullaby.

FARMER. Very nice. And now to bed.

ROOSTER. I'll never be able to sleep. It's too early.

FARMER. I'm tired of arguing with you . . . no more of this nonsense. You will crow on time or into the stew pot with you. I'll give you one more chance, and that's all. No crowing until tomorrow morning, and you'd better be on time! (*Exit*)

CHICKEN 3. Now you've gone and done it.

ROOSTER. What did I do?

TURKEY 2. You talked back.

ROOSTER. I did?

TURKEY 3. And besides that . . .

TURKEY 1. You crowed . . .

PIGEON 2. and snored . . .

PIGEON 1. in the middle of the *Opus*.

PIGEON 2. He's coo-coo.

CHICKEN 1. Your goose is cooked.

CHICKEN 2. One more mistake and you're done for.

CHICKEN 3. If I told him once, I told him a hundred times . . .

CHICKEN 4. Just plain stupid.

CHICKEN 5. No, there's something wrong with the time-keeper in his head.

CHICKEN 6. So what do we do?

CHICKEN 5. Maybe he needs an operation.

TURKEY 1. Or vitamins.

TURKEY 3. Or liver shots . . .

PIGEON 1. What he needs is a new head!

ROOSTER. Well, it looks as if I'm going to lose the old one.

CHICKEN 5. Listen gang, he's not much, but he's all we've got. Every herd of chickens needs a rooster.

CHICKEN 6. (*Correcting 5*) Every *flock* of chickens needs a rooster.

114

PIGEON 2. What can we do to help?

CHICKEN 5. We can keep watch . . . we'll take turns . . . one each hour all night long. One at a time we'll patrol. If Rooster wakes up, we'll shush him before he can crow. And the last one will wake him at dawn.

ROOSTER. Gee, I really would appreciate it. And maybe I'll get the hang of it.·

ALL. Agreed!

CHICKEN 5. All right. I'll take the first watch. (To 1) You take the second, and so on down the line. Everybody else to the roost. Attention! (All the birds perch) Ready, set, sleep!

(All the birds fall asleep immediately)

ROOSTER. This sure is nice of you.

CHICKEN 5. (Getting into position) Think nothing of it. Go to sleep.

ROOSTER. No thanks I'm not tired.

CHICKEN 5. (Yawning) I am.

ROOSTER. Would you like to play a little pinochle?

CHICKEN 5. (Yawning) No thanks. (Falls asleep)

ROOSTER. (Continuing to talk, not noticing chicken is asleep) Insomnia is a terrible thing. It's probably just nerves. Maybe I should try tranquilizers. (Sees chicken asleep) Hey, don't fall asleep! Wake up! Oh, dear, now what do I do? Wake up! Please wake up. (Chicken sleeps on) Well, might as well try to sleep. Nothing else to do.

(The lights dim to suggest a full moon night. Rooster and chicken sleep on. The two wolves enter with large sacks)

Wolf 1. Look, there they are.

Wolf 2. A perfect set-up.

WOLF 1. They look so peaceful. You'd never believe they're the ones who sing all day and keep us awake.

WOLF 2. I just couldn't take it anymore. (Shivers) How that squawking goes right through me.

WOLF 1. My nerves are simply shattered.

WOLF 2. And I'm not against the thought of chicken stew, turkey pie, and pigeon dumplings, are you?

WOLF 1. Yum! Let's get to work.

(The wolves circle the birds, sneak up on each one, and bop them lightly on the head. They put pre-arranged loops of rope around each bird's neck, ready to haul them off. The rooster wakes, but does not see the wolves. They do not hear him)

ROOSTER. (Yawning) Well, that was a nice sleep. Gee, it's light. It must be dawn. I'd better crow. No, wait, maybe it's only moonlight. Farmer would be furious if I woke him up in the middle of the night again. But if it's dawn . . . let's see, the sun rises in the East . . . no, the West. No, the East . . . now which way is East, I wonder? Oh, dear . . . it looks like the stew pot for me. (Pause) Uh-oh. I feel a crow coming on . . . oh, dear, I can't stop it. Here it comes . . . (Loudly) Cock-a-doodle-do! Cock-a-doodle-do! (He continues several more times)

(At the first crow, Wolf 2 yelps and leaps into the arms of Wolf 1. They both fall flat. The birds all wake up and start making sounds of panic. The birds in the nooses see what is happening and try to get the nooses off)

WOLF 1. Get off of me!

WOLF 2. That noise! It's hurting my ears!

WOLF 1. We've got to get out of here. Hurry!

WOLF 2. My nerves will never be the same.

WOLF 1. (*Shouting*) What did you say?

WOLF 2. (*Shouting, too*) Nerves!

WOLF 1. Can't hear you! Which way do we go?

WOLF 2. I beg your pardon?

WOLF 1. (*Frantic*) Out! Out!

WOLF 2. Out? Oh, yes. (*Leads the way to the fence*)

WOLVES. Let's get out of here!

(*Just as they begin to run, the farmer, with flashlight and gun, enters shouting, and all the animals freeze*)

FARMER. Quiet! What's going on? Where is that rooster? Where is that confounded bird? I'll wring his neck. Waking me up in the middle of the night!

WOLF 1. (*Whispering*) Do you see what I see?

WOLF 2. Yes, I do.

WOLF 1. Shall we depart?

WOLF 2. Yes, let's!

(*They now begin to tiptoe off as the farmer turns toward rooster. He points his shotgun at him*)

FARMER. There you are, you confounded idiot. You've crowed your last!

ROOSTER. I didn't mean it? I couldn't help it! Please!

ALL BIRDS. (*To farmer*) Stop! Stop!

(*At the word stop, the wolves also stop and turn to see*)

FARMER. What?

ALL BIRDS. Wolves!

FARMER. Where??

ALL BIRDS. (*Pointing to wolves*) There!

(*The farmer fires at the wolves. They grab their tails and run off yelping!*)

ALL BIRDS. Hurrah! Yea! Hurrah! Whoopee!

FARMER. I guess they won't be back for awhile.

TURKEY 1. That was a close call.

TURKEY 2. My tail feathers stood right up on end!

TURKEY 3. They do anyway.

CHICKEN 1. Rooster crowed.

CHICKEN 2. Just in time.

CHICKEN 3. That's right.

CHICKEN 4. He did.

CHICKEN 5. He saved us.

CHICKEN 6. He's a hero!

FARMER. Rooster, old buddy, I owe you an apology.

ROOSTER. But I didn't do anything.

PIGEON 1. You crowed.

PIGEON 2. And farmer came running,

PIGEON 3. And shot the wolves . . .

PIGEONS. right in the tail!

ROOSTER. But I couldn't help it . . . the crow, I mean. It was an accident.

FARMER. Then it was a lucky accident.

CHICKEN 6. Then he still doesn't crow at the right time.

FARMER. Rooster, I'm going to get you the biggest, fanciest alarm clock in the world. May even have a coo-coo clock—and we can use it in the chorus. Can't waste a good rooster in the stew pot.

CHICKEN 1. Rooster, you . . .

CHICKEN 2. almost got in the stew . . .

CHICKENS 3 AND 4. We are glad you are not . . .

CHICKENS 5 AND 6. In that great iron pot!

ROOSTER. You and me both!

(*All grin at rooster and he beams*)

CURTAIN

PRODUCTION NOTES FOR CHARACTER DEVELOPMENT

Cock-a-Doodle-Oops! is a light, humorous piece which is very dependent upon good characterizations and pantomime for an interesting and effective performance. With so much repetition of animal-types, individual characterizations are imperative to maintain interest and capture the humor in the lines. If each animal is given a specific personality, helpful props, ideas for characteristic rhythm patterns, and personality traits and gestures, then characters can become clear and each bit of dialogue more meaningful.

When speaking in chorus, the group must work for variety in volume, rhythm, level, texture or tone quality, and attitude. Individual lines should not always be given "in character" when part of a group reading, for personality may have to be subordinated to the idea of the words and the group as a whole. At other times, however, a switch to character interpretation can give a comic touch to an otherwise plain reading. To assist in visualizing the characters, each one is described as follows:

THE FARMER is energetic, authoritative, and temperamental. He takes his conducting seriously and is very methodical in his habits. He is dressed like a farmer except for one item: his hat. Each time he comes to the barnyard to conduct, he wears a tall silk hat. He doesn't think a conductor is a real musician with just a baton; he must also wear a black, silk hat.

CHICKEN 1 is the leader, always first to react and comment. She is aggressive, alert, and takes things in hand. The others usually follow her leadership.

CHICKEN 2 is a tag-along to 1. She always agrees with 1 and seldom ventures out on her own.

CHICKEN 3 is a pessimist. She doubts everything and always sees the dark side.

CHICKEN 4 is abrupt and tactless. She calls a spade a spade and doesn't care whose feelings she may hurt in the process. She is very practical.

CHICKEN 5 is bossy and loves attention. She is a busy-body, very outspoken, and always knows the latest gossip. A perfectionist in some things, she sometimes ignores her responsibilities in other things.

CHICKEN 6 is a dreamer. She has a wild imagination and usually says the first thing to come into her head, regardless of whether it is appropriate or not. Usually her head is in the clouds and she gives the appearance of being sleepy all the time.

TURKEY 1 complains constantly. If she has nothing to gripe about, she complains about that. She is a regular "Chicken Little."

TURKEY 2 doesn't openly complain like 1; she just accepts things as they are but knows nothing good will come of it.

TURKEY 3 has a dry wit; she is sometimes funny because she states things so plainly. Usually carries on a running commentary to a conversation or event.

PIGEON 1 is aristocratic; she thinks she can trace her family back for many generations. When she comments, she does it more to get attention than anything. She is very conscious of her appearance and anyone's reaction to her or what she says.

PIGEON 2 is a little one who always feels he is going to be stepped on. He is very self-centered.

PIGEON 3 doesn't like confusion or fusses and is constantly trying to get people to be quiet and speak only when spoken to. Wants little attention for himself and is easily embarrassed by Pigeon 1.

ROOSTER is really pure of heart. He sees no evil, speaks no evil, and thinks no evil. But with all his goodness, he still has a most irritating trait; he never crows when he should. His intentions are good, though. He is kind and gentle and wants to do well but just can't quite make it.

WOLF 1 is sly, quick, and full of plans and ideas. He can easily talk Wolf 2 into something but he is really a coward at heart.

WOLF 2 is dependable and loyal. He never questions 1 and is always willing to go along with his plans. Wolf 2 is really a better chicken thief because he has had the practice; he always does the work while Wolf 1 "watches."

THE PURPLE TIGER WHO LIKED PANCAKES

a play in one act

written by 11-and 12-year-old children

supervised by Jearnine Wagner and Ruth Byers

The Purple Tiger Who Liked Pancakes was written and produced by Baylor Children's Theater, Waco, Texas, in the spring of 1957. The original cast were also the student playwrights.

Chorus	PAM BAILEY
	PAM DIETER
	CYNTHIA RIDGEWAY
	JACKIE DRUM
Bumpy Grump	JUDY JOLLEY
He	FRED BEAN
Him	ROY BUTLER
Papa Brown	LARRY MAHON
Amelia Ann	VIRGINIA SEGAL
Hubert	BARRETT MOORE
Purple Tiger	JACKIE DRUM
Octapussy	CYNTHIA RIDGEWAY
Bop-ups	PAM DIETER
	PAM BAILEY

PLACE: The Castle, The Village, The Forest

TIME: Once upon a time

The stage scene is divided into three locales: the castle, the village, and the forest. There is an additional acting area downstage center and down left which is void of scenery but used by the chorus and by Amelia Ann and Hubert when they make their journey.

The castle is stage right. A seven-fold flat suggests a room in the castle, but at the top it becomes the exterior and is cut out to represent the castle outline. In the center of the flat suggesting the room area, there is a cupboard or series of shelves with bottles, test-tubes, and glass boxes which contain ingredients for Bumpy Grump's magic pot. To the right is a peg in the wall where HE places his bat. To the left of the cupboard is a bell sash which Bumpy uses to ring for HIM and HE. In the downstage center of this area is a large black pot. To the right of the pot is a low bookstand from which Bumpy reads from her magic book.

The village is stage left and center stage. Cut-out houses are used for the village in stage center. Stage left is Papa Brown's Tailor Shop. A single flat may be painted to suggest the interior of the shop with threads, fabrics, and finished clothes hanging on a rack. At the top of the flat painted in Old English letters are the words "Papa Brown's Tailor Shop." In the center of this area is a stool on which Papa Brown sits to sew. This is the largest flat in the group. The other three or four are painted to represent the exteriors of gingerbread-type houses, each in bright colors and with interesting accessories such as flower-boxes, windows with cloth curtains, doors with peep-holes, etc. The chorus will not walk through the doors of the houses when they become townspeople but walk from behind each flat.

The forest is also in center stage. Houses used in the village are reversible to become trees with hanging pieces to give them dimension. Additional trees are added to the scene by the chorus members who have hanging green gauze over their heads and arms so they can become moving trees.

When the play begins, the chorus members are hiding behind the village houses. Each enters with a movement to fit the sound of his entrance:

CHORUS. (Individually) Ping
                 Bang
                      Pong
                          Poosh!

(Together) We're going to tell you a story.

(They all begin laughing as though they have been discussing the story offstage. The following lines are divided among the chorus as they talk to the audience and then among themselves)

      It's a funny story.
      But it isn't all funny.
      No, it isn't all funny.
      Some of it is sad,
      And scary,
      And fantastic!
      It's the story of an old man who lived on the moon.
      It's the story of an old woman who traveled on a broom.
      No! You're both wrong; it's about an old lady who lives in a house.
      A castle,
      With squeaky steps,
      And bangy doors,
      And broken shutters,
      And cobwebs.

(Together) Oh, you know, the usual old things.

      (Divided again) We've all read about them,
      And we've certainly seen enough of them on television,
      And those late, late movies.
      A castle sitting waaaaay up on a lonely hill—
      A dead tree stretching its crooked fingers up against a black sky——

The sound of the old house stretching and moaning with the wind—
And a black hawk high on a tree limb watching and waiting.
An old woman lives in this castle . . .
With her two brothers.
Her name is Bumpy Grump.
Their names are Him and He.

One day Bumpy Grump woke up early in the morning, the sun was shining and the birds singing . . .

(All together) No!

(Divided again) One day Bumpy Grump woke up early in the morning . . .
The sky was dark and no birds were singing . . .
None were even in sight!
She decided that this was the day for opening the book that had been closed for 100 years. For 100 years a curse had been placed upon the book so that no one dared open it until the time had passed.

(Together) Today was the day. Bumpy Grump stole up the dark stairs to the old library . . .

(Chorus now look toward the castle and move in close to watch the scene. Bumpy Grump is heard laughing offstage as though she is getting the book)

There she took the large black book from the top shelf, brought it into her laboratory . . .

(Bumpy Grump comes from behind the flat into the castle-room)

blew the dust away . . .

(She blows the dust away and coughs furiously when it gets into her lungs)

and opened the cover:

(Bumpy Grump takes the book to the stand and opens it to her marked page and reads)

BUMPY GRUMP. (Reading) "How to make 10 World-Conquering Animals." (Begins to cackle with joy. Just as suddenly, she stops and calls) Him! He! This is it. This is it. Something we've always wanted to do . . .

(HE enters with his bat on one finger followed by HIM who is shining his fanged front tooth)

HE. What is it now? Can't you see I'm feeding my bat?

HIM. And I'm shining my tooth.

CHORUS. (To the audience) Horrible monsters, aren't they? Oooooooooh!

BUMPY GRUMP. Well, never mind that, now. I've found a way to conquer the world . . .

HE. A way to conquer the world? (Places bat on peg)

HIM. Huh?

(HIM and HE began to crowd around Bumpy to see what she is reading)

BUMPY GRUMP. Look here! A recipe for an octapussy.

HE. And a Bop-up.

HIM. What's a Bop-up?

BUMPY GRUMP. Ah—look, a tiger.

CHORUS. So, being very fond of animals, Bumpy Grump began to conjure up—(They suddenly stand up with fear)—the tiger! Ooooooh! (They scatter and hide behind the houses again where they now change accessories to become townspeople)

(Bumpy Grump begins to stir her pot and as she calls for the ingredients and begins to cast her spell, HIM and HE bring them from the cupboard and put them into the brew)

BUMPY GRUMP. One cup of camel's hair.
                    He! Put it in with care.
                    Five glasses of ground bugs.
                    Be sure they're freshly dug.
                    A two-nosed wart
                    With some chicken-hearts.
                    Put in some glums one or two . . .
                    Be sure to stir the precious brew.
                    Put in the whiskers of a bat . . .

(HIM starts to take the whiskers off of HE'S bat when HE sees HIM and swats HIM off)

HE. Not my bat, stupid!

Bumpy Grump. *(Continuing)* Make sure they are not skinny but fat.
                    A tiger we will make
                    So put in a tooth of a snake.
                    All is nearly through . . .
                    So let him stew and stew and stew . . .

(A sudden whiff of colored smoke and the three with great excitement and anticipation move close to look into the pot)

                    Let him fully dry
                    Our tiger will then be very spry . . .

(The Purple Tiger sticks his head out of the pot, licks his lips, and smiles up at Bumpy)

You Glups! You Glumps! You've conjured up a purple tiger. Who ever heard of a purple tiger.

HE. *(To HIM)* I didn't put the color in; you did.

HIM. No, I didn't. You did.

HE. Didn't.

HIM. Did.

HE. Didn't.

HIM. Did.

HE. Oh, what's the difference what color he is as long as he's a tiger.

HIM. But he doesn't have any stripes either.

BUMPY GRUMP. Let's see how we add the stripes. *(Reads)* "recipe does not include stripes for tiger and stripes do make the tiger." Humph!

HE. Well, we'll just have to make some stripes.

BUMPY GRUMP. But I can't sew.

HIM. And I can't sew.

HE. And neither can I.

BUMPY GRUMP. Our plans are foiled for awhile, but we'll think of something . . .

The scene changes to the center stage area of the village. Chorus members have now donned accessories to suggest people of the town and are looking around the sides of their houses, through the window or peep-hole.

CHORUS. Now the people in the village heard about the old woman and her purple tiger; for every night at 13 o'clock she walked the streets looking in all the store windows to see if she could find some stripes.

(Lines now divided among chorus members)

122

She never found any stripes but the tiger found some pancakes;
And he discovered that he liked pancakes;
He liked them so much that every night he would inhale all the pancakes in the baker's window.

One night the baker forgot to put pancakes in his store window and the tiger inhaled the whole store!

After the baker rebuilt his store, he never forgot to put pancakes in his front window.
The people were afraid to be out in the street at that time of the night,
But it didn't keep them from looking through their shutters,
And peeking through their keyholes.
Now, I don't blame them. I'd be looking too.

(*Chorus now steps out to form line as they introduce the next scene. As each character is mentioned, he enters and begins pantomiming the scene. Papa Brown is sitting on the stool sewing. Amelia Ann and Hubert are watching him, Amelia holds the scissors to cut the thread*)

(*Spoken as a group*) As in all villages of this type, there lived a timid, tactful tailor, whose name is Papa Brown. Papa Brown is an old-fashioned Papa. And he has two old-fashioned children: an old-fashioned girl and an old-fashioned boy.

PAPA BROWN. Amelia Ann. Hubert. Now, you go home and lock the door. It's almost 13 o'clock.

AMELIA ANN. But, Papa, aren't you coming too?

PAPA BROWN. No Amelia, I still have more patching to do before tomorrow. Now, Hubert, you take care of your sister.

HUBERT. Alright, Pa, but don't you stay out too late. Come on, Amelia.

AMELIA ANN. Goodnight, Papa. (*She hugs him*) Don't worry. I'll take care of Hubert.

(*The children go out a pantomimed door and go home—behind the shop. The chorus has begun to make the sound of a clock ticking. They all begin to look around for the old woman, fearful that they might see her, while continuing to make the clock sounds and individually saying the next lines*)

CHORUS. Time passes (*Several clock beats*)
　　　　Time passes (*Several more clock beats*)
　　　　She's late. (*Clock beats*)
　　　　Time passes. (*Clock continues*) Time passes.

(*There is the sound of footsteps*)

　　　　Suddenly! Footsteps!
　　　　Footsteps!
　　　　Footsteps!

(*Chorus members run behind their houses as Bumpy Grump and the Purple Tiger make their nightly round through the town. The chorus nervously watch as Papa Brown puts away his sewing and, unaware that the old woman and tiger are near, opens the pantomimed door and reaches for his keys to lock it*)

　　　　Don't come now, Papa Brown.
　　　　She's still in town.
　　　　Look behind you.
　　　　Look around you.

(*The old woman has suddenly seen Papa Brown. She stops*)

BUMPY GRUMP. A tailor! Stripes!

(*She motions to the tiger to inhale Papa Brown, now locking his door and having his back to the tiger. The tiger begins to back away behind one of the houses and Papa Brown is pulled by suction behind the house. The chorus members supply the sound of the suction, while watching with fear the complete action*)

CHORUS. Oh . . . oooooooooooooo . . . oooooooooooh . . . ooooooooooooh GLUMP!

(Bumpy Grump cackles and follows them off stage)

      Poor Papa Brown
      The tiger inhaled him.

(The chorus now runs to the side of the shop which is the entrance to Amelia and Hubert's house. They call desperately)

      Amelia Ann!
      Hubert!
      Open the door!
      Open the door!
      Help!

(Amelia Ann comes to the door with Hubert behind her)

AMELIA. What is it? What's happened?

CHORUS. (Individually) Poor Amelia
      Oh, Amelia Ann.
      The tiger—

AMELIA ANN. (Understanding) Papa? Oh, no. (Cries) Not Papa.

HUBERT. (Suddenly becoming very brave and answering the call for help) That's all right, Amelia Ann. I'll go after them.

AMELIA. And I'll go, too.

HUBERT. It's too dangerous—for a girl.

AMELIA. But the tiger likes pancakes. If I made some . . .

HUBERT (Suddenly not so brave after all) That's a good idea. Well, hurry. (He goes back into the house to get his knapsack, cap and walking stick)

CHORUS. I'll bring you some of my pancakes.
      I have some.
      So do I.
      And I have a big basket to put them in.

(As each chorus member says her line, they run to their respective houses and bring back pancakes and the basket. While they are getting them, Hubert has come out with his gear and Amelia Ann helps him shoulder it all. Then she runs to get a shawl for herself. As chorus members bring their pancakes, they put them into the basket supplied by another)

HUBERT. We're ready. Now, on to the castle!

(Hubert leads Amelia with a sweep of his arm, so brave and strong. The chorus members wave goodbye and Amelia follows Hubert as she waves goodbye to them)

AMELIA. Goodbye——

CHORUS. Goodbye.
      Goodbye, Amelia Ann.
      Goodbye, Hubert.

(The chorus members now drop their character roles and make a straight line as they become narrators for the journey ahead. As they describe the scenes, they add appropriate sound and movement while Hubert and Amelia Ann pantomime the journey in the down center and left areas)

CHORUS. And so Amelia Ann and Hubert started their journey.
      They walked and walked and walked.
      Down the dusty road,
      Over the icy mountain tops,
      Through boiling desert sands . . .
      And into the deep dark forest—forest—forest—forest . . .

(As the chorus members repeat "forest" in different levels and rhythms, they turn the house flats around to represent trees and cover their heads and arms with green gauze material, spacing themselves in such a way as to suggest trees that move and stretch toward the children as they wander through them. Once in place they begin to make the haunting sounds of the forest. Amelia Ann, now leading Hubert, winds her way through the trees, not ever sure they are going the right way. Hubert is getting slower and slower with fatigue and hunger)

HUBERT. Let's take a break. I'm tired.

AMELIA. We'll stop for lunch.

HUBERT. Good. I'm starving. Those pancakes sure look good.

(As Amelia Ann takes some pancakes out, Hubert begins to grab a hand full)

AMELIA. Well, we can't eat too many now. Remember the tiger.

HUBERT. Oh, these are good.

(Hubert starts to help himself to more)

AMELIA. Hubert! Don't take any more now.

(Hubert puts them back and begins to eat more slowly. Amelia Ann finishes her pancake, gets up to stretch and look around. As soon as she does, Hubert reaches over for a final handful of pancakes)

I wonder where Papa is. Poor Papa. Well, it's time to go. *(She turns and sees the basket almost empty)* Hubert! You've eaten all but three.

HUBERT. *(Stretching out for a short nap)* Oh, well, three's enough.

AMELIA. I hope so. Let's hurry. It's getting late.

HUBERT. Let's rest a while. I'm too full to move.

(Amelia begins to clean up and put the last three pancakes carefully back into the basket)

AMELIA. We're too near the old woman's castle, Hubert. It isn't safe to rest here.

(Hubert has fallen asleep. He doesn't hear the octapussy which now appears through the trees meowing like a cat. Amelia does and begins to look for him)

AMELIA. Oh, a cat. Here kitty, kitty, kitty . . . *(Suddenly sees the octapussy)* The Octapussy! *(She runs to Hubert and tries to awaken him)* Hubert! Wake up. Wake up.

(Hubert only moans and rolls over. The octapussy chases her but each time she manages to get away. He then suddenly sees Hubert and begins to try to wrap his arms around him. Amelia Ann quickly begins to hit him. Suddenly she stomps on his feet and he lets out a yell and begins to squeeze Hubert in anger. Hubert is now wide awake and petrified with fear. Amelia Ann, who doesn't like to see anyone in pain and is oblivious to Hubert, sees that the octapussy has a corn which she has stepped on)

AMELIA. Oh, you poor thing. You have a corn. Here, I have a warm pancake. That will fix it up.

(She puts the pancake on his foot and the octapussy purrs in comfort and gratitude and begins to hobble off. Hubert is hazy-eyed)

AMELIA. Come on, Hubert, let's get away now.

HUBERT. What in the world was that?

AMELIA. The Octapussy. That means the old woman knows we're coming. Hurry, now, Hubert.

(Amelia Ann and Hubert begin their journey again. The trees are becoming more hostile and the sounds deeper and more fearsome. The sound of the bop-ups are faintly heard. As they grow in volume, Amelia hears them . . . Steady, almost electronic sounds . . . "bop, bop, bop, bop" and as they come closer they become louder and higher in tone level)

AMELIA. What's that, Hubert?

HUBERT. I don't know. Listen to that sound. It's like something from another world.

AMELIA. I'm frightened, Hubert. Do you think it's another animal the old woman has sent to get us?

HUBERT. I'm sure it is. Wait. I brought my book on supernatural animals in the Black Forest; maybe it can tell us something.

AMELIA. Hurry. It's getting closer.

(The bop-ups are now in sight. They are square-shaped, armless, metal forms with two metalic green legs. They each have one eye and seem to be electronically mobile creatures. They destroy by crushing an object which is trapped between them. They now spring up and down as they move in on either side of Amelia and Hubert)

HUBERT. (Paging through his book and not seeing the animals) I can't find anything on it.

AMELIA. (Who can't take her eyes away from the one coming in toward her) Well, do something! Don't depend on the book now.

HUBERT. (Suddenly looks up and sees the bop-up on the other side of him) Help! Help!

AMELIA. Just yelling isn't going to do any good. Nobody would hear you.

HUBERT. Look at his eye. He's watching me.

AMELIA. (Backing up to Hubert) Do you think he would like a pancake? The tiger was one of the old woman's animals, too.

HUBERT. Run, Amelia, Run.

AMELIA. Where? (Sees the bop-up coming toward Hubert) He's coming in on both sides.

HUBERT. Well, back up.

AMELIA. (Trying desperately to think of something) Here, you want a pancake. Pancake?

(Hubert and Amelia are now back to back with the bop-ups closing in on them. Hubert, upon hearing her, gets an idea and takes the pancake from her, tears it in two and gives her half of it)

HUBERT. Here. When I say three, throw it over his eye; maybe we can blind him until we get away.

AMELIA. I never was a good pitcher.

HUBERT. Well, you'd better be now. Okay, one, two, three!

(They both throw and hit the animal over his one eye. They both freeze with fear, waiting to see what will happen next. The bop-ups stop. There is a deadly silence. Then slowly they begin to back away and go out the way they came. Amelia runs to the edge of the clearing)

AMELIA. We've got to hurry to the castle before she has time to send another animal after us.

(Amelia and Hubert begin their journey through the forest again. It is getting darker and the sounds they hear are from the wind, owls, and creaking limbs. It is quieter, too. They move slower and with more precaution)

HUBERT. Hurry, Amelia.

AMELIA. It's getting so dark that I can't see.

HUBERT. (*Offering Amelia his hand as he leads the way*) Hold my hand.

AMELIA. (*After walking hand in hand a few minutes, she shutters as she hears the wind*) It's getting cold.

HUBERT. It shouldn't be too far now. Come on.

(*As the children make their way in and out of the trees, the chorus begins to speak like the sound of the wind, elongating each word and speaking on different levels and in slow rhythm*)

CHORUS. (*Together*) Deep, deep, deep in the forest. Don't be afraid.

AMELIA. Ooooooohhhhh. I'm scared. Do you think we'll ever get out?

HUBERT. We couldn't go any deeper. I know we must be near.

CHORUS. (*Individually*) Amelia Ann . . . Hubert . . . Amelia Ann . . . Hubert.

AMELIA. Hubert, someone's calling us.

(*At this point the trees on one side call and then those on the other so that Amelia and Hubert move from side to side trying to follow the voices*)

CHORUS. (*One side*) This way, Hubert.

(*the other side*) No, this way, Hubert.

HUBERT. Don't listen to them Amelia Ann.

CHORUS. Sorry to frighten you, Amelia Ann, but this is the way the story goes . . . and goes . . . and goes.

AMELIA. Oh . . . oh . . . (*She begins to cry*)

HUBERT. I see a light.

AMELIA. Where?

(*Hubert points in the direction of the castle off up right*)

AMELIA. It's the castle.

HUBERT. So big . . .

AMELIA. And dark . . .

(*Unseen by the two children, HIM and HE have been watching them through the trees as they look at the light. Now they come up behind them quietly*)

HE. What are you doing here?

AMELIA (*Turning around quickly*) Oh!

HIM. Who are you?

HUBERT. We . . . uh . . . we . . .

AMELIA. We're from the village.

HIM. The village???

HE. What you got in the basket?

AMELIA. We——we brought some pancakes for the purple tiger.

HE. Who ordered them?

AMELIA. (*Thinking Quickly*) Uh . . . the old woman . . . Bumpy Grump.

HIM. I'm hungry, He. What about us having some of them?

HE. How do we know that's what you've got in there?

HIM. Yeah, I want to taste them.

HE. Let's see what they look like. (*Amelia Ann draws back as HE starts to take the napkin off the one remaining pancake*)

HUBERT. Oh, no.

AMELIA. Th——They'll get cold if you take the napkin off. Just take a whiff of them. (*She lifts the napkin. HE takes a whiff*)

HE. Ummmmmmmmmmmmm.

(*Then HIM takes a whiff*)

HIM. Hummmmmmmmm. I'll take them in. (*Reaches for them*)

HE. No, you won't. You'll eat them all.

AMELIA. Why not let us go in. We have to collect for them anyway.

HE. Well, alright. But don't stay too long.

(*They allow Amelia to pass but HE stops Hubert. Then, after getting his kick out of scaring Hubert, HE lets him go*)

HE. Alright. You, too.

(*The children exit up right and HIM and HE follow*)

As soon as the others exit, the chorus members remove their head drapes and continue narration, speaking straight to the audience and in a straight line.

CHORUS. (*Together*) And so, Amelia Ann and Hubert get into the castle.

(*Individually*) You knew they'd get in all the time, didn't you?
  My, this is a good story, isn't it?
  And no commercials.
  I think it's one of the best stories I've ever heard.

  Hey, little boy! (*Pointing to the audience*), don't go out to get a soda pop yet.
  We're right at the climax. Who ever heard of going out to buy a soda pop
   at the most important part of the play!

(*Together*) Well, you never can tell about some audiences!

Now, the last scene of our story takes place in the castle. Papa Brown is seen sewing the stripes on the tiger. One more stripe and the tiger will be a full-fledged tiger.

(*Lights come up to reveal Papa Brown sitting on stool in area where pot was for first scene. He is sewing stripes on the tiger and now picks up the last one, realizes it will be the last and he begins to think about what he can do to stall his work*)

He won't like pancakes anymore. Real tigers don't like pancakes. You know what they like, don't you? Ohhhhhhhh, let's find a place to hide. (*Chorus exits behind trees*)

(*As the scene in the castle continues in pantomime with Papa Brown, Bumpy Grump comes in. She is agitated because of her impatience.*)

BUMPY GRUMP. Can't you sew any faster? I can hardly wait to call all of my animals together.

PAPA BROWN. Those poor animals. What makes you so sure you can conquer the world with three animals?

BUMPY GRUMP. You weren't brought here to ask questions, but to sew.

PAPA BROWN. And what will you do with the world after you've conquered her?

BUMPY GRUMP. (Suddenly stops pacing) Well, I hadn't thought about that. But I will do something. Now, you sew!

PAPA BROWN. One more stripe and I'll be through.

BUMPY GRUMP. (Petting the tiger) And my purple tiger will be complete. Are you hungry? You won't want any pancakes in a few minutes, but if you want some now, I'll get them for you. I'll call Him and He to bring you some. (She rings the bell) He wants pancakes now but after that last stripe, he'll eat the world!

(Upon hearing this, Papa Brown stops sewing)

PAPA BROWN. (To himself) I must not finish this stripe. (He hides the thread and then speaks to Bumpy) I seem to be out of thread.

BUMPY GRUMP. What? Out of thread? Impossible! I brought you a whole bolt of thread. That's the seventh time you've given out of thread in three days. I haven't seen you use that much.

PAPA BROWN. (Showing his needle and empty hands) See for yourself. I have no more.

BUMPY GRUMP. We must get some more thread. I will have this tiger finished, and finished tonight!

(She rings the bell again. HIM and HE appear)

HE. What now?

HIM. We heard the bell.

BUMPY GRUMP. It's about time! I need more thread. This tailor is using it up too fast. I must have this tiger completed so buy the whole village if necessary, but get the thread! Now, hurry!

(The two helpers turn to leave)

Oh, and bring some pancakes, too. The purple tiger is hungry again.

HE. Has he eaten those pancakes up already?

BUMPY GRUMP. What pancakes? We're out. Why do you think I asked you to bring more?

HIM. But you have some . . .

HE. Didn't you order some children to bring you pancakes from the village?

(Papa Brown looks up quickly and then tries to hide his interest)

BUMPY GRUMP. What children? You glups, you clumps! Did you let children in this castle?

HIM. You haven't seen them?

BUMPY GRUMP. Of course I haven't seen them. Where are they? Find them. Hurry!

HIM. That's something. I never thought of it. How did they get through the forest?

HE. You never think.

HIM. You let them in.

BUMPY GRUMP. Don't stand there jabbering. Find them!

(HIM and HE search the room. Bumpy Grump follows them. The children are seen peeking around the door)

AMELIA. There he is, Hubert. (Whispering) Papa. Papa. Over here.

(Papa Brown hears the call and turns to see the children. He motions them back and points to his chains)

HUBERT. He's chained.

AMELIA. Poor Papa.

HUBERT. Let's get him out of here.

AMELIA. Suppose they see us.

HUBERT. They won't if we're careful. Now you follow me. Stay close.

(Hubert and Amelia Ann prepare to make a dash to Papa Brown when HIM, HE, and Bumpy come close to them. They stiffen and stand close)

HE. They've disappeared.

HIM. Maybe they've gone home.

BUMPY. Nonsense they're here. You aren't looking.

HE. Maybe they're somewhere else in the castle.

BUMPY. They're bound to wind up in this room sometime so keep looking!

(Bumpy Grump, HIM and HE exit. Amelia Ann and Hubert inspect the chains and Hubert tries to break them)

PAPA GROWN. Careful, son, don't strain yourself.

AMELIA. Hurry, Hubert. They'll find us any minute.

(Hubert tries one more time and there is a loud snap as the chain breaks)

HE. (Offstage) What was that?

HIM. (Leading the three onstage) There they are!

BUMPY GRUMP. Catch them, you clumps. Don't let them get away.

AMELIA. Oh, what are we going to do?

PAPA BROWN: The tiger, Amelia Ann. Make friends with the tiger.

AMELIA. The tiger? Why?

(Bumpy Grump, HIM and HE begin to close in with great glee)

PAPA BROWN. Just do as I say and hurry.

HUBERT. The pancake, Amelia. Do you still have the pancake?

AMELIA. (Taking the last pancake out of her basket) Here, pretty tiger. A nice pancake.

(The tiger takes the pancake. Amelia Ann pats him. He purrs)

BUMPY GRUMP. Stop her. She's feeding the tiger.

PAPA BROWN. Wait! One more step and the tiger will inhale you.

HIM. Inhale US?

HE. She's got us, Bumpy.

BUMPY GRUMP. He wouldn't inhale us. Come on!

HE. But they just fed him.

AMELIA ANN. Pretty tiger. Open your mouth and inhale the ugly people.

(The Purple Tiger slowly opens his mouth. Bumpy, HIM and HE stop where they are. Silence. Slowly the inhaling sound is heard as the tiger prepares to inhale them)

HE. He IS going to inhale us!

HIM. Run!

BUMPY GRUMP. Ungrateful tiger. (*The tiger moves toward her and she turns to follow the other two*) Run faster, you gloops, you glumps.

(*Bumpy Grump, HIM and HE run out—perhaps through the audience. Amelia and Hubert hug Papa Brown and the Purple Tiger licks his paws and purrs. As the lights fade from the castle scene, the action continues down stage center as the chorus pick up the narration of the story*)

CHORUS. And so, Bumpy Grump, Him and He fled from the dark castle, past the dead tree with its crooked fingers and down the lonely hillside, never to be seen again.

(*Amelia Ann, Hubert, Papa Brown and the Purple Tiger enter as though taking an afternoon stroll*)

While Amelia Ann, Hubert, and Papa Brown adopted the purple tiger—who really wasn't a tiger after all, for he had no stripes—

(*They stop stage center as Hubert begins to feed the Purple Tiger more pancakes, Amelia takes them from her basket and hands them to Hubert, and Papa Brown pats the tiger and looks on*)

And he loved pancakes—lots of pancakes!

That ends our story

(*Individually*) A funny story
           A sad story
           A scary story
           A fantastic story

(*Together*) It was a good story, a very good story—with no commercials!

(*All wink and look smug as a picturization is made of the entire cast and the Purple Tiger himself holds up a large box with the words: "Amelia Ann's Pancakes"*)

CURTAIN

PRODUCTION NOTES

The Purple Tiger Who Liked Pancakes makes use of both representational and presentational drama, for although all of the characters play to one another, the chorus members are also narrators and they speak directly to the audience. One of the most delightful qualities of this play is in the chorus. With a slight change of accessories and a complete change of character, they become trees, townspeople, narrators, and they can be used as the supernatural animals in the forest. The unity, strength, and flexibility of the chorus is one of the most important aspects of the play.

Purple Tiger can also challenge a director in his range of imagination, for the play moves quickly from scene to scene and the transitions by the chorus can be done before the eyes of the audience yet be so integrated into the style of the presentation, that the audience is never fully aware of the many changes taking place.

Selectivity and pacing of sounds (particularly in the forest scene), dialogue and movement are most important in establishing the mood which is so important in the progression of the play, and in capturing the many changes of attitude and style which is imperative if the production is to be consistent with the script.

Although there is much room for inventiveness in the production of the play, the characterizations are quite definite.

THE CHORUS members must be the most flexible. They should move well, have good diction, be imaginative, and clear in pantomime. Always the narrators of the play, they are constantly having fun with the story and they tell it to the audience with much elaboration and excitement. They often disagree among themselves but once they agree, each is eager to tell his part of his story. They are both narrators and audience for as they tell the story, they are also reacting to their own words; even to the extent of relating what happened while they act it out.

As townspeople, they may decide upon specific personalities which will help them in line reading and in the costume accessories, for it is only at this point that they can become distinctly different. When they are trees they act as a group, though they may be different kinds of trees with different movements. And if they also double as the supernatural animals of the forest, they completely divorce themselves from the chorus.

BUMPY GRUMP is a temperamental witch. She is unpredictable, bizarre, yet the wickedest of witches. She is shrewd, yet likes to make plans and then have Him and He do the dirty work. She uses people for her own convenience and she enjoys making them her personal puppets. She is an original witch; for although she wants to conquer the world with supernatural animals, they are a little different from the norm. She may live in the castle but in spots here and there, she has added an individual touch to the decor that sets hers apart from the rest of the castles.

HE is both taller and smarter than Him. Although both are Bumpy Grump's helpers, they are the witch's "Mutt and Jeff" characters and typical "end men of vaudeville." HE makes all the decisions for the two but they are not always the wisest. He is the weaker of the two and is particularly kind-hearted to bats and winged creatures of the underworld.

HIM is He's sidekick. He is mentally slow and simple. He enjoys pranks, jokes, and is very proud to be the witch's helper. The uglier and meaner he can become the more he likes it, though he isn't really mean at heart. He takes great pride in his big tooth and anything else that may make someone fearful of him.

PAPA BROWN is an old man, kind, gentle, but shrewd and wise. He is really too old to be considered the immediate father of Hubert and Amelia Ann, but he is their Papa and his wife died many years before. She was much younger than he and the children barely remember her. Papa Brown is well-known in the village and is considered the finest tailor in the country. His interests are mainly three: Hubert, Amelia Ann, and his tailor shop.

AMELIA ANN is a little girl who loves flowers, animals, and people. She trusts everyone and does not like to see them unhappy or ill. Amelia Ann is very attached to Papa Brown and would rather sit in his shop and watch him work than do almost anything. She does most of the work at their house behind the shop and is both resourceful and responsible. She is friendly and well-loved by all. Happy and carefree, she usually has to shoulder some of Hubert's responsibilities and even though she is younger than he, she acts like his older sister.

HUBERT is lazy but has good intentions. He wants to be brave and strong and all the things that most boys admire but he has to battle his own fears and laziness. He wants to do what is right and usually begins to, but somehow he is distracted along the way and Amelia Ann is the one to finish the job. He loves Amelia and Papa Brown and wants more than anything for them to be proud of him.

THE PURPLE TIGER is tame and lovable. He enjoys comfort and comfort is pancakes. Since he was not given stripes to make him a full-fledged tiger so that he would enjoy meat, he was given the power to inhale anything he wanted. Usually he inhaled pancakes, but if encouraged by someone who had befriended him, he would inhale buildings or people. It was this trait that made him fearsome, not his personality.

THE OCTAPUSSY has a face like a cat and a body like an octopus. She is very feminine and likes frilly things but she is trained to attack all living creatures and this she can do with her long and numerous arms. Feminine though she is, her embrace is sure death.

THE BOP-UPS are electronic boxes which appear to move and react by mechanical devices. It is surprising, then, when Amelia and Hubert blind it with pancakes that it reacts so sensitively. Perhaps its eye is the sensitive area and only when this is affected, can the Bop-up be stopped. The sound of the Bop-up can be made by each side or it can be taped from electronic sounds. There is more control in the vocal sound, however, and this is especially important in the build in level and volume when the two close in upon Amelia Ann and Hubert.

COSTUMES

CHORUS. Leotards and tights all in the same color with each member using accessories in a different color, or leotards and tights in different colors for each chorus member with accessories to blend. Accessories suggested are skating skirts over the basic costume for scenes as chorus. Additions of hats, collars or stole, purses, and elected handprops when seen as townspeople. Green gauze stoles that can cover the head and arms gracefully when seen as trees.

BUMPY GRUMP. Long black dress with monogramed "B" in purple and green on front. Chair belt, black or colored gloves, pointed shoes in purple or green or other similar color; colored wig, variation of the pointed hat or maybe a jeweled headband, long nose with usual wart or twist, pointed and bushy brows, and many rings on her fingers.

HE. Black tights and bulky, long shirt with a turtle-neck and a large monogramed "B" on front. Bald-head and general appearance of being muscle-bound. Men's dance slippers.

HIM. Identical to HE but with long, bushy hair. General appearance of being thinner and weaker than HE. False tooth.

PAPA BROWN. Brown suit with men's knickers, stockings, buckled shoes, vest, bow tie, pocket-watch, apron, white hair and mustache, rosy cheeks.

AMELIA ANN. Quilted floral-patterned skirt, long-sleeved white or colored blouse with draw-stringed neck, laced midriff, knee-socks, flat shoes, bandeau with trim. Shawl for the journey.

HUBERT. Short pants, white long-sleeved shirt with tie at neck, suspenders, knee-socks, lace shoes, cap. Papa Brown, Amelia Ann, and Hubert all suggest Swiss villagers in costume and colors.

PURPLE TIGER. Purple tiger costume with built head opened around the face so that the face may be painted and more flexible expressions used . . . or
if using one of the chorus members, purple leotards and tights, complete built-head to cover face, purple gloves with claws attached, purple shoes with claws, and tail. For easiest attachment of stripes, use adhesive cloth strips.

OCTAPUSSY. Yellow and orange costume with green and red accents. Tights, octopus top with wired arms and cat face.

BOB-UPS. Green tights, square boxes with one luminous eye in each, antennae, metallic color.

PROPS

Big black magic book
Spoon for stirring
Ingredients for brew
Bat
Coat to be mended
large needle and thread
basket
12 or more pancakes (10 eatable, 2 with adhesive backing)
knapsack
walking stick
shawl
stripes (with adhesive backing)
chain with breakable ring
large cereal box with "Amelia Ann's Pancakes" on front

LIGHTS AND SPECIAL EFFECTS

Stage divided into four lighting areas. (1) the castle with direct and indirect lighting in blue-green-pink color mediums; (2) the village with cross lighting and area spots in blue-green-magenta and follow-spot for children (4) and the down center area for the chorus and the journey which can be covered with follow spots or area lighting in pink color mediums.

Naturally the more variety in lighting effects, the greater the mood and visual support the play will receive. If necessary, the lighting design can be simplified but general illumination would completely destroy the effect.

Special effects include one smudge pot with colored smoke.

SETS AND FURNISHINGS

7-fold flat for castle, with peg on right end and bell sash on left
large black pot
low book-stand
cupboard or shelves for brew ingredients
stool
3 or 4 flats in various shapes and sizes to double as houses in the village on one side and trees of the forest on the other side. Flats should be light for lifting by chorus.
large flat backing for Papa Brown's shop
work stool

THE TIN MAN AND THE PAINTED TOWN

a short play in three acts

written by junior high students

supervised by Ruth Byers

The Tin Man and the Painted Town was written and produced by Baylor Teen Theater, Waco, Texas, in the spring of 1956. The student playwrights were also *the original cast.*

Boy	BUD GARGILL
Mr. Fizzle	JOHN WHERLE
Pixy Purple	DARBY BOYD
Atomic Green	JOHN WHERLE
Whisper Blue	HARRIET HALEY
Mayor Plumed White	JOE RILEY
Doctor Plasmic Red	BUD GARGILL
Mrs. Powdered Poosh	RHETTA BAKER
Miss Petty Pink	PAT GENTRY
The Tin Man	KAY DENNARD
Mr. Painter	RHETTA BAKER
Brushes	JANE SMITH

PLACE: Junior High Study Hall—The Town of Pure Colors

TIME: During a Quick Nap

ACT I

As houselights dim, the sound of a clock is heard ticking away in the background. Light comes up on a boy in studyhall. He is sitting at a desk surrounded by books, magazines, papers and pencils, and appears to be working on a report of some kind.

BOY. *(Throwing his pencil down)* Oh, how I hate to write reports. If I don't get this in by tomorrow though, Mr. Fizzle will sure get on me.

(He begins to write again. The face of Mr. Fizzle is seen speaking in time with the clock and shaking his finger)

MR. FIZZLE. Get that report. Get that report. Get that report, boy. Get that report.

(The boy now speaks in syncopating rhythm to Mr. Fizzle as he continues to speak)

BOY. Gotta get it in; gotta get it in; gotta get it in; gotta get it IN! *(In exasperation)* Oh, I just don't understand this. *(Reads from one of books)* "The Production of Tin in 19___. Tin is produced primarily in the——turn to page 11" Hmmmmmmmmmmm *(Opens a large folder)* Well, what's this? *(Reads)* "New Experiments in Paints. Bold, exciting new colors for 19___. Plumed white." *(To himself)* Looks like ordinary white to me. *(Reads)* "Plasmic red——

(One by one a chorus of voices join him as he continues to read)

BOY AND CHORUS. Pixy purple, whisper blue, hysterical yellow, atomic green, powdered poosh!

(Mr. Fizzle appears again)

MR. FIZZLE. Get that report. Get that report. The report, boy! *(Disappears).*

BOY. *(Yawning and stretching)* Ho-ho-hum. *(Thinking)* Tin.

CHORUS. Oh, such a shame.

BOY. Tin——tin——

CHORUS. The use of tin.

BOY. *(The more he thinks, the drowsier he gets)* The use of tin.

CHORUS. Powdered blue tin—

BOY. Powdered blue tin.

CHORUS. Plasmic red tin—

BOY. Plasmic red tin.

CHORUS. Pixy purple tin——

BOY. Pixy purple tin.

BOY AND CHORUS. *(Building in volume and tempo)* Pixy purple tin, atomic green tin, plumed white tin, petty pink tin!

(Boy is now asleep and chorus continues their orchestration of words and sounds beginning low and building to a climax)

CHORUS. *(Lines divided)* Plumed white
Plasmic red
Pixy Purple
Whisper blue
Hysterical yellow
Atomic green
Powdered poosh, poosh
Poosh
Poosh!

(The lights fade on the boy and come up on the remaining stage area where an outline of a town suggests the imaginary town of pure colors. The chorus, consisting of the people of the town, are in a speaking composition at the other side of the stage. As they speak, the tin man enters. He is painted chartreuse)

ALL OF CHORUS. *(Continuing)* And clashing chartreuse!!

CHORUS. This is the story of a tin man.
    A painted tin man.
        A tin man painted chartreuse.
Clashing, clashing, clashing, clashing chartreuse!

We are the people who live in a painted town.
    A painted town of *pure* colors.
        Red
                and white
                    and green
                        and yellow
Backed by traditions, customs and heritage
    Pure Heritage of Pure colors.

This is our Mayor, Mayor White

MAYOR WHITE. Plumed white, my record—yes sir, plumed white. When you vote at the polls—plumed white record!

CHORUS. And these are our children.

(Hysterical giggles. Atomic Green pinches Pixy)

PIXY. Ouch!

DOCTOR. Did someone call me?

CHORUS. Oh, and our Doctor———Doctor Plasmic Red.

CHILDREN. Oh, no Doctor Red, we were just playing.

(The children run off stage)

DOCTOR. *(Tipping his hat to the ladies)* Well, excuse me, ladies. I have an emergency case. *(Exits)*

PETTY PINK. Goodbye, Doctor. *(She waves and then turns to Mrs. Powdered Poosh)* Now, about that tin man—

MRS. POOSH. He just does not go with our town.

PETTY. Mixed colors, you know.

MRS. POOSH. Someone said it was called "chartreuse." A mixture of———

PETTY. I don't care what it's a mixture of. It clashes with our colors.

MRS. POOSH. Our pure colors. I just don't know what we are going to do.

PETTY. Someone said he was a member of the Neutralist Party.

MRS. POOSH. They always come in strange colors.

PETTY. Look, Powdered Poosh, there's Frisky Orange. I must tell her about the tin man——— *(Calls)* Oh, Frisky! *(She exits)*

MRS. POOSH. *(Looks at the tin man)* Humph! *(She turns up her nose and exits)*

(During this scene the tin man has been in a "frozen" position on the other side of the stage. He comes to life. He moves and gives forth a lonesome sound. Atomic Green runs in)

ATOMIC GREEN. *(Whispers to the Tin Man)* Don't worry, Mr. Tin Man. Something will happen to you, just wait and see. *(Runs back out again)*

(As the Tin Man slowly begins to walk off, making his "lonesome sound" as he goes, the chorus is heard offstage)

CHORUS. This is the story of a tin man———
      The story of a tin man———
         (Getting fainter) a tin man——a tin man
            A tin man———
               Painted———sssssssssh!
                  Chartreuse!!

(Lights fade as Tin Man exits)

Scene 2

As the stage lights come up, the town slowly comes alive, first with sounds to suggest late afternoon and then with movement. Finally school is out and the children enter and begin to play ball. Mrs. Powdered Poosh is heard in the distance and Pixy, her daughter, scurries to hide behind a bush nearby)

MRS. POOSH. *(Calling offstage)* Atomic! *(Enters)* Atomic Green. Have you or Whisper Blue seen my daughter since you left school?

ATOMIC GREEN. *(Crossing his fingers and putting them behind him)* No ma'm, I haven't. Have you Whisper Blue?

WHISPER BLUE. *(Crossing her fingers and putting them behind her)* No Ma'm. Come on, Atomic Green. Let's play over here.

(They move away from Mrs. Poosh to an area closer to Pixy behind the bush)

MRS. POOSH. Well, if you see Pixy Purple, kindly tell her to come home at once. *(Turns to leave)*

PETTY PINK. *(Calling from offstage)* Powdered. Powdered Poosh!

(Petty Pink enters)

POOSH. Yes. Oh, hello, Petty Pink. Have you seen anything of my Pixy? I declare, she never comes home until after dark and then it's too late to do any chores around the house.

PETTY. No, I haven't. Isn't that just like a child? Now, like I was telling——*(She continues in pantomime)*

WHISPER. Psssssss! Pixy. Pixy! Your mother is still here. If you don't stay behind that bush, she'll see you and you'll have to go home.

PIXY. Okay. But tell me when she leaves.

PETTY. *(Continuing her gossip)* And Mrs. Black——Cannibal has a terrible taste for clothes! Did you see that bold leopard skin she wore Sunday.

PIXY. Pssssss! Atomic!

PETTY. Mixed colors!

PIXY. Psssssssst! Atomic!

ATOMIC. Yeah! You'd better not talk so loud.

PIXY. Is she still there?

ATOMIC. Who?

PIXY. Mother. Is she still there?

WHISPER. Yes. She's talking to Petty Pink right now.

(Mayor Plumed White enters. He is jolly and stout)

MAYOR. What are you little fellows up to? Pixy, what are you doing behind that bush?

PIXY. Shhhhh! Just a game, Mayor White. Please don't give me away.

MAYOR. Well, I just wanted to be sure you aren't up to any tricks. You want to keep your record white, you know. Yes sir, plumed white——er, er—like my name. You know, that's why my mother gave me this name. She knew it would influence me to keep a plumed white record. And I have. Why I——

PETTY. Why, Mayor White. What brings you over our way?

POOSH. Out campaigning again, Mayor?

MAYOR. Well, not exactly. I was just telling these youngsters here—plumed white my record—yes sir, plumed white.

PETTY. Like I say, Mayor, you sure have kept our city clean. No new-fangled colors been clashing in our town. Nice and quiet.

MAYOR. Proud of that record. Yes sir!

POOSH. And our children are not influenced by any new, "modern" colors. Why, these colors have been here since my great-great grandfather.

MAYOR. Yes sir. We may not have the hues and shades of a big city but we've got a pure past——a pure heritage and it dates all the way back to——

(The children have thrown the ball and it hits Pixy)

PIXY. Ouch!

(Dr. Plasmic Red comes running on stage)

DR. RED. Did someone call me?

POOSH. What?

PETTY. It's Dr. Plasmic Red. Hello, Doctor.

DOCTOR. Did someone call?

CHILDREN. No, sir. We were just playing.

DOCTOR. Strange. I was positive I heard a cry of pain.

POOSH. Oh, I'm sure it was just your imagination, Dr. Red.

DOCTOR. Well, might be right. Could be my imagination. I've had a very hard day—a very hard day.

PETTY. Oh? Uh . . . uh . . . (Inquisitive) Any——uh—troubles?

POOSH. Any new baby——colors?

DOCTOR. Oh no. Nothing like that. It was a case of a strange mixture of paint.

MAYOR. Oh?

DOCTOR. The painter's dog got into his oils again. I don't see why he doesn't either quit painting or get rid of that dog.

MAYOR. Dogs are a menace in the town. Yes sir.

POOSH. I don't mind the dogs as much as I do that Painter. He's a threat to society.

DOCTOR. Strange man. Mixing paints all day. Seems he is looking for something.

MAYOR. Really?

DOCTOR. Says he wants to discover a new color. Ridiculous!

MAYOR. We have all the colors we need in this town.

PETTY. Yes. WE don't need anymore!

POOSH. The idea of that man!

(They merge into group talk with words like "painter," "menace," "new colors," "pure town," etc. Sounds of late evening begin)

VOICE. *(Offstage calling)* Suppertime! Children!

(Unseen by the adults, all three children now hide behind the little bush)

PETTY. It's about my suppertime, too. Now, where did those children go?

POOSH. Oh, they'll pop up when you call them to eat.

MAYOR. *(Tipping his hat)* Well, good evening to you, ladies. Plumed White Record. *(Exits)*

DOCTOR. *(As though agreeing with the slogan)* Plumed White Record. *(Calling to the mayor)* Just don't let that painter get hold of that record. *(He laughs at his own joke. Then turns to ladies)* Well, goodnight all. *(Exits)*

(The ladies nod and all go their separate ways)

ATOMIC. *(Looking up from behind the bush)* Are they gone?

WHISPER. Not so loud, Atomic. I think so. Look and see, Pixy.

PIXY. *(Looking around bush)* They're gone.

ATOMIC. Come, on, then, let's play. *(Throws the ball)* Catch!

(They throw the ball back and forth a few minutes. Then Atomic throws it over Pixy's head)

PIXY. You threw it too high.

(The Tin Man enters unnoticed. He picks up the ball and begins to move toward the children as though trying to return it to them. They turn and see him and become afraid)

PIXY. Oh, *(Runs to the others)* What's that?

WHISPER. I don't know. He's such a peculiar color.

ATOMIC. He doesn't look like any of us. I haven't ever seen anyone like him before.

PIXY. Neither have I.

WHISPER. I'm scared.

PIXY. Look, he's got our ball.

ATOMIC. You take it, Pixy.

PIXY. No. I'm scared to.

WHISPER. You're the only boy here, Atomic. You've got to go.

VOICE. *(Calling from offstage)* Atomic Green! Atomic! Supper.

ATOMIC. *(Relieved)* Phew! My mother's calling. I've got to go eat. Bye. *(He runs out)*

WHISPER. Wait and I'll walk that way with you.

PIXY. Don't leave me.

(They all exit. The Tin Man walks a few steps after them, then realizes they aren't coming back. He stops and sits down on a stump, and makes his lonesome sounds again. The painter enters with his dog, Brushes. He is whistling and at first does not see the Tin Man. He stops and looks . . . is curious . . . begins to walk around him to get a better look and slowly becomes excited. He and Brushes attempt to make friends with the Tin Man)

PAINTER. Hello.

TIN MAN. *(Hello sound)* Squeak.

140

PAINTER. Taking my dog, Brushes, for a walk. Just came over to see if you were friend or enemy. *(Laughs nervously)*

TIN MAN. *(Trying to be friendly)* Squeak. Squeak.

PAINTER. Friend, huh? *(laughs)* Well, that's good. *(Pause)* Real interested in the color you have there. Sure is different from any I've seen around here. *(Begins to examine him more closely)* Let's see. *(He begins to take notes)* It could be a mixture of———

TIN MAN. *(Sad sigh)* Squeak.

PAINTER. What's the matter, Pal?

TIN MAN. *(Lonesome sound)* Squeak.

PAINTER. Lonesome, eh? Haven't you met any of the people around here?

TIN MAN. *(Nods and repeats lonesome sound. Then he points toward direction of children's exit)* Squeak.

PAINTER. Oh, you like children? Well, it is rather hard to make friends. They ran away from you, hum? Well now, that's too bad. But don't worry, maybe I can be of some help. I'm a painter, you see, and just between the two of us, I think your main trouble is your color. People around here are very conscious of color. They haven't had a change of color in anything for the past 50 years. They never want a change. And your color—well, er—it kinda clashes with the colors they do have. *(He pauses and looks at the Tin Man who has been listening attentively)* Now if I had my paint and brush—let's see, *(Looks in his pocket)* I usually carry a few things around all the time—just in case I need them, you know.

(The painter pulls his paints out of his pockets and holds a sample of each color up against the Tin Man)

You've got to blend in with the town; else they won't like you. *(Suddenly not so sure he is doing the right thing)* You're sure this is what you want?

(The Tin Man nods)

Well, let's see. Red? Nooooo. Dr. Plasmic Red is the only red blood we have in town and he doesn't like competition. Blue? No, that wouldn't do. White? Well, that's the Mayor's color. I know! We'll paint only your face white and then he can't complain—he'll think you are advertising for his campaign!

(He begins to prepare his materials)

Let me see. Palate———er, right here; a little terpentine———and now brushes. Come over here, Brushes.

(His dog Brushes goes over to the painter and wags his tail)

I'll need the finest brush of all.

(He takes his tail and from it he finds a brush. He begins to paint the Tin Man's face)

There. A masterpiece if I do say so myself.

(The Tin Man begins to feel gay and makes happy sounds)

Now you come over to my house for the night and I'll oil your joints and tomorrow you can show off your new color. All the children are going to love you.

(They begin to walk off when the painter stops and speaks confidentially to the Tin Man)

Uh—by the way, I'm real interested in the color you do have. You wouldn't mind if I tried to find the right combination of paints that make that color, would you?

(The Tin Man shakes his head that he wouldn't mind)

Good! Then we're off for home. Come, Brushes, away for the experiment. We might have found something at last.

(They exit as the lights fade)

ACT II

It is early morning and the children are on their way to school. Miss Petty Pink is hanging out her morning wash. Pixy walks down the street and stops at the blue house to call for whisper Blue.

PIXY. *(Calling)* Whisper, you ready for school?

(Whisper comes out)

WHISPER. All ready. Where's Atomic?

(Atomic comes running in, out of breath)

ATOMIC. *(Calling)* Wait for me. Hey, Pixy, did your mother whip you for playing that trick yesterday?

PIXY. No, she just fussed a little.

ATOMIC. Say, what's that?

(The Tin Man enters. He is all smiles for he is confident that the children will accept him this time)

WHISPER. Remember? We saw him yesterday.

PIXY. Looks like he's made out of tin.

WHISPER. Yes, and he's so strange looking.

PIXY. *(Giggling)* He's painted his face white.

WHISPER. But look at the rest of him. What an odd color.

ATOMIC. I like it.

PIXY. I do, too, but——

WHISPER. But what?

PIXY. Why has he painted his face white?

WHISPER. He really isn't so scary looking in the daytime.

ATOMIC. No, and I really like his color. *(Walks around the Tin Man, admiring him)*

WHISPER. *(To Pixy)* Let's go over and talk to him.

(They all walk around the Tin Man, inspecting him)

PIXY. What color would you say he is? He doesn't come from my neighborhood.

WHISPER. Mother said I wasn't to have anything to do with colors I'm not acquainted with.

ATOMIC. But your mother hasn't seen him. He wouldn't hurt you. *(Speaks to the Tin Man)* Hello.

TIN MAN. *(Friendly sound extending his hand)* Squeak.

PIXY. *(Taking his hand)* Look. He wants to play.

WHISPER. Do you think it would be alright?

ATOMIC. Sure. Come on. Let's play.

(They then take the hands of the Tin Man and begin to play. Powdered Poosh enters and sees the children with the Tin Man)

POOSH. (Calling) Pixy! Pixy! Who are you playing with?

PIXY. Oh, Mother. We're just having so much fun.

POOSH. Stop that immediately and come over here. Pixy, Atomic, Whisper, all of you. I want to talk to you.

142

(The children leave the Tin Man and come to Powdered Poosh)

Who is that you are playing with? What's his name? Why aren't you on your way to school?

PIXY. Oh, Mother. He's so nice. He came out to play with us.

WHISPER. And it isn't time for school yet.

ATOMIC. I like him. I've never seen anyone like him before.

POOSH. That's just it. You shouldn't be playing with strangers.

PIXY. Why can't we play with new colors?

POOSH. It just isn't done that's all. Besides, he may try to fill your heads with strange ideas. *(To Atomic)* Does your mother know you're here?

ATOMIC. No ma'm. But she wouldn't care.

(Petty Pink comes out with another load of washing and sees the group talking)

PETTY. What's all the commotion about?

POOSH. Petty, do you know who that stranger is?

(They all turn to look at the Tin Man who now smiles no more but slowly begins to back away)

PETTY. Why, no. Huuuuummmm. What an odd color. You don't think he could be a Neutralist, do you?

POOSH. I don't know. Do you suppose he——he's dangerous?

PETTY. I bet he belongs to the Neutralist Party. They always come in strange colors.

POOSH. It's really unsafe for these children. Suppose he fills their heads with strange ideas?

PETTY. Just trying to overthrow the government, that's what. Call the police! If only the Doctor were here.

POOSH. The Mayor should be able to do something.

PETTY. *(Calling)* Oh, Mayor.

POOSH. *(Calling)* Doctor Red.

PETTY. Better get these children away.

POOSH. Pixy, you children go on to school. And remember, don't stop to talk to any strangers.

(Children look apologetically at the Tin Man and run out. The Tin Man is again in a "frozen" position)

PETTY. They may be invading the town.

POOSH. *(Begins to cry)* Oh, what are we going to do?

PETTY. Call for help. Oh, Mayor! Doctor! Police! Come quickly.

(The doctor enters, bag in hand)

DOCTOR. Did someone call for me?

POOSH. *(Running to him)* Doctor! Oh, Doctor!

(Mayor enters)

MAYOR. What's the matter. What's going on? Plumed white record. Yes, sir, my record is plumed white.

POOSH. Mayor! Look! *(She points to the Tin Man and they all stare at him, then slowly walk around him, keeping their distance)*

143

PETTY. It's him. He's come to invade the town.

DOCTOR. Now calm——calm down, ladies. Let's discuss this calmly.

PETTY. But don't give him time. He may be dangerous.

POOSH. He *is* dangerous. We must protect ourselves.

MAYOR. Hummm. Does have an odd color, doesn't he?

DOCTOR. I've never see anyone quite like him.

PETTY. Of course you haven't. He's dangerous!

POOSH. We must save the children! Our color heritage must be preserved.

PETTY. Our traditions must not be disturbed by someone like this.

DOCTOR. What can we do?

MAYOR. We must investigate——investigate——must investigate.

(The Mayor begins to walk slowly toward the Tin Man. The Tin Man moves toward him, hand extended)

MAYOR. *(Turning away quickly)* He looks too dangerous to investigate. Suppose he should attack me?

DOCTOR. That must not happen. We must protect ourselves. Gather the children up and seal their ears with wax. I'll get the wax. *(Exits)*

(The Tin Man begins to walk toward the group, hand extended)

MAYOR. Look! He's coming at us. Run!

PETTY. *(Running)* Help! Help!

MAYOR. Protect yourselves.

(They all run into their houses and begin to throw things at the Tin Man. Petty Pink throws her washing at him. Then she throws some of her wash water. The Tin Man begins to squeak again)

MAYOR. Lock your windows and doors. Stop up your ears.

(All slam their doors and windows. There is silence. The doctor enters with the children and a box in his hand. He tries to steer them toward their houses but they walk slowly up to the Tin Man)

ATOMIC. Look, somebody's thrown water all over him.

PIXY. He's squeaking again.

WHISPER. Oh, Mr. Tin Man. Please don't look so sad.

TIN MAN. *(Sad Sound)* Squeak.

DOCTOR. Now, children, children. You must get into the house. You don't know who this creature is. He's probably very dangerous.

ATOMIC. He is not, Mistor Mayor. That's all our mothers' ideas. He wouldn't harm any of us.

PIXY. That's right.

WHISPER. Right.

DOCTOR. *(Impatiently)* Now you children listen to me. I had orders to bring you home to your parents. You must go in . . . seal your ears with this wax; you don't know what this man may try to do to you. *(He begins to give each a wad of wax from his box)*

ATOMIC. Oh, please, Mr. Mayor. Let us stay with the Tin Man. He's our friend.

TIN MAN. (In agreement) Squeak. Squeak.

PIXY. Yes, we like him.

WHISPER. We think his color is beautiful.

DOCTOR. Now, listen. What would your mothers———

ATOMIC. We don't care what our mothers say. We're old enough to make up our own minds and we think he's tops.

PIXY. Check!

WHISPER. Check-check.

DOCTOR. But———

(The painter enters hurriedly)

PAINTER. Pal! Are you alright?

TIN MAN. (Answering) Squeak.

PAINTER. What happened? Didn't they like you?

ATOMIC. Sure, we like him. It's our parents.

PIXY. Yes, they think he's dangerous.

WHISPER. Just because he has a new color.

PAINTER. I know how you feel. You know. I kinda think people are always afraid of something they don't understand. They get kinda set in their ways. (To Tin Man) Never want anything new. But look. Look what I brought? My suitcase. And you and Brushes and I are going to pack up and leave. The whole world is waiting for us.

(The painter takes the Tin Man by the hand and they exit with Brushes following)

PIXY. They can't do that to us.

ATOMIC. No, we won't let them.

WHISPER. But what can we do.

ATOMIC GREEN. I don't know but we'll think of something.

DOCTOR. Humph. If you children would excuse me, I would like to add a word . . .

WHISPER. Ahhhhh.

DOCTOR. I think you would like to hear what I have to say.

PIXY. We're in a hurry, Doctor Red.

ATOMIC. Yes, they may be leaving right this minute!

DOCTOR. (Excitedly) That's what I'm trying to say. I think they shouldn't leave.

PIXY. You do?

DOCTOR. Exactly. I've been diagnosing this case and have come to the conclusion that there may be something to this idea of new colors. Statistics show that 205 out of every 500 children dislike eggs intensely; however, on an Easter-egg hunt, not one child refuses to eat the egg that he or she may find. Conclusion: colored shells add flavor to the mind's taste—now why couldn't this principle apply to pills and shots and hospitals?

ATOMIC. I don't know, Dr. Red. I don't think anything could change my feelings toward the hospital.

DOCTOR. No, no, son. It wouldn't change basically. It would merely change its face . . . become more attractive. That's it! More attractive—attractive—attractive—hummmmmmm. *(Exits)*

WHISPER. Well, he thought of something but it doesn't keep the Tin Man and Mr. Painter here.

PIXY. Let's think. A-B-C-D-E-F——

ATOMIC. Oh, that won't help. Pix—Pix! Say, I've got it!

PIXY. What?

ATOMIC. Well———

(The three children go into a huddle with exclamations of "oh" and "ah" and "sweeeeellll." Then they break)

ATOMIC. Gee, you know I'm pretty smart sometimes.

(They exit as lights fade)

ACT III

The children are walking up and down the city street with large picket signs reading:
"Color or Duller"
"Old Colors Always Dye"
"Colored Streetlights Give You Christmas Every Night"
"New Colors Make a More Progressive Community"
"We Want Our Town More Colorful"
"Hurrah For The Tin Man"
"The Painter For Mayor"
"If The Tin Man Leaves, Our Future Leaves, Too"

GENERAL SHOUTS. Hurrah for the Tin Man. We want the Painter for Mayor. We want a change. Let's be more progressive the colorful way. We like chartreuse. Down with the old and up with the new.

(In choreographed movement, the children begin to speak and move to the following lines:)

CHILDREN. We're for the new: *ta-ta-ta-ta!*
   A new me; a new you *ta-ta-ta-ta!*
   A change in our pace—and in the whole human race
   We want the new: *ta-ta-ta-ta-ta!*

ATOMIC. My mother feeds me caster-oil; it has a terrible savor.
   If only they would change the name; it might could change the flavor.

CHILDREN. We're for a change: *ta-ta-ta-ta!*
   No dogs with the mange: *ta-ta-ta-ta!*
   A change on our face and in the whole human race
   Oh, we want a change: *ta-ta-ta-ta-ta!*

WHISPER. My friends all call me bashful; cause Whisper Blue's my name
   But if I changed my color, I might not be so tame.

CHILDREN. Oh, we want a change: *ta-ta-ta-ta!*
   Yes, we want a change: *ta-ta-ta-ta!*
   Mixed colors, new friends
   New beginnings—no ends
   Oh, we want a change: *ta-ta-ta-ta!*

PIXY. My mother wants a new spring hat.
   Says she "Something that's different and untame"
   But how can she like something different
   When all of her differents are the same?

CHILDREN. Oh, we're for the new: *ta-ta-ta-ta!*
A new me; a new you: *ta-ta-ta-ta!*
A change in our pace and the whole human race
We want the new: *ta-ta-ta-ta-ta!*

(*Miss Petty Pink comes out of her house*)

PETTY. What's all this commotion? Pixy, what's the meaning of this?

(*Powdered Poosh enters*)

POOSH. My word! I wonder if the Mayor has seen this.

PIXY. Mother. We want a change in our town.

POOSH. A change? What kind of change, Pixy. You don't know what you are talking about. Now, put that pole down and come in the house right away. What will the neighbors think if they see you———

PIXY. I don't care what they think. We've decided—

PETTY. Did you hear that? *They've* decided!

POOSH. I don't care what you have decided. You can tell me about that once you are in the house. Now come on.

PIXY. Aw, Mother—

ATOMIC. Just a minute, Mrs. Poosh. Pixy and all of us have signed a petition and—

POOSH. A petition? What on earth for?

PETTY. That's what I say. You're too young to be doing things like that.

WHISPER. We live in this town, Miss Pink, and we have a right to express our opinions.

PETTY. Oh, you do, do you?

(*The mayor enters, his usual jolly self*)

MAYOR. Good morning, everyone. Beautiful day for the polls, yes sir, couldn't be a lovelier day.

POOSH. I'm glad you're here, Mayor. Will you please explain to these children why they can't go around signing petitions to change the town overnight?

MAYOR. Petitions? What kind of petitions?

ATOMIC. We've signed a petition, sir, to make some changes in our town and we have agreed, sir, that if you don't back us, we'll get Mr. Painter to run for mayor.

MAYOR. Why, you can't do that. He couldn't possibly run. No one has run against me in the past 12 years. Why, Mrs. Poosh, tell them they can't do this.

PETTY. Tell them? That's what we asked you to do. *You're* the Mayor.

ATOMIC. Yes, sir. You're the Mayor, but if you don't do something to let us know you're for a change in our town, we're going to get the Painter into office. Come on, fellow citizens.

(*The children go out marching and shouting with their signs*)

MAYOR. Wait! Wait! You can't do this. Why, I've been your Mayor for the last 12 years. You can't do this to me. Petty, Powdered, what am I to do?

PETTY. Don't worry, Mayor. We'll think of something.

POOSH. Look, here comes the Doctor. Maybe he will have an idea.

(*The doctor enters, not as hurried as usual*)

DOCTOR. Good afternoon, ladies, Mayor.

(*General exchange of greetings*)

I'm sending out announcements concerning my new office and I want you three to be the first to be my guests.

MAYOR. Why, thank you, Doctor. But I didn't know you were going to move. Where is your new location?

DOCTOR. Oh, I haven't moved, Mayor. I've just made a few new and vibrant changes. Please bring your children, ladies. Even they will find my office pleasant now. (*He exits cheerfully, tipping his hat as he goes*)

PETTY. Why, whatever did he mean by that?

POOSH. I don't know. You don't think he's gone in for this new change deal, do you?

MAYOR. I'm sure he has probably purchased new furniture or maybe some new pictures for his office. Perhaps we should go and investigate.

PETTY. Yes, maybe we had better. Come on, Powdered Poosh, this may be developing into something bigger than we thought.

(*They all exit. The Tin Man enters, and looks around to find no one in sight. Soon Brushes rushes in to the Tin Man, pulls him up on the tree trunk and begins to bark as if announcing his nomination for the office of Mayor. The children come running in*)

PIXY. There he is. Atomic, Whisper, I've found him. Where were you, Mr. Tin Man? We've been looking everywhere for you.

ATOMIC. We thought you had gone.

WHISPER. We were afraid you had left without telling us goodbye.

ATOMIC. He isn't going to leave us, Whisper. We're going to keep him here.

WHISPER. Did you hear that, Mr. Tin Man? We're going to keep you here.

TIN MAN. (*Joyfully*) Squeak.

WHISPER. What did he say?

PIXY. I don't know. Did you hear, Mr. Tin Man? We're going to keep you here.

ATOMIC. He looks happy.

(*The painter rushes in*)

PAINTER. There you are, Pal. I couldn't find you. Why did you run off? We'd better get an early start if we're going to leave. Come with me while I get my suitcases.

ATOMIC. Please, Mr. Painter, don't take him away from us. Not now.

PIXY. We're trying to run you for Mayor.

WHISPER. Yes, and you can't leave us now, either.

PAINTER. What? What's this?

ATOMIC. We're trying to run you for Mayor.

PAINTER. Me? Why? I don't want to be Mayor.

WHISPER. But you're the only one we know who could make our town a nicer place for us to live.

ATOMIC. Besides, you would let us keep the Tin Man.

PIXY. Wouldn't you run for Mayor, Mr. Painter?

PAINTER. Well, I don't know. I haven't thought about it.

ATOMIC. Oh, please do. We'll be your right hand men and whatever you want to do to our town, we'll help you.

148

PAINTER. Well, now, that's mighty nice of you, but you must remember that you kids aren't old enough to run this town entirely by yourselves. Your parents have a lot to say about it.

WHISPER. I'm not sure that they would like all of our ideas.

PIXY. I'm not either.

PAINTER. Maybe you haven't approached them the right way. I have a feeling that some of them feel just the way you do but they know that a quick change without any thought behind it isn't always the best change after all.

ATOMIC. I hadn't thought of it that way.

PAINTER. Besides, I don't know anything about being mayor of a town and your parents know it. They'd never vote for me and since they are the ones to vote, there just isn't a chance for me.

WHISPER. Oh.

PIXY. Ooooh.

PAINTER. (Cheerfully) Besides, to run for Mayor I'd have to go around kissing babies and greeting everybody on the street. I'd hate to have to worry about my campaigns every two years, too. I'm just not cut out to be a Mayor. (To the Tin Man) I'll be back in a minute. (Exits in a hurry)

ATOMIC. Well, we have to think of something.

PIXY. Yeah. We just gotta.

(They all sit down to think. Petty Pink and Powdered Poosh enter)

PETTY. Well, have you seen the like? The doctor's office is a sight if I've ever seen one.

POOSH. What did he call that new color on the walls—fuchsia?

PETTY. And the idea of changing his color name. Did you notice the sign on the door? Dr. Flagrant Fuchsia!

POOSH. And did you hear what Cannibal Black did?

PETTY. No.

POOSH. She got some more vitamin pills from the doctor this morning and when she got home, she didn't have any trouble getting Jet to take them. And do you know why?

PETTY. Why?

POOSH. Because they were all like colored polka-dots!

(They both begin to laugh)

PETTY. It's that tin man. He's the one who caused all of this. And there he is, listening to us.

(The children, hearing this, run over and stand in front of the Tin Man as if to protect him)

POOSH. Now children listen to me. We've had just about enough of this fuss. It's time you were all at home behaving yourselves.

PETTY. (To Brushes) And you go home, too. We'll be by to see the Painter in a few minutes.

PIXY. But Mother.

POOSH. Don't "mother" me, Pixy. Now come along.

ATOMIC. But, Mrs. Poosh, you said yourself that the Tin Man had done wonders for this town.

POOSH. Did I? When did I say that? Did I say that, Petty?

PETTY. You certainly did not.

ATOMIC. But that was what you meant. You said Mrs. Black didn't have any trouble getting vitamin pills down Jet now that they are in such pretty colors.

POOSH. That's true.

ATOMIC. And that's good, isn't it?

POOSH. Well, I suppose so, but—

PIXY. And you know you like his office color, Mother. Remember how you used to talk about how ugly and dingy his waiting room looked?

POOSH. Pixy, you should never repeat in public what I say in private.

PIXY. You did say it, though, didn't you?

PETTY. That's beside the point.

POOSH. No, it isn't, Petty. If we have seen only good things to come out of these changes, then the changes couldn't be so bad, now could it?

PETTY. Well, no, I guess not.

POOSH. Now, Petty . . .

PETTY. I guess we must admit that these children have a point. If there had been any harm done, we wouldn't see so much improvement. I guess you might say these changes are a sign of—a sign of progress!!

POOSH. That's it. A sign of progress.

MAYOR. Humph! You mean that you are going to back the painter for Mayor, is that it?

ATOMIC. Oh, no, Mr. Mayor. Besides, Mr. Painter said he didn't want to be mayor. He wouldn't have time to paint anymore.

PETTY. No, and he wouldn't make a very good mayor, anyway. He's really a very good painter.

POOSH. And you have been such a good Mayor these last 12 years. I'm sure you would want to lead out in some new changes for our town.

MAYOR. A—er—oh—I see, I see. Well, kids, I have been thinking about your petition and after intense consideration I have decided that maybe you have something to add to our town . . . a new color——sense, and I just think it might be a sign of genuine progress. Yes, sir, a sign of real progress.

ATOMIC. Oh, boy, Mayor White. Just wait until we tell Mr. Painter.

PIXY. You're really terrific, Mr. Mayor. I'm sorry we tried to get you out of office.

MAYOR. That's alright, Pixy. I know you were only thinking of what is really best for our town.

POOSH. I'm really very proud of you children. You are beginning to show some real interest in the community and that itself is a sign of progress.

PIXY. But what about the Tin Man?

POOSH. You might ask him home for supper tonight. Perhaps we should get to know him better. Ask him if he will. I'll be waiting for you. (Exits)

PETTY. I didn't really have anything against the Tin Man. It's just that he's so different. Perhaps I was mistaken.

(Mayor Plumed White walks up to the Tin Man)

MAYOR. Mr. Tin Man, we are very happy to welcome you into our city. May I be the first to ask you to become one of the healthy citizens of our community.

(The Tin Man extends his hand and the Mayor takes it)

Now, I must be on my way to see Mr. Painter. I have been thinking what a real contribution he can make to the City Beautification Board. *(To Petty as they exit)* I know he will have a lot of good ideas. *(Turns back to the Tin Man)* Anytime I can be of service to you, please feel free to call. I have a plumed white record of service.

(Petty and the Mayor exit while discussing their plans. The children run up to the Tin Man)

WHISPER. Did you hear that, Mr. Tin Man? They all want you.

TIN MAN. *(Happily)* Squeak. Squeak.

(Atomic and Mr. Painter rush in)

ATOMIC. Now see, Mr. Painter. I was right. Here is the Tin Man and he hasn't been out of town.

WHISPER. Mayor White has just gone to your house to ask you to join the City Beautification Board.

PAINTER. *(Excitedly)* He did?

ATOMIC. See! You were right. Our parents did consider our ideas and they are going to make some changes. Now you and the Tin Man won't leave us, will you?

PAINTER. I don't suppose we can now. There's just so much that needs to be done.

CHILDREN. Can we help?
        I'll help paint.
        I'm a good worker.
        We'll help change our town. We'll have a progressive city!

CHILDREN. *(In choreographed movement as before)*

        We're for the new: ta-*ta*-ta-ta-*ta*!
        A new me; a new you: ta-*ta*-ta-ta-*ta*!
        A change in our town to stay the whole year around,
        Yes, we're all for the new: ta-*ta*-ta-ta-*ta*!

(They all exit chanting as the lights fade)

        We're for the new: ta-*ta*-ta-ta-*ta*!
        A new me; a new you: ta-*ta*-ta-ta-*ta*!
        A change for the best that will stand every test,
        Yes, we're for the new——the new——the new——the new . . .

(As lights fade out, the spot comes up again on the boy in Study Hall. He is waking up and realizes he has been dreaming)

BOY. Gee, I must have been dreaming. Boy, what a dream! There couldn't be any real people like that, could there, Mr. Fizzle?

(He looks up to where Mr. Fizzle has been appearing and suddenly realizes that Mr. Fizzle is not there but all the people of the town of pure colors are. They rush out and chase him off stage saying:)

        "Who says we aren't real?"
        "Oh, yes we are. We're as real as you are!"
        "See us! See us! See us!"

                    CURTAIN

PRODUCTION NOTES

The Tin Man and the Painted Town is a fantasy. Although light and whimsical in character and situation, it is also an idea play. Each character is a caricature of a specific type of personality. The color name of each suggests a certain quality of personality; further imaginative ideas might suggest that each color-character have a costume of a certain shape and texture. Character portrayal may emphasize basic rhythms of movement, mannerisms and gestures, and level and patter of voice.

Since the major plot of the play takes place in the boy's imaginative dreams, to present the play realistically would lose the magic and primary intention of the script. Since Paul Klee inspired the basic idea for the play (*Discussed in the text*), perhaps Klee and even Jean Miro might serve as a stimulus for ideas on production style.

The characters are clearly drawn:

BOY is an average teenager who hates to get reports or do anything that does not engage him in activity. As usual, he really tries but because his heart isn't in the project, he falls asleep. It is only the memory of his teacher fussing at him that provokes him to work at all. But he is a most imaginative lad; perhaps his talent lies more in his creative ideas than in the mechanics of a report on the production of tin.

MR. FIZZLE is a thin, dried-up, kinky-headed old man with a scratchy beard. He has been teaching too long and is almost too old for his job. He does speak with authority, however, and if nothing else——he scares his students into working for him.

PIXY PURPLE is an impish wisp of a girl who is gleefully happy, doesn't have a care in the world, and is constantly mischievous. She has bangs and maybe pigtails, moves well for she would be an excellent cheer-leader. She always has the best of intentions but her joy in tricks and games usually tempts her away from what she knows she should be doing. She is not a trouble-maker for her tricks are never detrimental to anyone . . . only "trying" to her mother.

ATOMIC GREEN is the bully of the neighborhood. He is strong and has a loud voice. He really wants to be looked up to by the girls and so always assumes a brave attitude though he may not feel so brave within. Atomic is all-boy and very athletic. He's a good sport and looks the outdoor type.

WHISPER BLUE is pretty, shy, and feminine. She is not as aggressive as the other two but she never wants to be left out. She is fawn-like and has a good sense of humor. Perhaps she is the most compassionate one of the group and her feelings for the Tin Man are very deep and real to her.

MAYOR PLUMED WHITE is round and jolly. A twinkle in his eye, he has a word for everyone and always a cheerful one. His happy attitude sets a good example for the town but his desire for everyone to be happy sometimes causes him to want to keep everything at a stand-still so that all will be calm and quiet. He is not a lover of friction or arguments. He is a Mayor beyond reproach as a citizen and person and gleefully reminds everyone of his "plumed white record" which he has developed into a rhythmical, sing-song slogan always accented by a characteristic wave of his hand.

DOCTOR PLASMIC RED is very business-like. He loves his work and takes it very seriously. Most of all he prides himself on always being near when needed and anytime he hears a cry of pain or anguish, he is quick to answer his "call." Dr. Red is perhaps the quickest to be aware of and accept new ideas. Perhaps it is because he is constantly trying to improve and keep up as a doctor. Nevertheless, it is he who starts the ball rolling by experimenting with the idea of new colors and changes of approach in routine things.

MRS. POWDERED POOSH is Pixy's mother. She is a good mother but sometimes too protective. Although she does engage in a certain amount of gossiping with Petty Pink, she is not a gossip at heart and does not like to repeat any unkind words. She wants only the best for her children and her community and will work very hard for what she thinks is right. But she is a wealthy woman, and this has caused her to feel special in her neighborhood and sometimes her snobbish attitudes are revealed too clearly. She loves clothes and material possessions but down deep she knows that these are the least important considerations.

PETTY PINK is an old maid who is in her last years of good looks. She is round, rosy, and talkative. She is also the town gossip for she has little to do but talk and listen and talk some more. She believes everything she hears and reads, and she is sometimes too quick to draw conclusions and dream up fantasy situations, but she is also easily apologetic if she finds she is wrong.

THE TIN MAN should be highly sympathetic. His facial expressions, sounds, and movement must tell much about him for this is all he has to work with. Where he comes from, one never knows, but they do know that he has a need to be wanted and accepted. He has a kind heart and holds no malice toward anyone. Basically he has a sad heart for few people have ever made him happy . . . few have ever cared.

MR. PAINTER is highly energetic, curious, and a hard worker. He has a lot of good ideas, is very creative and experimental and likes everyone. It is somehow easy for him to over-look the smallness in people for he is much larger himself. He understands human nature and is wise in his interpretations of actions and attitudes. He is somewhat of a sage but he is also a pioneer for he is interested in anything new and exciting. He has no relatives and so has no attachments which hinder him from taking a trip whenever he desires. His one pal is his dog Brushes—who also doubles as his source of paint brushes. He does not find the people of the town particularly stimulating and longs for a pal with a desire for knowledge and new experiences.

BRUSHES is the Painter's dog. He is frisky but always posing with a human viewpoint. He is not like a real dog—more like a human-being in dog's clothing.

COSTUMES

Costume suggestions might include leotards and tights for all characters in the color of their role. Then basic shapes in colors and textures of the character can be attached so that the fantasy quality of the characters is a visual one also. Suggestions for shape, color and textures are as follows:

PIXY PURPLE—Zig-zags or series of curves, purple and shades related, net-cheesecloth-organdy-cellophane, elf-like features in makeup with purple and lavender highlights.

ATOMIC GREEN—Explosive-mushroom characteristics, combination of hard/soft mate-rials like chain and cotton, shades of green, muscle-man makeup features in shades of green and yellow highlights.

WHISPER BLUE—Flowing material in shades of blue, chiffon, velvet cording, feathery ac-cessories, ballerina features in makeup with blue and purple highlights.

MAYOR PLUMED WHITE—All white with accents of black. Shaped like a plume and yet suggestions of dignity and importance in paper, velvet and tassels. Clown-like face with happy look.

DOCTOR PLASMIC RED—Red and shades of red, shaped like a droplet—even his bag is a droplet—but his stethescope is real but colored. Accessories to suggest plastics and other antiseptic materials. Red makeup with black bushy eyebrows and goatee . . . serious and important expression.

MRS. POWDERED POOSH—Yellow and shades of gold. Materials of elegance and wealth: fur, velvet, jewels. Perhaps a diamond or octagonal shape. Hat and gloves. Overly made-up face with emphasis on light pink cheeks and gold eyelashes.

MISS PETTY PINK—Pink and shades related. Shaped like a powder puff—with cotton, cellophane, tinsel and glitter material. Apron; purse; pink, round makeup with accent on round eyes and arched brows with bowed lips.

THE TIN MAN—Chartreuse costume with metalic painting on boxes combined to give a square-shaped tin man. Head square with opening only for face. Idea for painting in shades of chartreuse could be inspired by Paul Klee's painting "WOMAN IN COSTUME."

MR. PAINTER—Multi-colored apron-shape like palette with "brush" hair.

BRUSHES—Obvious dog costume in brown only but should be stylized to blend in with other costumes. Ideas can again come from Klee or Miro.

SET

The set includes a desk, chair and backing for the study hall scene. The town can be suggested by an abstract line-drawing of the town. The outline can be made from 1 x 2 boards, pipe, or other thin materials. Portions can be filled in to give solid color and depth to the outline. See paintings by Piet Mondrian for ideas.

The set should also include a tree stump or something that would give a level for standing or sitting but should be in the style of the rest of the set.

DON'T CROSS THAT LION!

a play in one act

written by 10- through 12-year-old children

supervised by Louise Mosley

Don't Cross That Lion! was written and produced by the Dallas Theater Center Children's Theater in the spring of 1963. The student playwrights were also the original cast.

Harriet (a monkey)	BECKY BOWEN
Cynthia (a monkey)	CINDY BOONE
Uncle Gorilla	STEVE McCARTY
Mockingbird	CAROL LUPTON
Bear	KEITH SLAUGHTER
Lion	ROGER BROWN
Judge Owl	CAROL GERHAUSER
Mrs. Squirrel	JANICE TILTON
Parrot	LINDA HUGHETT
Fox	SUSAN GOODELL
Miss Mink	SARAH OSBURN
Miss Chinchilla	SHANNON TAYLOR
Mrs. Rabbit	HERMA ROSENBACH
Missy Rabbit	ANN CUNNINGHAM

PLACE: The Forest

Scene I: Tree in the Forest
Scene II: Home of Mrs. Parrot
Scene III: The Bear's Cave
Scene IV: Center of the Forest
Scene V: Home of Mrs. Parrot
Scene VI: Center of the Forest

TIME: The Present

SCENE. Although each scene suggests a different area of the forest, the stage may be set for all scenes at once with the action continually flowing from one scene to another with no break throughout the play. In such case the set consists of a minimum of five trees: Uncle Gorilla's tree downstage left, which can be climbed, the Bear's tree upstage left center which has an opening for entering, Mrs. Parrot's tree upstage center which can be climbed, Judge Owl's tree upstage right which can be climbed, and the Mockingbird's tree downstage right which has a limb with a hive of honey hanging from it and may or may not be climbable.

AT RISE. The animal kingdom is asleep. Judge Owl only is wide awake and hoots occasionally to remind all he is on watch. The Bear, seen in his opening, is snoring loudly, as is Uncle Gorilla. The others stir only as they shift positions or respond to their dreams. From the distance (made offstage by the Fox, Misses Chinchilla and Mink and Mrs. Squirrel) come the sound of birds in early morning activity. Harriet hears them, stirs, yawns, stretches and hops down to Cynthia on the ground below her.

HARRIET. *(To Cynthia)* Good morning.

(Cynthia now awakens and looks at Harriet)

Do you know what I'm thinking about?

CYNTHIA. *(Wide awake now and enthusiastic)* Yes.

HARRIET. Breakfast!

CYNTHIA. *(Suddenly remembering what she will have to sat and dreads it)* Tiger milk, you mean.

HARRIET. And rice gruel sprinkled with mace.

CYNTHIA. *(Begins to moan)* Oh for the days when we ate bananas like other monkeys. *(Remembering and rubbing her stomach)* The wonderful coconuts we used to eat . . mmmmmmmm.

HARRIET. But that was in the days before Uncle discovered health food.

(Uncle Gorilla comes awake at the sound of his name. He yawns, stretches, and begins exercising)

UNCLE. What a useful looking day. I'll have to have the girls run fifty miles before breakfast. *(Begins to exercise again)* One, two, three. One, two, three. *(Suddenly he stops and looks around to see Harriet and Cynthia watching him from behind the tree)* There you are. I see you. Come out and begin your warmups.

(They back away from him)

Just what do you think you're doing?

HARRIET. Nothing, Uncle.

UNCLE. Well, good. I have a special breakfast for you—banana . . .

HARRIET AND CYNTHIA. Ah!

UNCLE. Peel cooked in yogurt.

HARRIET AND CYNTHIA. *(Sudden disappointment)* Ooooh.

UNCLE. *(Grabbing vine and starts to swing)* No, I guess I'm too old to swing down.

(The Bear and Mockingbird enter and do not see Uncle and the girls)

MOCKINGBIRD. *(Following the Bear to downstage right)* You idiot, now listen to me. Say "I the bear." *(Waiting. No Answer)* Repeat that.

BEAR. *(Puts his toys down and begins to play with his blocks)* Yeah, yeah, yeah.

MOCKINGBIRD. Listen! "I, the bear, challenge Lion to an election for king of the forest. The Lion is an unworthy office-holder."

156

BEAR. *(A little interested)* Why ain't de Lion wort'y?

MOCKINGBIRD. Numbskull! After all the trouble I go through to write this speech for you, you ask questions. *(Pause)* It's because he's a coward. He hasn't killed anything since he's been in office. Now repeat. "I, the Bear, ...

BEAR. I da Bear . . . . . . but my name ain't Ida!

(Mockingbird looks at him hopelessly. During the preceeding scene, Uncle, Harriet and Cynthia have moved behind their tree so they could listen but not be seen. Now they begin to move out to get a better look while the Mockingbird begins to take the Bear's blocks away from him. He puts them behind his tree and out of sight)

UNCLE. What are they doing here?

HARRIET. Shhhhhh! Listen. They're going to challenge the Lion to an election.

UNCLE. *(Very pleased)* And run me, no doubt.

CYNTHIA. *(Disgustedly)* The Bear!

MOCKINGBIRD. *(As he arranges the Bear's hat and general action of preparing him to be king)* I can see it now———when you are King of the forest *(To the audience)* and I rule everything. You'll sit on the throne and I'll make the decrees. You can have the crown and I the treasury. You can have banquets but I'll tell you how and when, when you are the King of the forest and I rule everything.

(The Lion enters as Mrs. Squirrel comes through the forest. She is bustling to market and he is making his morning stroll through the forest. They stop to chat)

MOCKINGBIRD. *(Whispering)* There's the lion. Now's the perfect time. *(Calling loud and clear)* Listen, everyone, gather around. We've got an announcement to make.

(The forest animals come down from their trees, and in from either side as they gather around the Mockingbird and the Bear)

MOCKINGBIRD. *(Whispers to Bear)* Say it.

BEAR. I da Bear . . .

MOCKINGBIRD. *(Still whispering)* That's fine . . . go on.

BEAR. I da Bear . . . . . . uh . . . uh . . .

MOCKINGBIRD. *(Impatient but trying to hide it)* What this modest, fearless, honest, intelligent, leader-type soul wishes to say is that——he challenges the unworthy Lion to an election for King of the Forest.

(General buzz of excitement as everyone begins to talk to everyone else as follows:)

MISS CHINCHILLA. Dear me, an election! That means free food!

MRS. SQUIRREL. Yes, and parties! Lots of parties!

MRS. RABBIT. New clothes, new hats . . .

MISS MINK. I must be sure that I'm in the Social Register.

MISSY RABBIT. Parades and Picnics!

FOX. And barbecue! YUmmmmmmmmmmmmmmmmmm!

CYNTHIA. Did you hear that, Harriet? Real food!

HARRIET. I can hardly wait!

UNCLE. Now if you want my advice . . .

PARROT. Honey, did you pay your poll tax this year?

MRS. SQUIRREL. I'll never get to see my favorite Westerns on television. They will always be interrupting to bring a special statement or public debate.

MRS. RABBIT. I haven't gotten all the posters out of my garden from the last election. My sweet peas have climbed all over them.

JUDGE OWL. As Supreme Court Judge, I'll preside and check all qualifications.

LION. But why? What have I done? Why do you want to have a new King?

(When the Lion asks this question, all quiet down, suddenly realizing that none of them knows the reason for a new king)

MOCKINGBIRD. Because you are a coward. You haven't killed anything since you've been in office.

(Outburst from crowd again: some saying "that's right" and others answering "he didn't need to kill anything")

MOCKINGBIRD. *(Quieting the crowd)* What should a REAL leader be able to do? Now, take this lion here, just look at him . . . he wouldn't hurt a fly, not even a mosquito if it were biting him! *(The timid, lovable lion just hangs his head in shame and embarrassment)* What we need in this day and time is a leader with real courage who won't be afraid to stand up and fight for what he wants. *(A few agreements)* Everyone else fights. If we have a king who is afraid of his own shadow and wants to just sit and talk about all our troubles and gripes, our enemies will be taking our back yards while we sit around the dining table. *(More agreements)*

Now, I propose as a real fighter and true leader, the Bear here. *(Harriet has come over near the Bear and has been irritating him by standing too close and watching him. He now takes a swat at her and she ducks)* Look, there he is fighting now. Come here, Bear. *(He does this only to get him away from Harriet and getting in trouble)* Get away from that monkey and come see the people. *(He drags Bear away and Harriet makes a face at him which almost gets another rouse from him)* Have you people of the forest ever seen such an upstanding citizen? *(Makes Bear stand up straight)* He knows what he wants and, what's more important, how to get it . . . by grabbing it, and fighting if the other fellow grabs, too. None of this sitting around the dining table and starving while we "talk over" who gets the best piece of meat! Good Folk of the Forest, are you hungry?

(General negative response)

Do you want to see all your food taken by the enemy while we do nothing?

(More response)

Then let's do something about it. Is the Lion fit any longer to be our weak leader?

(Crowd begins to look at the lion and back away from him as they shake their heads and mumble "No")

Do you want a strong leader to fight for your rights?

CROWD. Yes!

MOCKINGBIRD. Then let's make the Bear our King!

CROWD. Yes!

MOCKINGBIRD. Hurrah for the Bear!

CROWD. Hurrah for the Bear!

JUDGE OWL. *(Who has been listening quietly all this time and now clears his throat to speak)* Just how do you intend to carry out this election?

MOCKINGBIRD. I thought we . . .

JUDGE. I suggest you have a series of contests after which everyone may vote.

LION. *(Grateful to the Owl for coming to his rescue)* That seems fair.

MOCKINGBIRD. *(To himself)* It's not what I planned.

158

CROWD. What's wrong? Are you scared? Let's have some contests!

MOCKINGBIRD. If that's what you want. But what kind of contests?

MRS. SQUIRREL. A pie-eating contest.

BEAR. *(Hungry)* Goody!

LION. *(Frowning)* Ugh! Ugh!

MRS. RABBIIT. A party-throwing contest.

BEAR. I luv parties.

UNCLE. A race!

BEAR. Oh, goody, goody, goody!

LION. That's not too bad. *(Hands his crown to Judge Owl)*

JUDGE. Then that's settled. *(Announcing in loud voice)* Two weeks from today we will have the election. A week from now we will start "Contest Week."

CROWD. *(Yelling excitedly)* Hurray! Rah!

(Buzz of excitement and activity as all leave but the Lion)

LION. *(To himself)* I really don't know much about this campaign business. What I need is a campaign manager, like the bear has. Now who . . . *(He looks around and sees the Parrot climbing into her tree)* . . . the Parrot. Would she do it? The only way to find out is to ask . . . so here goes.

(He walks over to the Parrot's tree and calls)

Miss Parrot? Miss Parrot?

PARROT. Yes? Who is it? Who is it?

LION. It's me, the Lion. I need someone to run my campaign for me. I thought you might like to.

PARROT. *(Agreeably)* Why certainly! Certainly!

LION. You will

PARROT. Will what? Will what?

LION. Manage my campaign.

PARROT. Campaign? What campaign?

LION. My campaign for king of the forest.

PARROT. King of the forest? You are the king of the forest.

LION. Don't you remember? The Bear challenged me to three contests——eating, party-throwing, and a race——to see who is most fit to be King of the Forest.

PARROT. Of course I remember, but I don't know about being campaign manager.

LION. The Mockingbird is going to help the Bear.

PARROT. Then it's a cinch you'll win.

LION. But suppose I don't. Just think what would happen if the Bear got elected.

PARROT. Then we'll make sure he won't be. *(Jumping down by him and putting her wing on his shoulder)* My boy, I think the first thing we ought to do in our campaign is to find people who will help us get each contest organized. What are those contests again?

LION. Pie-eating.

PARROT. Like pie?

LION. Hate it. Party-throwing—

PARROT. Like parties?

LION. Too shy. And a Race.

PARROT. What kind of shape are you in?

LION. (Holding his tummy out) Flabby.

PARROT. You need a coach for the contest, someone who will get you in shape.

LION. What about Uncle Gorilla?

PARROT. Perfect, Perfect! He hates the Bear. Now, who can give the party?

(The Fox quietly slips onstage and hides behind a tree as he listens)

LION. If we get someone good, they can take care of it and it won't matter if I'm shy.

PARROT. That's good thinking! (Lion grins, proud of his contribution) The Mink and Chinchilla. They're the most sociable animals in the forest.

LION. Yes, but why would they want to help me?

PARROT. You might offer them the post, of say——Minister of Culture.

LION. Well . . . .

PARROT. We're going to have to do something about this pie business You must like pie—everyone likes pies. You've been eating pies that aren't good. Who makes good pies?

LION. (In low voice, hopefully) Mrs. Squirrel?

PARROT. (Jumping up and down) Mrs. Squirrel! Perfect! What do you think of having Mrs. Squirrel?

LION. I think she's perfect.

(The Fox sneezes and the Parrot and Lion turn and catch him hiding behind the tree)

PARROT. Well, what do you want? What do you want?

FOX. I—uh—uh—just wanted to tell the Lion that I'm on his side all the way.

LION. Thank you very much.

FOX. Uh . . . uh . . . I guess I'd better be going.

PARROT. Goodbye.

(The Fox leaves in a hurry)

See? The whole forest is falling our way already. Yes, unusual I'd say. (He begins to think and become suspicious. He seems at a lost for words suddenly) Uh—uh—well, we ought to have a committee meeting with all the people who are going to help us. You write invitations and tell them to come tomorrow at four.

LION. Everything's working out perfectly, isn't it?

PARROT. (Leading him offstage as a real buddy) Perfect! Just perfect!

(The Fox comes running onstage to the entrance to the Bear tree and knocks on the door. Mr. Mockingbird sticks his head out and the Fox whispers something)

MOCKINGBIRD. You say they're having a committee meeting tomorrow?

FOX. Yes.

MOCKINGBIRD. (Coming out of the tree followed by the Bear) We don't need Mrs. Squirrel anyway. That glutton will eat everything—Miss Chinchilla, I mean. And Mrs. Squirrel would break us by putting so much butter in her pies. She uses butter like she were trying to use up all the surplus in one pie. I do wish we could get Miss Mink, though. She's an important and wealthy woman.

FOX. We still can get her if we play our cards right. Pardon the term of the trade. Why don't we sort of watch that meeting from a distance?

MOCKINGBIRD. Good! We still need other people. Do you know anyone? What about your family——any relatives with a leaning toward politics?

FOX. All my friends are up the river——dam project, you know.

MOCKINGBIRD. I'm no good either——none of my relatives have been to Harvard.

(The Bear begins to throw his blocks in the air)

MOCKINGBIRD. Stop that! Here. (Hands Bear large sheet of paper) Draw a poster. Make yourself useful.

FOX. We need some slogans and some posters. Make the public aware of the Bear. Hey, that's good. Advertise, visualize!

MOCKINGBIRD. Vote for the Bear——he's unbearable. (Pause——looks at the Bear as though he might consider it) No, that would never do.

FOX. We could change sides. "Don't cross that lion!"

MOCKINGBIRD. What?

FOX. Just a thought.

MOCKINGBIRD. What are you doing now?

BEAR. Makin' da poster. (He holds poster up)

MOCKINGBIRD. My gosh! What's that a picture of?

BEAR. Me!

(Blackout)

(In the forest Mrs. Rabbit and Missy Rabbit enter carrying signs saying "Vote Bear" and meet Miss Mink and Miss Chinchilla with signs saying "Vote Lion." They all four tack them up on different trees, then notice one another's signs and go off in a huff)

(Blackout)

(Miss Parrot and Lion are preparing for the committee meeting. The setting may be in Miss Parrot's house or at the bottom of her tree. In either case, a rug covers the acting area and five stools are being placed by the Lion as the scene begins)

PARROT. There's a spot on the rug.

LION. They will be here any minute now. It's too late to get it up.

PARROT. I can try. (Gets on floor to clean spot when Mrs. Squirrel enters and knocks on the door or tree)

LION. Someone's at the door. I'll get it.

(Mrs. Squirrel enters)

Hello, Mrs. Squirrel.

MRS. SQUIRREL. Look what I brought——pies. I just know you'll love my pies.

PARROT. Now isn't that nice? (Takes them and puts in window of house or on limb of tree.

MRS. SQUIRREL. I thought you could serve it this afternoon.

(Another knock, Lion answers it and Mink and Chinchilla enter)

LION. Hello Miss Mink, Miss Chinchilla.

MISS MINK. I can't begin to tell you how flattered we are to have been asked to serve on this worthwhile project.

(Chinchilla has "smelled" her way over to the place where the pies have been placed)

PARROT. It's we who should be flattered to have two women of your talents to assist us. (She sees Chinchilla almost sampling the pies) Mrs. Squirrel brought those for us to have later, Miss Chinchilla. Wasn't that nice?

(Mrs. Squirrel beams)

CHINCHILLA. How lovely, but you see, I can't have any. I'm on a diet.

MRS. SQUIRREL. Tch, tch. What a shame.

(Knock at the door, Lion answers and Uncle enters)

LION. Hello, Uncle. How are you?

UNCLE. Fine, a little stiff. (Puts hand to his back as he begins to walk even stiffer) How are you, Ladies? Miss Mink?

(The ladies smile and nod their heads except for Miss Chinchilla who is now eating a small piece of pie)

MISS MINK. Fabulous! Utterly fabulous!

UNCLE. Mrs. Squirrel?

MRS. SQUIRREL. Still baking.

UNCLE. Miss Chinchilla?

CHINCHILLA. (Surprised, she tries to hide her mischief) Uhh! Who me? Oh, just fine. Just fine, thank you.

PARROT. Well, that's just fine. Now, I think we can start the meeting. (In lower voice to Miss Chinchilla) Mrs. Squirrel will serve you later, dear.

CHINCHILLA. Of course, but I can't touch a bite. Must watch my waistline.

(Parrot smiles knowingly)

PARROT. Shall we start with the race? (All sit)

UNCLE. I'll have to get Lion in shape. He looks pretty bad. (Sees Chinchilla eating again) Say, you don't look so good yourself, Miss Chinchilla!

(Miss Chinchilla turns—caught)

PARROT. Now that we're through with the race . . . Miss Chinchilla, we'll serve pie later.

CHINCHILLA. (Refusing to admit she has been caught) Uh . . . uh . . . not for me, really. I'm on a diet, thank you. (She mumbles the latter part)

MISS MINK. I have the most fantastic plans for the party. Chinchilla dear, shall we tell them?

CHINCHILLA. Yes, of course. (Now meek and quiet)

(As the conversation continues, the Fox and Mockingbird are seen sneaking in and stealing the pies. No one sees them)

MISS MINK. We can invite everyone in the forest . . .

CHINCHILLA. We can serve lots of little sandwiches.

MISS MINK. . . . except the Bear and Mockingbird.

CHINCHILLA. Honey punch would be nice.

MRS. SQUIRREL. *(Standing up)* You didn't have to eat all my pie!

LION. What?

MRS. SQUIRREL. She ate all of my pie!

PARROT. Chinchilla, you didn't have to do that!

CHINCHILLA. I didn't.

MISS MINK. I'm quite certain that Mrs. Squirrel is mistaken.

MRS. SQUIRREL. You glutton you. You even ate the pan!

CHINCHILLA. Glutton! I'm on a diet *(She storms out)*

MISS MINK. My dear! *(She follows Miss Chinchilla)*

LION. *(Trying to stop them)* Oh, no!

(Lion looks at Parrot and Uncle with a long face. They are all bewildered)

PARROT. Who can plan the party now?

UNCLE. I will! I'll take over from here.

(Blackout)

(The scene begins with a parade led by Judge Owl and followed by the Lion and the Bear, the Mockingbird and the Parrot, and all the other animals. They carry signs, carry balloons, posters, have noise instruments and wear festive hats. They march around the stage and through the trees, keeping time with recorded band music. Finally the Judge holds up his hand and stops the parade and calls for attention)

JUDGE OWL. As Supreme Court Judge of this forest, it is my duty and privilege to officially open "Contest Week." As citzens of the forest we must attend all of the contests so that we may vote as intelligent and informed citizens. First, there is the party, then the pie-eating and finally the race. Ladies and Gentlemen, let us begin CONTEST WEEK!!

(The crowd cheers and the parade continues until all are led offstage but Uncle who goes to the area near his tree and begins pulling out his party surprises: weights, a jump rope, boxing gloves, and small hand weights which he takes for himself and begins to exercise. Lion and Parrot also remained behind and began exercises with him but soon became weak and collapsed on the floor)

UNCLE. It's a good thing you let me take care of the party. Boy, is this going to be a whing-ding! That's all right. You two can stop now.

UNCLE. *(Placing his equipment in various areas)* Boy, have I got some games planned! Boy, oh, boy!

(Harriet and Cynthia enter)

HARRIET. We're the first ones here.

CYNTHIA. Oh, we didn't see you. Hello, Mr. Lion, Miss Parrot.

LION. Hello girls.

(Miss Parrot can only wave)

UNCLE. *(Rushing over to put the girls near the weights)* You girls are lucky because you're the first ones here. I'm going to let you lift weights. Go on——start. *(They groan and begin tugging their weights)* You're going to have lots of fun!

(Judge Owl enters)

LION. *(Standing up and helping Parrot to her feet)* How are you, Judge?

UNCLE. I'm glad you're here, Judge. Here's something special for you. You've been putting on a little weight lately. Put on these gloves and box with Parrot.

(Parrot does a double-take to Uncle, then tries to grin and bear it as she begins to spar with the Judge. Then Mrs. Rabbit and Missy enter.)

MRS. RABBIT. Our fur looks so nice since we got it back from the cleaners. Don't get it dirty, now.

MISSY. I'm going to hardly move all evening.

LION. Good . . . . . .

UNCLE. Just what I need. *(Uncle takes them by the arm and leads them away)* You two can jump rope together. This is going to be a great party. *(He picks up a bell and rings it)* That means for everyone to change places. Judge, you and Parrot can lift weights. Rabbits, you box. Girls, you can jump rope. Ready? *(He rings bell as everyone changes places)* Change!

(Miss Mink and Miss Chinchilla enter)

UNCLE. *(Getting to them before Lion even sees them)* I know, you saw what fun everyone was having and decided to come back over to the Lion's side.

MISS MINK. No. We've come to invite everyone to the Bear Barbecue. And from the looks of everyone here, it will be a welcome invitation. *(Louder)* We have lots of rocking chairs.

CHINCHILLA. You can also throw darts at pictures of the Lion and guess who. *(She looks coyly at Uncle)*

(Everyone turns and looks at Uncle)

CROWD. That's right!

(All begin to leave except Lion, Parrot, and Uncle)

JUDGE. After all, we must be impartial!

UNCLE. Wait! You can't leave now. You haven't eaten yet. The games were to work up your appetite.

CROWD. *(Stopping and turning back)* Food?

UNCLE. Yes, I've lots of things to eat. *(They all begin to walk toward him)* There's piles of wheat germ flavored with blackstrap molasses, gallons of yogurt . . . . . . *(All turn and run)* Why, what's wrong? *(Turns back to Lion and Parrot)* What's wrong with them? Don't they like parties?

(Blackout)

The scene is the forest a few hours later. Banners are flying to establish the beginning line for the race, posters are everywhere, and balloons are held by several. Everyone is on stage talking in small groups except the Fox, Lion, Parrot. The Fox follows the Lion and Parrot. The Lion has eaten so much he can hardly walk. He goes to the tree down left and sits down.

LION. Ohhhhhhh.

PARROT. Yes sir. Maybe we didn't win the party, but we certainly won the pie eating contest. How do you feel? *(Lion belches)* Well, we won!

LION.———with no thanks to Mrs. Squirrel.

PARROT. You know, it's odd, very odd. There was pepper in the pie but Mrs. Squirrel says she didn't do it.

LION. Who else could have?

FOX. *(Standing close by)* Yes———*(Grinning)* I wonder.

(The Mockingbird enters in his usual confident style)

MOCKINGBIRD. I hope you're ready to lose the race, Lion. My candidate is going to win, you know.

164

PARROT. Ha!

FOX. When you think about it, this is the most important contest of all. Whoever wins the foot race will win the election because it is the most important contest. Our king must be physically fit. He who can run the fastest can get out of trouble the fastest and everyone will vote for the one who wins the most contests.

PARROT. Goodness, he's right! *(To Lion)* Are you all right?

LION. I don't feel so good!

PARROT. Try walking. *(Lion and Parrot walk to other side of stage leaving Fox and Mockingbird alone)*

MOCKINGBIRD. You didn't pepper the pies enough. He can still walk.

FOX. I peppered and peppered Mrs. Squirrel's pies. How was I to know that Uncle brought pies, too. They used his pies when they found out the others were peppered.

MOCKINGBIRD. The Bear must win the race. Don't fail me now. *(The Fox turns to leave when he sees the Bear entering and Harriet pestering him again. Fox tugs Mockingbird's sleeve. Bear gives a swing at Harriet and misses. Cynthia giggles and so he turns on her)*

BEAR. You gonna vote for me?

CYNTHIA. *(Proudly)* No.

BEAR. You better or I'll bash you in.

CYNTHIA. *(Still touting him)* No.

(The Bear knocks her down and she looks up with surprise. The crowd now becomes concerned and begins moving in)

BEAR. I'll give it to you good so you can't vote for nobody.

(The Lion hears this and sees what has happened. Without thinking, he goes over to the Bear in great anger)

LION. You leave her alone.

BEAR. Aw, shut up.

PARROT. All is fair in love and elections. You know, we might get a few votes that way, too.

(Lion turns to look at her and she backs away)

BEAR. *(To Cynthia)* Who you gonna vote for?

LION. Leave her alone.

BEAR. Aw *(Raises his hand to hit her again)*

CYNTHIA. *(Running to Uncle)* Help, Uncle!

LION. *(Stepping between the Bear and Cynthia)* Stop it now or you'll be sorry.

MOCKINGBIRD. Don't be silly. You won't hurt a fly.

LION. *(Turns upon Mockingbird with a roar which frightens him to hide behind a tree)* No one is going to hurt my animals while I'm here to protect them.

PARROT. Save your strength for the race.

LION. *(Paying no attention to Parrot)* Come over here. *(He grabs the Bear by the neck and leads him away from the crowd down right)* Listen . . . . . . *(He whispers)*

BEAR. *(Suddenly pale with fright)* Yes sir! *(Backs away and runs off to the astonishment of the crowd. Mockingbird comes out from behind the tree)*

MOCKINGBIRD. What's going on here? What happened?

CYNTHIA. I'll tell you. Your candidate was going to bash me in but the Lion has stopped him.

MRS. RABBIT. But where is the Bear?

MISSY RABBIT. He's down somewhere hiding because the lion told him . . .

JUDGE. (Looking at his watch) It's almost time for the race.

PARROT. What did you tell him?

LION. (Proudly but no tattle-tale) Nothing.

MISSY. He told him to leave her alone or he'd have bear meat for supper.

UNCLE. Well, it surely scared him away.

CYNTHIA. Thank you for protecting me, Mr. Lion . . . uh . . . I mean *King* Lion.

LION. I have to protect my animals. It was nothing.

UNCLE. I say give the crown back to the Lion. Who says he can't rule the forest?

CROWD. I never said he was a coward.
I was only for the bear because I was scared of him.
Now look who's scared! (Laughter and cheers)

MOCKINGBIRD. (Stepping forward) But you can't do that.

JUDGE. The Bear isn't here to race and it's time to begin.

UNCLE. Do you have the crown?

JUDGE. (Motions to Cynthia to get the crown) Right here.

(He places the crown on the Lion's head. As the animals make a circle around the Lion to cheer their King, Lion shyly puts his hands over his head and shakes them together—He is the winner)

CURTAIN

PRODUCTION NOTES FOR CHARACTER DEVELOPMENT

Don't Cross That Lion! is a simple one-set play that can become as detailed as desired in costumes and business. Good characterizations bring even more life to the play and there are several exercises which might be of assistance in obtaining clear and imaginative personalities among the animals.

Before scripts are given to the performers, the story can be told and presented through creative dramatics. A scene may be taken out of the script and elaborated upon. These exercises will stimulate each child to begin thinking from his character's viewpoint, and character attitude and understanding can be developed.

Creative exercises in the personality and animal rhythms, movements, business characteristics, and character traits will be helpful in reaching distinct characters through movement or pantomime.

Involving the child in various art expressions of his character—painting or drawing what he looks like, where he lives, or collages of his clothes or his personality—may stimulate him to think more specifically about the creation of his character.

With the exception of only a few scenes, most of the script is written in segments so that the directing involves only a few people at the same time. During those times when all of the cast is onstage, such as at the beginning, each character should be motivated to business in keeping with his portrayal and the scene itself.

If the tempo of the play lags, it will lose much of its excitement. Each scene should find its own rhythm and mood, yet be continuous to its final build when the Bear runs away from the Lion.

To assist in visualizing each character, personality sketches are as follows:

HARRIET and CYNTHIA are sisters and are young monkeys that have much energy, curiosity and are always full of mischief. They are spending some time visiting their Uncle and though they love him dearly, they also love to eat and do not like his diets and exercises.

UNCLE GORILLA is middle-aged. He is a bachelor and a very meticulous "old maid." He is a stickler for his health food and exercises and thinks he should help everyone else become healthier, too. He is somewhat self-centered, confident, and opinionated.

MOCKINGBIRD is a salesman: egocentric, fearing no one, confident, intelligent and a born talker. He can sometimes become a pest with his schemes and plans. He moves fast, is going somewhere all the time and each activity is more important than the last.

BEAR is dumb, slow-thinking and slow-moving. He is perfectly content with his blocks. He is big and does not like to be pushed around or be stared at. He likes compliments and due respect given an animal of his size and reputation for fierceness. He plays easily into the hands of the Mockingbird and never really knows too much about how he has been or is being used. He is naive and trusting.

LION is kind, gentle, modest and lovable. He is usually smiling and wants most of all for everyone to be happy. What people of the forest do not know about him is that if once he becomes angry, he can be vicious and unmanageable. Lion is a very sensitive person and is popular with everyone because he does care about them and leaves them alone to their own affairs.

JUDGE OWL has been a judge for many years and he has great pride and security in his position. Everyone looks up to the Judge for his age and wisdom for he is easily the oldest in this part of the forest. He talks slowly and deliberately, with great authority and pride. He loves to pronounce, announce, and make decisions . . . and often takes it upon himself to carry out this activity when it is neither desired or needed.

MRS. SQUIRREL is very busy and tidy. She gets up at the crack of day and goes to bed as soon as it is dark. She works constantly and has no respect for those who do not carry out their responsibilities. She is known as a good housekeeper and excellent cook.

PARROT is lively and dependable. She loves pretty things and loves activity. Parrot has a strong sense of justice and does not like to see anyone taken advantage of . . . especially someone she likes as well as the Lion. She is a manager and can be clever and imaginative if it is required of her.

FOX is a snooper. He makes his living by spying on others. He is lazy, a loafer, and spends all of his money on clothes and accessories to keep himself looking snazzy. His tastes are loud and bizarre. He changes his loyalties easily and can be dependable in one thing only, snooping and following orders for a profit to himself.

MISS MINK was lovely when she was young. She is older now but still tries to keep her beauty by wearing fancy clothes, much jewelry and too much makeup. She is a lady of wealth and influence.

MISS CHINCHILLA is much younger than Miss Mink but is also a younger person of means. She is rather giddy, a little overweight, and always going on a diet.

MRS. RABBIT is motherly, matronly, and very serious and responsible. She is a good mother and a good citizen of the forest.

MISSY RABBIT is Mrs. Rabbit's youngest and only girl and she is very dependent upon her mother. Shy and delicate, she is not aggressive but will do always what she is told.

THE TRAGEDY OF ORPHEUS AND EURYDICE

adapted from the Greek myth

written by 10- through 12-year-old children

supervised by Don Davlin

The Tragedy of Orpheus and Eurydice was written and produced by the Dallas Theater Center Children's Theater in the spring of 1964. The student playwrights were also the original cast.

Chorus	SALLY DACUS
	LINDA HAYDEN
	DARLENE DAVISON
Eurydice	KIM PAULEY
Orpheus	BILL WOODBURN
The Snake	JACKIE DEAR
Messenger, Hermes	PATTY O'CONNOR
Death	DANNY YATES
Hades	ART GREENHAW
Persephone	ALLATIA HARRIS
Fire	JACKIE DEAR
Agony	KAREN KRAFFT
Torture	BARBARA POPE
Revenge	GILBERT TRAVIS
Jealousy	KIM PAULEY
Hate	DARLENE DAVISON

The entire play takes place on a bare stage. Variety and change are dependent upon direction given the performers and in the lighting. It is most effective if no curtain is used. When lights come up, Eurydice is on stage miming the picking of flowers. The chorus enters from stage right. Harp music is heard in the distance.

CHORUS. Eurydice is out picking flowers in the meadow. She is so happy.

EURYDICE. I am so happy. Orpheus and I are to be married today. Listen! Orpheus is playing his beautiful music on his lyre. He enchants the forest with his beautiful music. He makes the flowers grow, the trees grow, the grain in the fields grow. The cows give milk, the animals are happy, people sing and dance all day long when he plays. When he plays, it is always spring and today Orpheus and I are to be married. I am so happy.

CHORUS. The trees are dancing.
The leaves are whispering in the breeze.
The people are singing.
Everyone is happy.
The sun is shining in the clear, blue sky.
Orpheus is playing beautiful music for the earth.
Eurydice is out picking flowers in the meadow.
Blue ones, red ones, gold ones . . .
Blue ones, as the sky.
Red ones, as the sunset.
Gold ones, as the sun.
The trees are dancing . . .
The leaves are whispering in the breeze . . .
The people are singing . . .
Everyone is happy.

(A snake begins to slither on stage. Weird music accompanies its movements as it makes its way toward Eurydice)

But wait. What is that in the green grass?
It's a stone.
No, it's a leaf.
It's a bird.
No! It's a snake!
Watch out, Eurydice!
Eurydice, watch out!
Eurydice, run.
Eurydice, watch out!

(The snake bites Eurydice. She falls, and dies. The snake slithers off and the chorus kneels beside Eurydice)

Eurydice! Wake up! Eurydice!
She's dead.

(As they turn to leave to go tell Orpheus, Death appears from upstage left, motions to Eurydice. She gets up, unseeing, and follows him off up left)

No! No! Come back, Eurydice!

(Death and Eurydice exit. Lights fade except for spot on chorus)

We must tell Orpheus,
Eurydice is dead.
We must tell Orpheus that Eurydice is dead.
It is a sad day for us, that we must bring him such terrible news.
Eurydice is dead!

(They run wildly across the stage shouting "Orpheus! Orpheus!" to downstage left where Orpheus is seen playing his harp. Lights fade on stage left and up on Orpheus)

ORPHEUS. Today is the day I marry.
　　　　　Eurydice is to be my wife.
　　　　　I will play my lyre forever
　　　　　And sing praises to Eurydice.
　　　　　My Eurydice, with hair of spun night,
　　　　　Lips of ruby red . . .

(Chorus interrupts him)

CHORUS. Orpheus! Orpheus!

ORPHEUS. What? *(He stops playing his lyre)*

CHORUS. Orpheus, there has been a terrible accident.
　　　　　In the meadow.
　　　　　Eurydice was picking flowers in the meadow.
　　　　　The trees were dancing
　　　　　Everyone was happy.
　　　　　Eurydice . . .

ORPHEUS. Eurydice? Did anything happen to Eurydice?

CHORUS. Eurydice is . . .

ORPHEUS. Where is Eurydice? Is she all right?

CHORUS. Eurydice is . . . . dead.

ORPHEUS. Dead? What are you talking about? She can't be dead.

CHORUS. Eurydice was picking flowers in the meadow.
　　　　　A snake
　　　　　A black snake
　　　　　A black ugly snake
　　　　　Large, long, and horrible,
　　　　　Hidden in the grass,
　　　　　A black ugly snake bit her.
　　　　　Eurydice is dead.

ORPHEUS. I was with her just a minute ago. She can't be dead. Where is she? *(Silence)*
Where is she?

CHORUS. She is gone . . . . . . down into the underworld.
　　　　　Death took her into the Underworld.
　　　　　Down, down into the darkness,
　　　　　Where no one returns.
　　　　　Eurydice is gone.
　　　　　Where the green grassy meadow is by the crystal stream,
　　　　　A black ugly snake bit Eurydice.
　　　　　Where the trees were dancing, and the flowers of red and blue and gold
　　　　　Cover the meadow.
　　　　　There in the meadow Eurydice died.
　　　　　She descended . . . down, down, down into the Underworld.

ORPHEUS. Show me where.

(They cross to the other side of the stage)

CHORUS. Here, Orpheus . . .
　　　　　Here the trees were dancing
　　　　　Here the flowers of red and blue and gold cover the meadow.
　　　　　Here in the meadow Eurydice died.
　　　　　Death came and took Eurydice
　　　　　In the Underworld——forever.
　　　　　Eurydice is gone forever.
　　　　　Poor Eurydice . . . Poor Orpheus . . . Poor Orpheus . . .

(Chorus exits and Orpheus falls to his knees)

170

ORPHEUS. Today the gods have been cruel to me. Oh, Zeus! King of the Gods. Why did you let this happen? Today was our wedding day——the day we were to be married. I vow now that I shall never play another happy song on my lyre. I break now my promise to you. I want the world to die as Eurydice died. Only sad songs of bitterness shall come from my lyre——only words of death and unhappiness shall come from my lips.

(The lights fade on Orpheus and come up on the chorus upstage left)

CHORUS. Poor Orpheus . . .
      The blue birds no longer sing their happy song.
      The song they sing is of sad days that are here.
      The trees whisper sad words back to the breeze.
      The flowers wilt and have forgotten to grow,
      Because they have forgotten the happy songs Orpheus used to sing.
      There is no more spring in our land . . .
      Oh, Orpheus, sing again your happy songs.

(Lights fade on chorus and come up on Orpheus playing his lyre)

ORPHEUS. There is no more happiness——it is gone.
      My songs are sad because my heart is sad.
      There is no more happiness——I am alone.
      My songs are sad because my heart is sad.
      There is no more happiness——Eurydice is gone.
      My songs are sad because my heart is sad.

(Chorus enters near Orpheus)

CHORUS. No more spring.
      Unhappy days. Grey, sad days are here to stay.
      Oh, Zeus! Take pity on poor Orpheus.
      His heart is gone——and we are doomed to die.
      The flowers wilt and have forgotten to grow.
      Oh, Zeus! Take pity on us.
      The grain in the field is dying.
      The cows give no milk.
      The fruit on the trees are dying.
      Oh, Zeus, help Orpheus so he will sing happy songs again.
      Poor Orpheus . . . *(Chorus begins to exit)* Poor Orpheus . . .Poor Orpheus . . .

(Orpheus continues to play his sad song. Suddenly the sound of trumpets far away is heard. Orpheus stops to listen. He starts to play again; then the trumpets sound again, closer. Hermes enters)

HERMES. Orpheus.

ORPHEUS. Go away.

HERMES. Orpheus.

ORPHEUS. Leave me alone.

HERMES. Orpheus.

ORPHEUS. Go away, I told you. Since Eurydice is gone, I can only play sad songs on my lyre.

HERMES. Orpheus, look upon my face.

(Orpheus turns to look. He sees it is Hermes and he falls to his knees)

HERMES. I am Hermes, messenger of the gods. Zeus is upset with you because you will not play happy songs anymore. Everything on earth is dying and it is your fault. You made a promise to Zeus that you would always play happy songs for the earth so it will grow. You have broken your promise. The anger of Zeus, mighty Zeus, ruler of all the gods, is mighty. He could destroy you for breaking your promise.

171

ORPHEUS. I don't care. Let Zeus destroy me. Eurydice is gone from me to the kingdom of the dead. She is gone forever.

HERMES. Oh foolish Orpheus. The power of Zeus is mighty.

ORPHEUS. His power is great, but he has no power in the Underworld.

HERMES. Zeus has taken pity on you and the earth. He has decided to help you.

ORPHEUS. Help me? How?

HERMES. The songs you play are sad. Perhaps Persephone, Hades' wife, will take pity on you when she hears you play. She once was a member of the living. She remembers music. She is moved by sad songs. Perhaps she will take pity on you and persuade Hades to give Eurydice back to you.

ORPHEUS. I will play my most beautiful music for her if only I can get Eurydice back.

HERMES. But you must be careful. Orpheus. The way to the Underworld is long and dangerous.

ORPHEUS. I don't care how dangerous it is.

HERMES. And you must not open your eyes in the Underworld or you will join the dead forever. You must wear this golden mask to the Underworld. Do not take it off. *(Holds mask for Orpheus to see)*

ORPHEUS. But how am I to get to the Underworld? No one knows the way.

HERMES. Zeus has decided to take you the secret way to the Underworld. Death will lead you there. *(Hands Orpheus the mask)* Put on the mask now and he will come. *(Begins to back away)* Remember, do not take off the mask in the Underworld. Remember . . . remember . . . remember. *(Exits)*

(Orpheus puts on the mask and Death appears. Weird music is heard suggesting the mood of the Underworld. Death begins to lead Orpheus away. As they wind their way across the stage, moving upstage as they go, the lights change in color and direction. It is more difficult for Orpheus to follow Death for the elements are pushing against him. Then he begins to hear moans. Looking behind him he sees the dead pulling themselves toward him with arms outstretched—snakelike—on the floor. This is somewhat frightening to Orpheus and he begins to walk backwards keeping his eye on the dead and trying to stay out of their reach. They seem to be reaching for his harp, too, and he holds it high above his head. The lights change to colors of red, magenta, and gold area lights. Hades and Persephone enter. They see that Orpheus is surrounded by the furies)

HADES. Death! *(The dead fall back)* Foolish mortal! You have no business in my kingdom. How dare you enter where you should not. *(Sneaky)* Would you like to see my subjects in action? Would you like to see the dead? Just take off your mask and you will see something that no one else, no other living person, has ever seen before. Take off your mask.

ORPHEUS. No.

PERSEPHONE. Oh, mortal, take off your mask . . .

DEAD. *(Hissing, whispering)* Take off your mask . . . take off your mask . . .

ORPHEUS. No! I can't take it off . . .

HADES. Why not?

ORPHEUS. Hermes told me . . .

HADES. So, Zeus has been at work I see . . . he has no business with the dead . . . but surely it will not hurt to take off your mask for just one little peek . . .

ORPHEUS. No, you can't trick me. I won't take off my mask.

PERSEPHONE. Ah. You are smart, aren't you? Well, then listen to me.

(Hades snaps his fingers and the dead begin to move again)

172

DEAD. We remember. Please don't make us remember the earth or how we died . . .

FIRE. I remember . . . the earth.

AGONY. The earth

TORTURE. The living

FIRE. I remember the earth

REVENGE. The trees, the shade, the whispering of the breeze through the leaves.

JEALOUSY. The cool breeze, the fresh, sweet air

HATE. The sun, the warm, friendly sun . . .

FIRE. The rich, warm wind

AGONY. making music through the strings of grass

JEALOUSY. the sweet smell of the flowers

FIRE. I remember——my mother

REVENGE. my father

TORTURE. family, home, love . . . . . . life.

JEALOUSY. the light

REVENGE. the light was bright

TORTURE. the light over the warm, friendly earth

HATE. star, night

FIRE. earth, light

DEAD. We remember the earth, the living. We remember how we died.

FIRE. I remember how I died.
I died in a hot, white fire.
The fire burned——pain, heat.
I remember how my skin burned and turned black
The fire burned white fire——pain, heat
DEATH!

AGONY. I remember how I died.
They tortured me.
Pulled my arms apart.
Broke my legs.
They destroyed me.
DEATH!

JEALOUSY. I remember how I died.
I fell from a high cliff into the sea.
Falling, falling, down, down, down . . .
I drowned.
DEATH!

TORTURE. I remember how I died.
I starved——no food.
Hunger——no food.
I starved——all bones.
I died——no food.
DEATH!

REVENGE. I remember how I died.
      In battle.
      The flashing sword cut into my chest.
      So sharp . . . flashing sword.
      Blood . . . my blood . . red, warm-like spilling out of me.
      The flashing sword cut death into my heart.
      DEATH!

HATE: I remember how I died.
      So old—not able to move.
      Old, tired . . .
      My poor heart was tired of beating.
      I died old, tired . . . I died.
      DEATH!

DEAD. We remember how we died.
      We remember life . . . and death.
      We remember the warm, good earth.
      We remember . . .

(As they say this, the dead begin to close in on Orpheus to touch him, perhaps to drag him with them. Persephone stops them)

PERSEPHONE. DEATH!

HADES. Fool! Why did you come to the Underworld?

ORPHEUS. I came after Eurydice. Please let me take Eurydice back to the living.

HADES. You know that once a person enters the Underworld he can never return.

ORPHEUS. But without her life is nothing to me. She died on our wedding day, before we were to be married.

HADES. That is no matter. She stays. Now leave before you are caught forever in the Underworld. My people will kill you if you stay much longer. (The dead start to rise and surround Orpheus) I warn you to leave while you can.

ORPHEUS. I cannot leave without Eurydice.

HADES. Then you choose to die. My people will rip you to pieces. Not a very pretty death.

(As the dead close in around Orpheus, Death motions him to begin playing his harp. At first he does not understand, and the dead come closer. Finally he does understand and begins to play. The dead stop moving toward him and begin to listen)

ORPHEUS. I sing of the happiness I once knew on earth.
      That is gone because Eurydice is dead.
      My heart is broken because she is gone from me.
      My song is of unhappiness, of sadness . . .
      Of days when I was happy . . . days that are gone . . .

PERSEPHONE. (Obviously touched by the singing) Such beautiful music. So sad. Play more. I beg of you.

ORPHEUS. I sing of my Eurydice.
      Who is gone from me forever.
      Please let me take her back to the green earth.
      The light, cool green earth . . .

PERSEPHONE. (To Hades) Let him have Eurydice.

HADES. What?

PERSEPHONE. Please let him take Eurydice back to the living. Anyone who plays such beautiful sad music should be made to sing once again the happy songs. I remember when I was on earth. And how happy the music made us feel. With this music there is only sadness. So let him take her. Let him take Eurydice.

174

HADES. Very well. You may take her . . . on one condition. You must not look at her or speak to her until you are in the Upperworld again. If you do, she will be lost forever, and you will suffer a punishment worse than death. I warn you, do not look at her until you are in the Upperworld. Now go, before I and my people become impatient with you.

(Hades motions to Eurydice to follow Orpheus and Orpheus turns to follow Death back to the Upperworld. The lights fade on Hades, Persephone and the dead. Cross lighting suggest the return to the Upperworld. As she follows, Eurydice cannot understand why Orpheus will not take off the mask and look at her or speak to her)

EURYDICE. (Calling) Orpheus . . . Orpheus . . . Orphus.

(Suddenly she gets an idea and just before they reach the Upperworld, Eurydice screams that she is falling)

Orpheus, help me! I'm falling!

(Without thinking, Orpheus removes his mask and turns to Eurydice. Death throws a spell upon Orpheus so that he cannot move and then takes his lyre away from him and leads Eurydice back to the Underworld. After they have disappeared, Orpheus slowly comes to his senses and begins to crawl to the Upperworld. He is moaning in grief until he gets to his feet in the Upperworld and as he blindly finds his way offstage to bemoan his fate)

ORPHEUS. Oh . . . oh . . . ooooooh . . . oh . . . . . .

(The chorus enter when he reaches the Upperworld. They know what has happened)

CHORUS. Poor Orpheus . . . poor Orpheus . . .
    Of all the creatures on the earth,
    He is the most unhappy.
    He has lost Eurydice . . . forever.
    He has lost his lyre . . . he cannot sing even his unhappy songs now . . .
    We are all doomed to be unhappy . . .
    No longer will we sing or dance . . .
    No more happiness . . .
    We will all die.
    Oh, Zeus! King of the gods, have pity on us.
    Have pity for poor Orpheus . . .

    Poor Orpheus . . . poor Orpheus . . . poor Orpheus . . .

(As the chorus repeats "Poor Orpheus" the lights fade to blackness)

END

PRODUCTION NOTES

Since *Orpheus and Eurydice* has been written to be produced as a Greek tragedy, the play is completely dependent upon the director for an effective and satisfying performance. The director should realize the importance of stage areas for the different scenes, entrances and exits of all characters, direction and rhythm and silhouette of movement, and be ever conscious of his stage picture by using composition and picturization techniques imaginatively.

The play begins in a spirit of lightness. Although the elements of death and tragedy are climactic to the play, they are treated poetically and in this way can be effective yet not too realistically strong for the child performer or the child viewer.

THE CHORUS is perhaps most important in this script, just as they were in the ancient Greek drama. They must move well, speak well, and be imaginative yet simple in both body and voice. It is not necessary that they look alike, though it is effective if they are dressed alike and have a similar hair style. Sometimes they speak together and move in unison and at other times they move and speak individually. The division of lines and the suggestion of movement and pantomime is left up to the director. He must be careful that the movement and speech is true to the spirit of the scene and that they do not detract from the idea of the moment; however, a constant static stance by the chorus makes the performance earth-bound and monotonous.

EURYDICE should be feminine and graceful. It is helpful if she is pretty and fair, but this is not imperative. She must have a feeling for beauty, however, and reflect the softness that Orpheus sees in her.

ORPHEUS is second only to the chorus in casting requirements. He must be sensitive yet manly. It is most important that he speak his lines with a feeling of their meaning, their poetry, and their emotion and beauty. He must be believable as a singer of songs and as a tragic figure. He must be a good actor.

THE SNAKE is a movement piece and this is the prime requirement for this part.

HERMES should be athletic. He should have a strong voice and a good build for he is a representative of the gods.

DEATH is a very important part because he must set the mood of the Underworld in his every movement and gesture. His is a part that requires sensitivity to mood, movement and to pantomime.

HADES is the god-figure. He must speak, move and suggest authority, both in his bearing and in his attitude.

PERSEPHONE should be dark-haired but pretty. She, too, is feminine, but with more dignity and mature posture than Eurydice. Although once a mortal, she is now a Queen and she moves and speaks with that authority.

FIRE, AGONY, TORTURE, REVENGE, JEALOUSY and HATE are parts which demand movement and speech most reflective of their title:

> FIRE: quick, darting, vertical.
> AGONY: slow, sustained, rolling.
> TORTURE: strained, progressively strong, horizontal.
> REVENGE: jabbing, elastic, multi-directional, hard.
> HATE: slow but constant, big, loud, all-encompassing.

COSTUMES

CHORUS. Greek chitons in off-white with yellow himation which can be versatile in use. Yellow, gold, or off-white sandals. Hair pulled back in "pony-tail" fashion with gold band around it. Straight makeup.

EURYDICE. Light blue Ionic chiton. Blue thonged-sandals. Hair styled in the ancient Greek fashion with usual accessories. Arm band. Straight makeup.

ORPHEUS. Beige Ionic chiton with Greek patterned band in blue and gold. Laced half-way to the knee, beige sandals. Straight makeup.

THE SNAKE. Green leotards and tights with spiral-stripes in red and yellow. Snake mask.

MESSENGER, HERMES. Grey Ionic chiton, wine or maroon chlamys and belt, black boots—Greek style—and a petasos, or traveller's hat. Straight makeup using a sun-tan color.

DEATH. Black Doric chiton with hood to almost cover face, black gloves, black tights and dance shoes.

HADES. Green Ionic chiton with gold himation, crown, gold arm-band, gold thonged-sandals, scepter. Character makeup.

PERSEPHONE. Lighter green Ionic chiton with orange-gold himation. Gold thonged-sandals. Hair in cone-bun with gold lacing, long-gold earrings and gold arm-band. Straight makeup, heavily applied.

FIRE, AGONY, TORTURE, REVENGE, JEALOUSY, and HATE. Leotards and tights with tattered pieces of chiffon or cheese cloth in colors suggestive of their title. Abstract makeup with color base to suggest the face of the emotion.

PROPS

A snake mask
A gold lyre
A gold mask
Character masks for Hades and Persephone in the style of the ancient Greek tragic masks
Scepter

LIGHTS

Although the play can be given without any change of lighting from beginning to end, effective lighting can add to the mood and imagination of the audience. The following presets are suggested:

>general illumination (blue cyc if possible)
>down right and center
>down left
>down left and center
>down center
>diagonal from down right to up left
>cross lights from downstage to upstage
>Underworld lights across upstage areas (red cyc)
>follow spot

Except for the cross lights for the journey to the Underworld and the area lights for the scene in the Underworld—and a follow spot with various color mediums for the lines of each of the Dead, other lights may not be in any colors other than the usual pinks and blues, when cross-lighting is used on each area, or the pinks alone if only one light per area is used. All lights should be controlled by dimmers.

WHERE IS MY GOLD?

based on the Roman Comedy *Pot of Gold* by Plautus

written by 10- through 12-year-old children

supervised by Synthia Rogers

Where is my Gold? was written and produced by the Dallas Theater Center Children's Theater in the spring of 1964. The student playwrights were also the original cast.

Household Gods:	No. 1	MARY SULLIVAN
	No. 2	LAURA DeBOLT
	No. 3	VICKI LYNN
Euclio, a miser		KEITH SLAUGHTER
Staphyla, his slave		LESLI GLATTER
Megadorus, a rich old man		CLINT VENABLE
Drusilla, sister of Megadorus		KITTY SMITH
Esmerelda, daughter of Euclio		BECKY BOWEN
Little Caesar, a famous cook		LUCY CROW
Asparagus, his assistant		RONA GLASS
Broccoli, a musician		JUDY LEEDOM

TIME AND PLACE: A street in Rome during Ancient Times

The stage depth is shallow. The upstage boundary is established by three doorways, the only set on stage. The doorways may be rounded arches with no visible supports or they may be square doorways in a wall. They may be identical or they may vary with decor or basic shape but they are all open with no doors attached and they are placed on the same plane with one another, in keeping with the early Roman stage.

The center doorway leads to the temple. The stage right doorway leads to the home of Euclio. The stage left doorway is the home of Megadorus. The imaginary street in front of these doorways leads from left to right. Stage right leads to the city and the forum while stage left leads to the country and the seashore.

SCENE 1

Household God No. 2 enters from the temple. He walks straight downstage and begins to talk to the audience.

NO. 2. *(Shyly)* Hello. I'm . . . I'm a household maid. *(Looks at the audience with great satisfaction)*

(Household Gods 1 and 3 run out of temple entrance as though trying to catch up with 2 and stop him)

NOS. 1 AND 3. No! You're not a household maid. You're a household god.

NO. 3. Well, all together everyone. 1 . . . 5 . . . 9 . .

1, 2, 3. We are the Household Gods of this house.

(1 and 3 point to the home of Euclio. Then they realize that 2 is pointing to the home of Megadorus. They glare at 2 and he quickly points to Euclio's house)

NO. 1. *(To 2)* Household God, tell these people the history of this house.

NO. 2. I'm not sure I can remember. Let me see . . . oh, yes, I am the good household maid.

NO. 3. No, you're not the good household maid. You are the *dumb* household god.

NO. 2. Oh, now I remember. I am one of the dumb household gods of Euclio's household.

NO. 1. Now tell the people how long you've lived here.

NO. 2. Now we have lived here from Euclio's grandfather to Euclio.

NO. 3. Euclio is the present master of the house.

NO. 2. Euclio is very greedy.

NO. 1. He's always searching for gold.

NO. 3. He knows that his grandfather hid the gold somewhere in this house, but he doesn't know where.

NO. 2. We know where the gold is hidden. But we will never tell Euclio because he is such a miser that he would keep it all for himself.

NO. 1. He is suspicious of everyone.

NO. 3 He is always listening for someone who might sneak in and steal his gold.

NO. 2. He listens so hard he even hears the slave when she plucks her eyebrows.

NO. 1. And he is always beating his slave.

NO. 2. That poor miserable slave.

(Slave is heard offstage right, screaming)

NO. 3. I hear them now. Come on. Let's go. Line up everybody . . . . . .

(The three household gods walk out in single-file)

SCENE 2

(Euclio is heard beating Staphyla, his slave. She is screaming and there is much noise)

EUCLIO. *(Offstage)* Come back here slave. Come back here, you skinny chicken. I'll catch you, you boney pig.

(Staphyla runs on stage through Euclio's doorway. Euclio follows, club in hand)

EUCLIO. Where is she? Where is that sneaky weasel?

STAPHYLA. Ye gods, help me. He's beating me again.

EUCLIO. You wretched old slave. You're always spying on me. I know you're after my gold.

STAPHYLA. Oh no, master. I was just dusting the furniture. I wasn't looking for your gold. *(Aside:)* Why should I be looking for his gold. He doesn't even have any. He's the poorest man in town.

EUCLIO. *(Beating her again)* Take that, you old bag of bones.

STAPHYLA. Oh, oh, oh . . . you're hurting me.

EUCLIO. How could I hurt you? Your skin is as thick as tar.

STAPHYLA. Ohhhhhhhhh . . .

EUCLIO. Now I am going to town. Don't let anyone in the house. Not even the Emperor of Rome. *(Aside:)* He might try to steal my gold, too. *(Exits stage right)*

STAPHYLA. Yes, master. Anything you wish master. Is he gone? Is he gone? *(Feels her body)* No bones broken this time. How could he beat me . . . an old woman like me, with all my miseries . . . my headaches . . . my backaches. The curse of the gods is upon me that I must serve such a master. He is so greedy. And he's always looking for that gold. He doesn't have any gold. He doesn't even have wood for the fireplace . . . I'll keep my eyes open . . . I might get back at him someday. *(Exits into house)*

SCENE 3

(Drusilla enters from stage left)

DRUSILLA. Oh, I can't wait to tell my brother. He's going to be so excited! I'm so excited. Everything's so exciting.

(Megadorus exits from his house)

MEGADORUS. Good morning, sister. What are you babbling about?

DRUSILLA. Oh, my dear brother, last night I dreamed you were going to get married . . . to Procefine, my best friend.

MEGADORUS. Not her!

DRUSILLA. The green grass and the blue sky will light their path on that glorious day. Oh, rapture, rapture, rapture.

MEGADORUS. Ye gods, she must be drunk.

DRUSILLA. Oh wonderful, glorious Porcefine.

MEGADORUS. *(Laughing)* I wouldn't marry that lard belly for anything. When she walks in a room she looks like a battleship going to war.

DRUSILLA. By the gods of Jupiter, how dare you insult Porcefine? She's such a charming person and cuts an elegant figure.

MEGADORUS. That fat slob.

DRUSILLA. Why there's not another figure in the world like hers. 9 at the top, 90 in the middle, and 900 at the bottom.

MEGADORUS. Unbelievable! And how about those big shiny warts?

DRUSILLA. Beauty marks. Two absolutely perfect warts right on the tip of her nose.

MEGADORUS. The hideous elephant.

DRUSILLA. But, brother, you should get married. You are such a lonely, rich, old man.

MEGADORUS. Well, I do get lonesome. Maybe you're right. By the power of Venus I will get married!

DRUSILLA. Yes, yes. You and Porcefine . . . a perfect match.

MEGADORUS. No, no, no. I shall marry Esmerelda, Euclio's daughter. Surely he will let me marry his daughter. I'd be a wonderful husband. I'm so rich and that old miser would love to get some money in the family. Oh, lovely, lovely Esmerelda. (Exits in a daze back into his house)

DRUSILLA. Oh, no, he can't marry Esmerelda. All my lovely plans. What will I tell Porcefine? I've already promised her the wedding. Oh . . . most UNglorious day! (Exits off stage right)

SCENE 4

(Euclio comes out of his house. He looks for his gold)

EUCLIO. Where can that gold be? (Sings) Oh where, oh where is my gold? (Gets down on floor and looks around) If I don't find it soon I won't be able to buy a crumb of bread. I'll starve. Oh, poor me.

(Megadorus comes to the door of his house and watches Euclio a minute, then speaks)

MEGADORUS. Hello there, Euclio. Are you looking for something?

EUCLIO. Oh, uh, no. I just enjoy crawling around like this. (Aside:) I can't let him know I'm searching for my gold. He's rich, but he's still greedy.

MEGADORUS. Nice day, isn't it?

EUCLIO. Uh, yes.

MEGADORUS. Nice weather lately..

EUCLIO. (Aside:) He is being too polite. He must want something from me. He probably has heard about my gold.

MEGADORUS. Euclio, I have come to ask you a very important question.

EUCLIO. (Aside:) Just as I thought! He knows about my gold. He wants some for himself. (To Megadorus) If you have come to borrow something, save yourself the trouble. I don't have anything.

MEGADORUS. No, my good man, I came to ask you for something you do have.

EUCLIO. (Aside:) The rich old pig. He has more gold than he needs. Why should he want mine too? (To Megadorus) Gracious sir, you have everything in the world you want. I am a poor soul who barely has enough clothes to cover his back. What could I have that you would possibly want?

MEGADORUS. Good Euclio, you have in your possession the most important and most precious thing in the world.

EUCLIO. (Aside:) As I suspected! He does know about the gold. (To Megadorus) No, I have nothing of such value.

MEGADORUS. Oh, please, Euclio. Let me have your daughter as my wife. I'll even pay for the wedding.

EUCLIO. What wedding?

MEGADORUS. Our wedding.

EUCLIO. (Shocked) Surely you don't want to marry me!

MEGADORUS. Good heavens, no! I meant the wedding of your daughter and me.

EUCLIO. What will you give me if I let you marry my daughter?

MEGADORUS. As much gold as you could ever need.

EUCLIO. In that case, you can marry her. And remember, Sir, you promised to pay for the wedding.

MEGADORUS. I did, and it will be a grand wedding. I know the most famous cooks and musicians. I'm so happy, and I know your daughter will be delighted to marry a rich, intelligent, and handsome man. I must go and tell my sister the good news. (Exits stage right)

EUCLIO. He isn't handsome or intelligent, but he is definitely rich. I can't wait to get my hands on his gold. Now to tell my daughter about the wedding. I'm afraid she won't be pleased about it. She just doesn't seem to love gold the way I do. (Exits into his house)

SCENE 5

(Esmerelda enters from stage left, singing)

ESMERELDA. Wonderful day. This is the happiest day of my life. Oh, where is Father. I can't wait to tell him the good news. Won't he be happy to know that Claudius wants to marry me. Claudius is the most handsome and intelligent man in town. I know he'll be famous someday even though he's only a blacksmith. Father, where are you?

(Euclio comes from his house)

EUCLIO. Oh, there you are, Esmerelda. I've been looking for you.

ESMERELDA. Father, have you heard the news?

EUCLIO. Yes, but how did you know?

ESMERELDA. I was the one he asked. But how did you know?

EUCLIO. He asked me first.

ESMERELDA. Then you approve?

EUCLIO. Of course. You have my permission.

ESMERELDA. I'm so happy, Father.

EUCLIO. I'm glad you are, daughter. I never realized you liked gold so much. I thought you would rather marry a handsome and intelligent man.

ESMERELDA. And so I am, Father. The most intelligent and handsome man in the whole town.

EUCLIO. I wouldn't say that, daughter. He's rich, yes. But handsome and intelligent, no.

ESMERELDA. How can you say Claudius is rich?

EUCLIO. Who said anything about Claudius?

ESMERELDA. I'm going to marry Claudius.

EUCLIO. You are not going to marry Claudius. You are going to marry Megadorus.

ESMERELDA. Not Claudius?

EUCLIO. No. It's Megadorus, and that's that! (Exits into house)

ESMERELDA. But Father . . . oh, why do I have to marry Megadorus? Why, why, why? That Megadorus is so old and ugly. He has nothing to offer except gold. I'm sure that's why Father wants me to marry him. Father cares more about gold than his own daughter. This is horrible. I'll go and tell Claudius. He will be so upset when he finds out he's losing me. (Exits stage left)

SCENE 6

(The cooks and musician enter from stage right: Little Caesar, followed by Asparagus and Broccoli)

CAESAR. Hurry up, Asparagus and Broccoli. We must not be late. Megadorus is one of my best customers and I can't disappoint him. Ah, this must be Euclio's house. It's the worst looking place on the street.

ASPARAGUS. This is where we must prepare the feast for Megadorus' wedding?

CAESAR. I had come to that conclusion. See that you do more work and less talking. Now, read the list of delicious dishes I shall prepare for the event.

ASPARAGUS. Yes, most great cook. For the first dish, you plan to serve cow peas, with one slice of bacon. Then you will serve asparagus, my favorite dish. And then, broccoli.

BROCCOLI. *(Licking Lips)* ummmmmmmmm.

CAESAR. Please, don't interrupt the reading of the menu.

ASPARAGUS. And the final dish will be . . . uh . . . fly eggs.

CAESAR. Oh, yes, my specialty.

ASPARAGUS. What do we do now?

CAESAR. Roll up the list, stupid. Now let's get the pots and pans and start cooking.

ASPARAGUS. Little Caesar, how can we get in?

CAESAR. Listen, Asparagus, we're supposed to knock. Knock, stupid.

(Asparagus knocks very loudly)

CAESAR. Not that way, stupid. This way. *(He gives a long curvy bang with one hand)*

ASPARAGUS. Nobody home, sir. How do we get in?

CAESAR. I'm thinking. I'm thinking.

ASPARAGUS. I've got an idea.

CAESAR. I'll tell you when to get your ideas . . . start getting ideas.

BROCCOLI. Door's open.

CAESAR. *(Startled)* Oh, the door is open. Why didn't you think of that, stupid. Well, don't just stand there. Let's go in.

(Asparagus starts to go in. Little Caesar pushes him aside)

CAESAR. Me first! Now, let's go get those pots and pans.

(Cooks start bringing the pots and pans out and Broccoli keeps taking them back into the house)

CAESAR. I have never carried so many pans. And I thought this Euclio was supposed to be a poor man. He certainly has a good supply of cooking vessels.

ASPARAGUS. Yes sir, he really does.

(Caesar notices Broccoli carrying the pans back into the house)

CAESAR. Broccoli, what are you doing? Will you please sit there and sing, and leave the work to us.

(Broccoli sings as Caesar and Asparagus arrange and rearrange pots and pans. Euclio walks up to see all of this)

EUCLIO. What are you doing here in my yard with my pans?

CAESAR. Are you Euclio, the master of this house?

EUCLIO. Yes, I am and who are you?

CAESAR. My name is Little Caesar. I am the famous cook in the city. This is Asparagus, my stupid assistant. This is Broccoli, a silly musician.

EUCLIO. Get off my land this minute.

CAESAR. But Megadorus hired us to prepare the wedding feast.

EUCLIO. (Aside:) He doesn't fool me. They're looking for my gold. (To Caesar) Get off my property or I'll pour boiling water on every one of you.

(Caesar, Asparagus, and Broccoli begin to scream)

CAESAR. Say no more sir. We are leaving. Come, Asparagus and Broccoli. Just wait until Megadorus gets my bill.

EUCLIO. Leave, all of you. (They exit)

SCENE 7

(Euclio begins to take the pots and pans into the house, mumbling as he goes)

EUCLIO. I hope they didn't find any of my gold. How dare Megadorus send those stupid people to my house when I'm not here. That horrible Megadorus. I'm sorry now that I told him he could marry my daughter. If only I could find my gold I wouldn't let her marry him. (Begins searching on the floor again and singing) Oh where, oh where is my gold? (Begins to cry as he continues searching)

(The three household gods appear. No. 2 begins crying and then 1 and 3 follow him)

NO. 1. (To No. 3) Why are you crying?

NO. 3. I'm crying because you're crying. (To No. 1) Why are you crying?

NO. 1. I'm crying because he's crying. (Points to No. 2)

NOS. 1 AND 3. Why are you crying?

NO. 2. I don't know. Oh, yes, I'm crying because Euclio is crying.

NOS. 1 AND 3. Well, why is he crying?

NO. 2. Listen.

EUCLIO. (Crying) Where is my gold?

1, 2, 3. The same old story. He wants his gold.

EUCLIO. If I could only find it, my poor daughter wouldn't have to marry Megadorus.

NO. 3. Did you hear that?

NO. 1. I can't believe my ears.

NO. 2. That's the first nice thing I've ever heard Euclio say.

NO. 3. Is it possible that Euclio is getting nice?

NO. 1. Impossible.

NO. 2. I think we should tell him where the gold is.

NO. 3. We haven't told him in all these years. Why should we tell him now?

NO. 2. Because if he finds the gold, he won't make Esmerelda marry old Megadorus.

NO. 1. For once I think you're right. I think we should tell Euclio where the gold is.

ALL. Let's do. (Calling) Euclio. Euclio. Your gold is in the fireplace.

184

EUCLIO. Where could my gold be? Wait a minute. There's one place I haven't looked. Maybe it's in the fireplace. (*He runs into his house and comes out with the pot of gold*) I found it! I found it! Oh, I'm so happy. (*Pause*) But now what shall I do with it? I must hide it. Where would be a safe place? I must think.

(*Euclio starts thinking and as he does, Staphyla comes out of the house*)

SCENE 8

STAPHYLA. (*Aside:*) So the the old miser finally did find his gold. Now's my chance to get even with him for all the beatings he's given me. I'll trick him and take that gold. (*To Euclio in a whisper for Euclio has not seen Staphyla*) Why don't you hide your gold in the temple?

EUCLIO. I know. I'll hide the gold in the temple.

(*He walks in a pattern on the floor as though the temple is further away than next door. Staphyla runs ahead and poses in the doorway as a statue*)

Here I am at the temple. But now where would be a good place?

STAPHYLA. (*Still posing as a statue*) Hide it here, by this graceful statue.

EUCLIO. That's a good idea. I'll hide it right here by the statue. (*He hides the gold behind the "statue"*) At last my gold is safe. Now I can go home and not worry anymore. (*Exits to his house—walking the pattern to the doorway—humming as he goes*)

STAPHYLA. That's what you think! (*Grabs the gold and runs off stage right*)

EUCLIO. (*As he walks home*) Oh, joyful day. At last I'm rich. Now Esmerelda can be happy, too. I must go tell Megadorus that the wedding is off.

SCENE 9

(*Staphyla hides and listens to the scene*)

EUCLIO. (*Calls across the stage to the house of Megadorus*) Megadorus. Megadorus. There will be no wedding.

(*Megadorus comes to the doorway of his house*)

MEGADORUS. No wedding? What are you talking about? All the arrangements are made.

EUCLIO. No, Megadorus. I'm as rich as you are. My daughter can marry the person of her choice now.

MEGADORUS. You? Rich? (*Laughs*) (*Aside:*) The old fool's crazy.

EUCLIO. Yes, I am rich, rich, rich! I've found my gold. I'm the happiest man in Rome.

MEGADORUS. I can't believe it. You're out of your head, Euclio.

EUCLIO. Come. I'll prove it to you. I'll show you my beautiful, golden gold.

MEGADORUS. (*Aside:*) This I must see with my own eyes.

(*They walk to the temple. Staphyla follows*)

EUCLIO. The gold is hidden here, Megadorus. Right behind this statue. (*He does a double-take for the statue is not there*) Right here . . . but it must be here . . . I put it here . . . Oh, where is my gold?

MEGADORUS. Come, come, Euclio. Calm yourself. You need to rest a little and then you will feel better. (*Nods his head knowingly to the audience*) Now we will have the wedding as planned, Euclio. I'll go and complete the arrangements. (*Exits*)

EUCLIO. All right, Megadorus. Whatever you say. (*Exits*)

(*Staphyla comes out of hiding and watches them leave*)

STAPHYLA. My poor Esmerelda. To have to marry such a rich old buzzard. She is a sweet gentle girl . . . and she has always been very kind to me. Yes, I must do something to help her. I shall give her the gold. *(She exits stage left)*

SCENE 10

(Everyone is on stage left waiting for the wedding to begin except Staphyla, Euclio, and Esmerelda. Staphyla runs in out of breath)

STAPHYLA. Wait! Stop everything. The wedding is off.

MEGADORUS. *(Angrily)* What do you mean?

STAPHYLA. There's not going to be a wedding. I gave the gold to Esmerelda, and now she certainly won't marry you, Megadorus.

(Euclio rushes in)

EUCLIO. You lazy cooks. Get up from there.

(The cooks, who have been sitting with their backs to stage right, now stand)

We're having a wedding this afternoon. Let's get started.

STAPHYLA. No, master, the wedding is off.

EUCLIO. Stay out of this, you old crow. The wedding is on.

STAPHYLA. Off, master, because . . .

EUCLIO. On.

STAPHYLA. Off!

EUCLIO. On!

(Esmerelda enters)

ESMERELDA. Father, Father. I don't have to marry Megadorus. Look. Look at the gold. I have the gold.

EUCLIO. Let me see. Oh, it is the gold! My beautiful, wonderful gold! Oh, happy day! I'm rich again.

ESMERELDA. *(To Megadorus)* Now I won't marry you, Megadorus, you fat old fool.

EUCLIO. Come, daughter. You can marry anyone you like . . . anyone. Let's go to town and tell Claudius. Come, Staphyla, I'll even buy you a new rag for your head.

(Exit Euclio, Esmerelda and Staphyla, happily)

DRUSILLA. Stand up there, cooks, and follow me! We will have a wedding today. *(Grabs Megadorus by the arm)* Come now, my dear brother. I know the perfect wife for you. *(Calling as they exit stage right)* Oh, Procefine . . . Procefine. Oh, marvelous day! Oh, most glorious, glorious day!

MEGADORUS. *(Looking upward)* Oh, ye gods . . . . . .

(Exit Drusilla, Megadorus, cooks following)

(The three household gods come forward and speak to the audience as at the beginning)

HOUSEHOLD GODS. And so our story is told.
    The play ends happily.
    Our miser, Euclio, has found his gold.
    Now he's the soul of generosity.

END

PRODUCTION NOTES

An effective production of *Where is my Gold?* should employ comedy techniques from both vaudeville and slapstick comedy. If these skills can then be refined and used economically, the charm of this production can be a priceless experience for both the performer and the audience.

There is usually some humor in the lines of a Roman Comedy, but the great fun comes with what is done with the line and the physical action inserted between lines and words. The more time a director and his cast can give to a basic study of comedy techniques, the more enjoyable and worthwhile the production will be. Books and films from a local library can be helpful in visualizing the methods used to achieve the techniques and style of universal comic techniques which are rooted in the Roman Drama.

Since much of the dialogue is directed to the audience, the cast should be made aware of the difference in representational (playing with one another) and presentational (playing to the audience) acting. Stock characters should be understood for each portrayal in *Where is my Gold?* should be a comment on a certain type of person. Variation of characters can come in rhythm patterns established in dialogue and movement, level and attitude of voice, silhouette of body, individual business, and costumes which use contrasting shapes, colors and accessories to establish style.

To assist in visualizing each character, the following descriptions may prove helpful:

HOUSEHOLD GOD NO. 1 is the leader of the three. He is strong-willed, bull-headed, loud, and a man of action.

HOUSEHOLD GOD NO. 2 is shy, lovable, naive and full of wide-eyed wonder. Simple of mind, he makes up for his weakness by his compassion for the under-dog.

HOUSEHOLD GOD NO. 3 is the most intelligent of the three. He is not as aggressive as 1 but his decisions are the wiser. He is intellectually smart but lacks common sense.

EUCLIO is a shriveled-up, prune-faced miser. He is sour on the world and has a one-track mind. He is clever and a contriver but he is also mentally slow but verbally quick. He has few friends and feels very insecure about everything, believing that all his troubles can be solved if he could only find the gold that no one else in his family has been able to find for years. His one softness is his daughter; and even though he is willing to marry her to Megadorus in order to get wealth in the family, he justifies this act by saying he is securing her future at the same time.

STAPHYLA is a shrill-talking, blabber-mouthed, shriveled hag. She is ugly and can be vicious but this is only to protect herself. She craves gentleness and kindness from others but seldom gets it. She is the shrewdest one of all and is physically agile and quick.

MEGADORUS is fat, fastidious, spoiled, and a snob. He wallows in his wealth but is very straight-laced and proper. Obviously, only a misfit herself would be interested in marrying Megadorus for his only asset is his money.

DRUSILLA is ultra-feminine, fluttery, easily excitable, and thinks only in superlatives. She is never still but constantly moving and talking, gesturing, batting her eyes and primping. She never listens and lives in her own world of fantasy and false hopes.

ESMERELDA is the sweet young thing. She is fragile, lovely and unpretentious. She appears quite out-of-place in relation to Euclio, Megadorus, Drusilla and Staphyla. The quicker she moves away from her present environment perhaps the better off she will be, though she loves her father dearly.

LITTLE CAESAR is pompous, pretentious, a "dude" of a cook, and full of confidence and egotism. He struts and gestures, never works, but always giving commands.

ASPARAGUS tries to be like Caesar but never quite makes it. He is stupid and can never think for himself.

BROCCOLI is forever in his world of fantasy. He is never "with it" in the actions of Caesar and Asparagus. It is questionable as to why Caesar allows him to be a part of his company.

COSTUMES

Although the basic style of each costume should be Roman such as using the basic tunica for both men and women, thonged sandals laced half-way to knees, a toga for Megadorus, a tunica interior or Greek chiton for Drusilla and Esmerelda, and bangs clipped for the men and hair up and entwined for the women—there can be other additions to the costumes which are not authentically Roman but characteristically contemporary and which make their own comment so basic to the Roman idea of comedy.

Colors and accessory suggestions are as follows:

HOUSEHOLD GODS: Off-white with purple and gold. A banana to be eaten by No. 2; a compass to be used by No. 1; and a book for No. 3.

EUCLIO: Shades of brown. A flower wired to the first finger for occasional sniffing a la Ferdinand the Bull.

STAPHYLA: Shades of dark green. A red mop-wig and an old broom. Grey, brown and black rags.

MEGADORUS: Yellow and blue. Rings on his first fingers on either hand, a handkerchief, and snuff-box.

DRUSILLA: False eyelashes, long silk handkerchief, excessive jewelry. Red and purple color scheme.

ESMERELDA: Light blue and greens. Arm-band and dainty handkerchief. Ribbons.

LITTLE CAESAR: White with red and greens. Variation of a cook's hat. A chef's apron and book. Gloves.

ASPARAGUS: Shades of red with green. Hat and apron inspired by the vegetable Asparagus. A belt of spoons of different sizes and shapes.

BROCCOLI: Shades of green with red. Hat and apron inspired by the vegetable Broccoli. A flute tied around his neck for he is usually playing for their entrances and exits.

Only Esmerelda has straight makeup. Character makeup exaggerated for each stock character should be used. Some of the costumes can be of print material and shape might be inspired by the character of the person, such as the shriveled-up quality of Staphyla, the roundness of Megadorus, etc. Wigs for the women would be appropriate.

PROPS

Pots and Pans
Pot of Gold
Cook book scroll
Flute
Broom
Banana

LIGHTS

General illumination may be used at all times. The stage curtain may be omitted from the production with only the stage lights to suggest the beginning of the play. For pacing and continuity, there should be no division of scenes in the running of the play. Such divisions should be only helpful to the actor and director in rehearsals.

MUSIC

Music should be used to set the mood and style of the production and used at the beginning and ending of the play. A single rhythmical instrument can be used such as a flute or a simple orchestral arrangement may be used. It is most important that the music itself suggest humor, slapstick, and variety of sounds and tempo.

Although not included in the script, a tune for the words below may be used at the beginning of the play and throughout. They do not have to be sung by a person on stage but can

188

be used as a comedy piece with sounds and moans at the beginning before the Household Gods enter.

Song: Where oh where is my gold?
       Where oh where is my golden gold?
       Where——where——where——where?
       Where oh where is my gold?

SET

The basic set consists of three doorways; however, the greater the imagination in interpreting these doors, the more fun can be suggested in the set design.

WHO IS CASSANDRA?

a play in one act

written by senior high students

supervised by Claudette Gardner

Who is Cassandra? was written and produced by the Dallas Theater Center Teen Theater in the spring of 1965. The student playwrights were also the original cast.

The Individual Voice	MELANIE HESTER
The Conformist Voice	SALLY REID
The Rebel Voice	SHERRY WIGLEY
Cassandra	DIANE MEE
The Teacher	JOANN SCHAIBLE
Student One	EMILY REYNA
Student Two	NAN SCHWALBE
Student Three	JO ANN MITCHELL
The Father	MARC LANG
The Mother	NANCY PERRY
The Singer	BARBARA KAMHOLZ
The Old Man	CHARLES WELLS

Guitar music by John Kamholz

It is late January, the day before semester holidays, in a modern-day public high school. The first scene takes place inside the mind of the girl Cassandra as she sits in her English class. It is the last period of the day. Cassandra is surrounded by her inner voices: the Individual, the Conformist, and the Rebel.

INDIVIDUAL. Who . . . is . . . Cassandra?

ALL VOICES. We are . . .

CONFORMIST. I am . . .

REBEL. No! I am!

INDIVIDUAL. Nobody is . . . yet.

GIRL. I wonder which one . . . I wonder which one I am.

INDIVIDUAL Funny how a person isn't just *one* on the inside, but many. Many faces, many voices . . . all trying to be heard . . . trying to be seen . . . trying to take over . . .

REBEL. *(Loudly)* It's no use! Why bother? Do what you want! Don't let anybody tell you what to do . . . or to be!

CONFORMIST. *(Softer)* No. Do what they tell you. Be what they want you to be.

INDIVIDUAL. *(Whispering in the girl's ear)* Look for Cassandra. She's here . . . somewhere . . . very . . . close by . . .

GIRL. Am I really Cassandra?

CONFORMIST. Or am I . . . Sandra?

REBEL. *I'm* Sandra!

INDIVIDUAL. Why is it no one calls me Cassandra?

REBEL. Why should they?

INDIVIDUAL. What is in a name?

CONFORMIST. Names are important!

INDIVIDUAL. A rose by any other name would . . .

GIRL. Wait! Mother calls me Cassandra . . .

REBEL. And she should. She thought of it . . . and gave me the name. Trying to trace our family back to the Greeks, I guess.

CONFORMIST. Wish I had a normal name. An everyday name, like Mary, or Jane . . .

REBEL. Mother thinks one of her great, great, great grandmothers was Helen! Social Clubs! Social status, social everything! Mother makes me sick!

CONFORMIST. But she usually knows what I should do. She knows how to get along with people, and that's important!

REBEL. Bet she doesn't know who the first Cassandra was . . .

INDIVIDUAL. I do. I looked it up. A prophetess in Troy, the daughter of a king. She heard voices inside her head, too.

GIRL AND INDIVIDUAL. Like me.

INDIVIDUAL. But nobody believed her . . . or believed *in* her. Nobody had any faith in what she said . . . not even her own family.

REBEL. *(With scorn)* A prophetess . . . in Troy!

GIRL. I'm no prophetess. I'm nobody.

INDIVIDUAL. Greece. The Golden Isles of Greece.

CONFORMIST. The first Cassandra went crazy. Wonder if I'm a little . . . crazy.

REBEL. Ridiculous!

CONFORMIST. Wonder if other people feel the way I feel?

REBEL. Nobody feels the way I feel . . .

INDIVIDUAL. Nobody *knows* the way I feel.

REBEL. And nobody cares.

INDIVIDUAL AND GIRL. Father cares . . . but he doesn't know . . .

REBEL. No. Parents don't care how you feel. They're too busy flying airplanes and going to club meetings and parties.

CONFORMIST. Wonder why Joe's staring at me . . . he's Elaine's boyfriend.

REBEL. Who cares? I like him. I'll date him if I want to.

CONFORMIST. But Elaine's my friend. I shouldn't even try.

REBEL. Aww, I wouldn't have a chance with him anyway.

GIRL. If only I were someone else . . . someone that was fun to be with . . . not shy . . . not afraid of anything . . . and everybody.

REBEL. Somebody exciting. And daring! A real swinger!

CONFORMIST. Popular! Well-liked! Someone who belongs!

GIRL. Maybe a nickname would help. Like . . . maybe . . . Sandy.

REBEL. Yeah!

CONFORMIST No. That's not as cute as everyone else's nicknames.

INDIVIDUAL. I am not . . . "Sandy" . . .

REBEL. I *could* be. I'll be "Sandy" if I want to be "Sandy" . . . and nobody is going to stop me. They'll have to call me that if I say so.

CONFORMIST. No, they won't. They'll call you what they want to call you.

INDIVIDUAL. It's getting crowded in here.

CONFORMIST. I can't let people know I'm this mixed-up. What would the rest of them think?

REBEL. Who cares what they think? Let's cool it.

CONFORMIST. Hide!

INDIVIDUAL. Make up my mind . . . must . . . make up my mind.

CONFORMIST. Mrs. Potter's looking at me . . . she can tell when you're not listening. Maybe I've missed something important.

REBEL. Ohhh, not likely. Anyway, I'm tired. And it's last period. Too tired to listen to Mrs. Potter.

INDIVIDUAL. *(With great wonder)* I . . . have . . . written . . . a . . . poem . . .

CONFORMIST. She'll ask for the term papers in a minute. I'm afraid she won't like mine . . .

INDIVIDUAL. My poem . . . my poem . . .

(The lights gradually come up on the rest of the stage, revealing Mrs. Potter and several students in the classroom. The lighting and general mood of this scene is more realistic than the preceding one)

TEACHER. All right, class. It's almost time for the bell. Get your term papers ready to turn in.

192

STUDENT 1. Hey, how do you spell "philosophical"?

STUDENT 2. Search me.

STUDENT 3. *(Spelling)* p-h-i-l-o-s-o-p-h-

TEACHER. Be sure you include your title page and bibliography.

STUDENT. *(Completing his spelling)* i-c-a-l.

STUDENT 1. Mrs. Potter, how much did you say this paper counts on our semester grade?

TEACHER. One-third.

(She moves among the students, picking up the papers. She takes Cassandra's last)

Charles, I hope your spelling has improved.

STUDENT 2. I hope so, too.

TEACHER. Sandra, did you mean to turn this in now? This is a poem.

GIRL. Yes m'am. It's my . . . term paper.

TEACHER. But Sandra, I can't accept this. You have no footnotes or bibliography or outline.

GIRL. But I worked just as hard as anybody else. It's a *long* poem.

TEACHER. That's beside the point, Sandra. I told you to write a theme, not a poem. I don't understand. You're always done what I assigned in the past. What in the world prompted you to turn this in instead of your research paper?

REBEL. Don't tell her . . . wouldn't understand.

CONFORMIST. Better answer her before you really get into trouble.

GIRL. Well, I was thinking about it, and I decided that most research papers are just organizing other people's thoughts. I wanted to do something of my own, to contribute something of myself for a change.

TEACHER. Your ideas aren't worth anything in this paper. Research papers are supposed to help prepare you for college. If you got to college and didn't know anything about research papers, you'd blame me, wouldn't you?

GIRL. I already know how to footnote and do all the other details. I've written research papers all through high school. The poem is on the topic you assigned; it's about poverty. Please, Mrs. Potter, won't you at least read it first?

TEACHER. *(As she reads)* Why, Sandra, this is the best thing I've ever seen you write. Would you read a part of this to the class? We only have a few minutes left.

CONFORMIST. Won't like it. Too different.

INDIVIDUAL. I worked hard. It's good.

GIRL. Alright, Mrs. Potter.

TEACHER. Quiet, class, Sandra has something to read to us.

GIRL. It's a poem I wrote.

> A small, dark, hungry child sits alone on the road-side
> And he lifts up his dirty hand to you
> As if to say: "You are my friend. Can't you help me?"
> And you hold his dirty little hand in your clean one.
> And you look deep into his eyes, and see all the sorrow and hunger
>   and dejection of the world.
> And you see his mouth slightly parted in hope of food.
> And his other hand trembling, so you grasp them both.
> And his heart throbs, longingly, and it cries out, only to be loved . . .

TEACHER. That's enough, Sandra. Let's have some class criticism. Susan?

STUDENT 1. I didn't get it. I mean, I couldn't understand what she was trying to say.

TEACHER. Betty?

STUDENT 2. Oh, it was okay.

STUDENT 3. Miss Potter?

TEACHER. Yes, Sally?

STUDENT 3. I don't think she's being realistic. I mean, how can anyone say that poverty is beautiful?

INDIVIDUAL. Listen to me, please . . .

GIRL. It's . . . well, it's like you see something bad . . . a play, or maybe read a book. Things can be beautiful and still be sad and ugly at the same time . . .

STUDENT 3. We're not talking about a beautiful play; we're talking about poverty. Dirt, and filth, and hunger.

REBEL. Ahhhhhh, she doesn't know what it's all about. Hypocrite?

CONFORMIST. I told you nobody'd like it.

TEACHER. Bob, do you have anything to add?

STUDENT 4. Well, I think that Sandra has made an interesting point in her poem on the complexity of human nature. As to whether there can be beauty in poverty itself, I rather. doubt it. But many people seem to think there is some beauty in pity.

GIRL. Not pity, but love and human . . .

(The bell rings)

TEACHER. Have a nice holiday everyone.

STUDENTS. Oh, boy. Two weeks of freedom. Did you understand what she was saying? I didn't. Old Sandra has really flipped her switch.

CONFORMIST. Take it back. Tell her you didn't understand the assignment.

REBEL. Don't let her tell you what to do.

CONFORMIST. You'll flunk the term. You know what that means.

REBEL. Show them all how cool you are.

CONFORMIST. No college . . . no sorority . . .

REBEL. Who cares?

TEACHER. Sandra, wait a minute. I'll tell you what: since yours is a special case, I'll let you write your research paper over the holidays. I can see you put a lot of work into this poem, but you must write a research paper.

GIRL. I did research. I walked around in the slums and talked with social workers and all kinds of people who lived there.

TEACHER. But you still must turn in a research paper. The rest of the pupils have done the required assignment. I have sixty-five papers to grade over the weekend before I can turn in the grades. I'll have to give you an incomplete, but if you will turn in the paper when you return from the holidays, I'll accept it. It's up to you.

INDIVIDUAL. Up to me . . . it's up to me . . .

(Sandra and the voices leave the classroom area, and the lights fade out. As they enter the area outside, suggesting the street, Sandra and her voices continue to talk)

CONFORMIST. Of course we'll write it over. Have to.

194

REBEL. No. Can't make me.

INDIVIDUAL. Can she?

REBEL. Of course not. Nobody can.

INDIVIDUAL. Master of my soul? "Invictus?"

REBEL. Yeah, but you're different. In a class by yourself.

GIRL. A lower class.

CONFORMIST. No college if you don't make good grades.

GIRL. Mother!

CONFORMIST. Have to tell her. Boy, a real boner today.

GIRL. What's she going to say? And father . . . wonder what he'll say?

CONFORMIST. You've let your parents down.

REBEL. You're more important. It's your life.

INDIVIDUAL. Mine.

REBEL. Sure. Do anything you like.

CONFORMIST. No, you can't! See what happened today?

GIRL. Wonder what else will go wrong today. (She waves to some friends) There goes Joe. He's walking Elaine home.

CONFORMIST. Why shouldn't he? She's the girl he cares about.

REBEL. He would like me, if he knew me better. I know he would.

INDIVIDUAL AND GIRL. I don't even know me. Joe, you don't know me at all. I wish you did.

GIRL. They look so happy. Everything Elaine does is so right. She makes good grades; she's the best one on the drill team, and she's got Joe Wilson for a steady. He's really crazy about her. I wonder what's wrong with me? Nothing ever goes right for me.

CONFORMIST. Let's go home . . . they're expecting us.

GIRL. Yes, I'd better not be late for dinner.

(The girl and the voices stop at the door to her home. The lights fade on them and come up on the interior of the girl's home)

MOTHER. (Offstage) Howard . . . is that you?

FATHER. (Entering the room) Uhhhhh-hhhmmm . . .

MOTHER. (Entering) Now, Howard, I told you Madeline has the night off tonight. We were supposed to have dinner promptly at six. She's in a terrible mood . . . and so am I. You know its opening night at the opera tonight.

FATHER. No. I'd forgotten.

MOTHER. Howard, how could you forget something as important as opening night. The first opera of the season. When I do so adore to arrive early and see everyone.

FATHER. And be seen by everyone . . .

MOTHER. I reminded you before you left this morning . . .

FATHER. Dear, I couldn't help being late tonight . . . even if I had remembered . . . we had very strong headwinds, and a little trouble with the . . .

MOTHER. You know I don't understand that kind of talk—those technical explanations. That's no excuse.

FATHER. *(Calmly, still not annoyed)* It's not an excuse. It's a reason.

MOTHER. Well, in any case, dinner's over and we have to hurry. The curtain goes up at eight.

FATHER. I'll just have a snack then. *(Exits to the kitchen)*

MOTHER. Now, Howard, you know you have to hurry and get dressed if we're going to be there early to mix and mingle. And remember, there's that reception for the cast afterward. I'm so proud of that invitation. *(She picks the invitation up off a table and holds it. He enters eating a chicken drumstick, and sits down, putting his feet up on the couch)* Howard. For heaven's sake, take your feet down. You know very well I've just had that couch redone in that expensive brocade!

FATHER. How about a little soothing music before the opera. *(He puts on a Miles Davis record)*

MOTHER. Must we listen to that horrible what's-his-name?

FATHER. Miles Davis is his name, I believe. No, we don't have to listen. I just thought it would be a nice appetizer for the heavier fare ahead.

MOTHER. I bought that stereo for classical records, so that Cassandra would grow up with good music. I don't particularly like having that . . . played on it.

FATHER. It's Miles Davis.

MOTHER. Well, whatever his name is, I still don't care for his kind of music.

FATHER. How long has it been since you played a record . . . one of your precious collections. Hummm?

MOTHER. Why, I don't know. A few days ago, I suppose.

FATHER. It's been at least two months since you touched this machine.

MOTHER. Now with fine records if you play them too much they get scratched. And I don't want that to happen. Mine are all in perfect condition.

FATHER. Still in the wrappers, some of them.

MOTHER. I wonder where Cassandra is. She didn't come home for dinner either. Sometimes I think she's more like you than *you* are. Always late . . . always with her head in the clouds.

FATHER. Literally. And figuratively, too, I suppose. Well, worrying and fretting isn't going to hurry her home. She'll be along.

(Cassandra and the voices enter)

MOTHER. You've missed dinner entirely, Cassandra. And you remember I told you this morning it would be early. You know we're going out tonight . . . and it's Madeline's night off.

GIRL. I'm sorry, Mother. I guess I just forgot.

INDIVIDUAL. I didn't want to remember.

MOTHER. Yes, I can very well believe you did. Well, how was school today?

CONFORMIST. Pulled a first class boner . . .

REBEL. Told them all off . . .

INDIVIDUAL. It was awful, Mother.

GIRL. It was . . . all right, I guess.

MOTHER. How did Mrs. Potter like your term paper? You turned it in today, didn't you?

GIRL. She didn't have time to read them, today. How was your flight, Dad? You went to New York today, didn't you?

FATHER. Yeah, Punkin, it was New York today . . . shining . . . beautiful as it always is.

INDIVIDUAL. I wish I'd been with you, Dad.

FATHER. I'll take you there someday.

GIRL. I'd like that.

MOTHER. Now, Howard, don't go putting notions like New York in her head. You know college is going to be difficult enough.

FATHER. There were some diplomats and ambassadors on board today . . . from the UN, I suppose. They were really splendid . . . in those flowing orange robes . . . Liberia, I think they said.

GIRL. Gee, that sounds exciting. Did you talk to any of them?

MOTHER. Howard, hurry and get dressed. We're going to be late.

FATHER. We have plenty of time.

GIRL. What opera is it?

MOTHER. *La Traviata.*

FATHER. *(Exiting to kitchen for more food)* More like "La Trivia" . . . *(Pretends to sing)* Ahh . . . ha . . . ha . . . ha . . .
(Cassandra laughs and the voices also as he exits)

MOTHER. Surely Mrs. Potter had some sort of reaction to your paper. Why didn't you ask her to just glance over it?

GIRL. She did, Mother.

MOTHER. Well. What did she say?

REBEL. Go on. Tell her now.

GIRL. She didn't like it much.

MOTHER. Why not? You did do the paper, didn't you?

GIRL. Yes, I did it. I wrote it, but it wasn't exactly what she wanted.

MOTHER. What did she want? What didn't you do?

INDIVIDUAL. I wrote . . . a poem.

GIRL. I wrote a poem about beauty . . about what I thought was beautiful. I wrote about poverty, and hunger, and war and death.

MOTHER. Beautiful? You think these things are beautiful? Haven't we always taught you that beautiful things are paintings . . . and literature . . . flowers . . . gardens . . . and opera?

GIRL. You just don't understand.

REBEL. Old-fashioned.

GIRL. You're just so old-fashioned, Mother.

MOTHER. All your little friends seem to like me.

REBEL. If she only knew!

GIRL. Don't you have to get dressed for the opera, Mother?

MOTHER. I'm already dressed, Cassandra. Why is it that you never tell me what goes on at school? You never tell me anything.

INDIVIDUAL. She never has time to listen.

MOTHER. It's not as if I didn't want to hear. I'm always interested in what you're doing.

But I think your grades are more important than your outside activities. Like that drill team you want to join. It's not as important as college, is it? And to get into a good eastern girl's school, you have to have grades! But . . . I suppose it's possible to do both. Now Marsha's little girl . . . what's her name?

GIRL. Elaine.

MOTHER. Now Marsha's little girl manages to be on the drill team and keep up her grades, too.

INDIVIDUAL. I'm not Marsha's little girl . . .

REBEL. Who cares about grades?

GIRL. Grades aren't the only thing in the world, Mother.

MOTHER. I didn't say they were. But they're very, very important. They measure what you learn.

GIRL. I don't think they do.

REBEL. Grades are what the teacher thinks of you . . . how much she likes you, or doesn't like you.

INDIVIDUAL. But . . . that isn't always true . . .

MOTHER. Well, it doesn't matter what you think, you've got to do what the teacher wanted you to do. You have to call her and tell her you'll do something about the paper . . . to make it right.

GIRL. It's semester holidays. I don't think she'd want to be bothered.

MOTHER. You're going to have to make a decision right now. You'll have to do the paper over.

CONFORMIST. Yes. Why not? Write it over. Nobody liked it. My friends are laughing at me behind my back.

REBEL. Who cares what my stupid so-called friends say. Who cares what anybody says? Let them say whatever they like.

INDIVIDUAL. I have my own mind.

REBEL. Own mind . . . HA!

CONFORMIST. And what good is a mind of your own if it causes confusion and keeps you from getting ahead?

MOTHER. I'm waiting, Cassandra.

(Father has entered and has been watching the argument)

FATHER. Let her make up her own mind, Helen. For heaven's sake, let her decide.

MOTHER. I am, Howard. I'm just telling her what she has to do.

FATHER. (Laughing) And that's not letting her decide. Take your time, Punkin. You can think it over while we're out feeding our souls on Puccini.

REBEL. No . . . no . . . I can't do it. I can't do the paper over again. She doesn't understand. She doesn't even remember what it was like to be young. Times are different now.

CONFORMIST. College. A good sorority. Dates with fraternity men. Football games.

REBEL. I won't let anybody tell me what to do. I'll do what *I* want.

INDIVIDUAL. What *do* I want?

MOTHER. All right, you think it over. You and your father both put things off until the last minute. No college. Nothing like I'd planned. (She exits)

FATHER. You decide, Punkin. You decide what you want to be.

MOTHER. *(Offstage)* Howard! We'll be late.

FATHER. Remember, it's your poem . . . and *your* life. *(He exits)*

GIRL. I'll try to remember, Dad.

CONFORMIST. I could write a nice, polite letter to Mrs. Potter. On my best stationery. And tell her I'll do a research paper like all the others over semester holidays.

INDIVIDUAL. But is that what I want to do? What I really want to do?

CONFORMIST. I guess I'd better get started now if I'm going to do a nice, neat job and get it mailed tonight.

REBEL. But what good's it going to do. She'll flunk you anyway. Or give you a "D." She hates you, you know that.

CONFORMIST. This letter might smooth things over.

REBEL. No, Mrs. Potter never has liked me.

CONFORMIST. It will be all my fault if I make another mistake. Here's my chance to make things right.

REBEL. Nothing's really my fault.

INDIVIDUAL. Sometimes it's my fault. I can't get around that. Sometimes things are my fault and sometimes they aren't.

CONFORMIST. Go on. Get the paper and pen and write Mrs. Potter. She might even forget about that other theme . . . the poem. Your mother wants you to write this letter. It will make everybody happy.

REBEL. Except me. And who's the most important. Who would I rather see happy: me, or Mrs. Potter?

CONFORMIST. Apologize . . .

GIRL. *(Writing)* Dear Mrs. Potter. I'm sorry I . . .

REBEL. Down on your hands and knees to that old fuddy-duddy . . .

CONFORMIST. But it's good. It'll fix things. Go on. Say you're sorry and you'll never do anything like this again.

GIRL. *(Writing)* . . . did not do the assignment correctly. I will write a research paper over the holidays. Sincerely . . ."

INDIVIDUAL. Where can we be different, Mrs. Potter? Is there anywhere on the earth we can be ourselves . . . and not a thousand other people . . .

CONFORMIST. There. That looks so neat. I'll go mail it and she'll get it the first thing in the morning. I could even stop by the library, check out some books, and get started on the paper tonight.

(The girl and voices exit from the house into the street area)

INDIVIDUAL. It's so cool and purple out here . . .

REBEL. You're not really going to mail that letter, are you?

CONFORMIST. Family . . . grades . . . future . . .

REBEL. Chicken!

CONFORMIST. Mrs. Potter holds my future in her hands.

REBEL. Walking in sand . . . not standing on my own two feet.

CONFORMIST. Everyone else is much wiser than you. They have so much more experience. They know what's best for you.

INDIVIDUAL. We know better than anyone what's best.

REBEL. Do what I want for a change. Tear that letter up. See how many pieces you can tear it into. Tear up failure; tear up Mrs. Potter; tear up all the stupid people who don't care.

(The girl hesitates a moment, then tears the letter up, and puts it into the trash container just beside the mail box. Suddenly she hears music from a nearby coffee house)

CONFORMIST. Tear up your future.

REBEL. Who cares about the future? Now! Look!

GIRL. It's one of those coffee houses.

CONFORMIST. I can't go in there. Mother's always told me not to go in places like that.

REBEL. I'm not scared. Come on, let's go.

(The girl and voices enter the coffee house area where lights come up slowly revealing a couple of tables with chairs. There are several people sitting at the tables listening to a folk singer)

CONFORMIST. Look how dirty it is.

REBEL. So what? Haven't you ever seen dirt before? It's still suave. Listen to that.

(The girl sits at a table alone and listens to the folk singer complete her song. The folk singer is singing The Times They Are A-changin'! by Bob Dylan or a song similar)

INDIVIDUAL. I've never been anywhere like this before.

REBEL. Really going to like this place. Great music. Wild people.

CONFORMIST. People with no future.

INDIVIDUAL. Maybe they're looking for their future.

INDIVIDUAL AND GIRL. Like me . . .

(The singer notices the girl and comes over to sit at her table and talk)

SINGER. I haven't seen you around here before.

GIRL. I've never been here before. What goes on here? I mean, what do you do? Was that you singing?

SINGER. Yes, that was me.

GIRL. I don't understand it.

SINGER. Haven't you heard that song before?

GIRL. No. What else goes on here?

SINGER. You mean besides singing and stuff?

GIRL. Yes.

SINGER. Well, there's always someone reading poetry or something. Do you qualify?

GIRL. Do I what?

SINGER. Qualify. What do you do? You must do something.

REBEL. Say it. I write. Go on and say it.

GIRL. I write.

SINGER. What?

GIRL. Poems, mostly. *(She hesitates)*

REBEL. Ask. Go on, ask. These people will love the poem.

GIRL. Could I . . . would it be alright if I read part of a poem I have written?

SINGER. Sure. Why not? Hey everybody! *(She turns her back to the girl and speaks to the others, then turns back to the girl)* Hey, kid, what's your name?

INDIVIDUAL. Cassandra.

GIRL. Cassandra.

SINGER. Cassandra here has got a poem. *(She turns back to the girl)* Go on . . . they're waiting.

CONFORMIST. See what you've got yourself into?

REBEL. They look friendly. They're your kind of people.

(The girl clears her throat. The group waits quietly. She reads a portion of the poem and stops in mid-sentence. The group is silent. They do not applaud, but simply return to their coffee and conversation. The girl returns to the table)

GIRL. What did they think?

SINGER. *(Kindly)* I guess they didn't dig it much.

GIRL. I guess not.

SINGER. What else?

GIRL. What do you mean?

SINGER. Well, what else do you do?

INDIVIDUAL. I think . . .

GIRL. I think a lot . . . is that good?

SINGER. Yeah. You've got to be able to think if you want to live in this world.

GIRL. What makes you different? I mean, what else do you have to do to qualify here?

SINGER. Well, mostly it's your life. How you live . . . what you do . . . how you feel . . . things in life that . . . affect you . . . are what put you here. Things people do to you.

GIRL. What do you mean *what they do to you?* Don't they like you much?

SINGER. It's not exactly that. It's like when you try all your life to be somebody and do something you can hold up and be proud of. Like . . . well, like your poem. And then nobody likes it or accepts it.

GIRL. Right. Nobody liked my poem.

SINGER. And you feel like you don't belong, and you can't fit. It gets to be where everybody's inside and you're outside, and there's nobody there to help you. You can't even find yourself. And then you find out there are people like you, almost . . . and they become your friends. And because you can't fit inside, you try and fit in outside. Only when you do fit in outside, you get the feeling like now you're *inside*, and you've found yourself, and you can express yourself and not be afraid anymore. When you're outside, you're always afraid.

GIRL. Are you afraid now?

SINGER. Not now. I guess I found out what I want.

GIRL. What is it?

SINGER. I want to be let alone . . . just to be let . . . alone. That's all.

(They sit in silence a moment)

GIRL. That's not what I want. That's not what I want at all.

(Someone in the coffee house calls out to the singer something like "Come on, there's a group going over to Jay's house. Hurry up!" and the singer stands to leave)

SINGER. So long, kid. See you around. Maybe the next time'll be better.

(The singer exits with the other people in the coffee house leaving the girl alone, sitting silently at the table. Old man enters, begins sweeping, putting the tables in order and the chairs on top of the tables. The girl suddenly crumples the poem and throws it on the floor)

REBEL. Worthless trash.

OLD MAN. Did you drop this? *(He picks the poem up from the floor and hands it to the girl)*

GIRL. Yes. Just get rid of it, please.

OLD MAN. Why should I do that? It looks like something that might be important.

GIRL. It isn't. It's just a piece of trash.

(Old man begins to read poem)

OLD MAN. Who says so?

GIRL. Everybody.

OLD MAN. Who is everybody?

GIRL. Why, everybody . . . my teacher, my friends, my parents, the people in this place. I thought sure the people here would like it.

OLD MAN. What made you think that?

GIRL. I don't know. I guess because no one else had liked it. These people just had to.

OLD MAN. So you thought that here, a place where the so-called non-conformists gather, that you would be accepted?

GIRL. Yes. How did you know?

OLD MAN. Oh, many people come here for that very same reason.

GIRL. And what happens to them?

OLD MAN. Some are accepted, some aren't. It all depends . . .

GIRL. You mean, this is a "group" too?

OLD MAN. Yes, these people have their own rules and their own little society. They're sort of misfits, outcasts, you might say, from the rest of the world . . . they gather and try to glorify themselves by calling themselves non-conformists . . . beatniks . . . any one of several labels. They stick to themselves. You see, everybody needs to be in some group, no matter who they are.

GIRL. But I don't belong to any group. Not at school, not at home, or here.

OLD MAN. I had the same problems when I was your age. Oh, I know this may sound like the same thing you've heard over and over again, but . . . I used to think I had the greatest set of ideals in the world, and that everyone else was too worldly and not interested in the "finer things" like I was.

GIRL. Yes. That's it. That's how I feel. Did you write poetry, too?

OLD MAN. Oh, yes. Poetry, and plays . . . short stories. I even started a novel once.

GIRL. When did you start writing?

202

OLD MAN. When I was young. When I started seeing the world realistically. When I knew I could do something about it instead of saying, "This is this," and "That is that" . . . I began trying to make my life mean something: to say something and set things straight.

GIRL. When people say things or do things that hurt you or upset you, and you don't know how you feel about it exactly, you write down what you feel. It's a poem, and it comes from inside you, and somehow you find . . . something important.

OLD MAN. You are your poem . . . and your poem is you.

GIRL. But doesn't somebody else have to like your poem?

OLD MAN. I don't think they have to . . . I have many poems stored away in my room, that no one ever liked except me. But I like them . . . they give me pleasure and peace. I read them sometimes when I'm lonely, and they keep me company. It doesn't matter to me if no one else ever likes them. I do.

GIRL. I'm not sure . . .

OLD MAN. You think it over. I have to close now. You'd better be getting home, hadn't you?

GIRL. Home? There's no one there. Can't I stay here?

OLD MAN. There's going to be no one here either in a little while. You have to face things sometime. You don't have to go back to the old way of thinking. Go home and rest. And tomorrow, try being just you . . . nobody else. Not completely *different* from everyone else, but not completely *like* everyone else, either.

GIRL. You said everyone needs a group to belong to. But where do I belong? Where are my people?

OLD MAN. Just be yourself and your friends will find you. Don't ever try to be what you're not . . . inside.

GIRL. It's getting late. I guess I'd better be getting home.

OLD MAN. Wait. Don't forget your poem.

GIRL. Oh, yes. I want it now.

OLD MAN. Incidentally, I like the poem.

GIRL. I like it more now . . . myself.

OLD MAN. I thought you would.

GIRL. Thank you.

OLD MAN. Goodnight, child.

GIRL. Goodnight.

(She exits from the coffee house into the street area. Her parents, the teacher, and the old man are seen in the dim background, perhaps lighted in separate areas to suggest the memory of the girl)

INDIVIDUAL. What was it he said . . . "it doesn't matter if no one else likes my poems . . . I like them."

GIRL. That sounds good to me, but I'm so mixed up.

CONFORMIST. Think it through.

REBEL. No good just thinking. Do something. Move. Run. Fight. Take a risk if you want to win the game.

CONFORMIST. But then you might lose.

INDIVIDUAL. I need help.

REBEL. No. I don't need anybody. You can't depend on anybody.

INDIVIDUAL. I'm alone.

REBEL. You can't depend on anybody. You're in a world by yourself and you've got to hold up on your own. You can't trust anybody.

CONFORMIST. But sometimes you can't depend on yourself either. Sometimes you've got to have other people.

REBEL. Running . . . begging to other people. Can't you do anything by yourself?

INDIVIDUAL. All discouraging me. All against me.

REBEL. I'm against them. Be different . . .

INDIVIDUAL. My poem . . . is good.

TEACHER. Footnotes, bibliography . . . research . . .

CONFORMIST. No use . . . can't fight city hall

CONFORMIST AND MOTHER. Take Marsha's little girl . . .

INDIVIDUAL. But I'm Cassandra . . . Cassandra . . .

ALL VOICES. Somebody help me . . . tell me what to do.

FATHER. Work it out for yourself, Punkin.

INDIVIDUAL. I can't.

REBEL. Was a good poem . . . write more . . . show them . . .

CONFORMIST. Keep quiet . . . keep mother happy . . .

MOTHER. Write it over . . .

REBEL. Won't write it over . . .

CONFORMIST. Grade lowered . . . term grade lowered . . . can't get into the . . .

MOTHER. . . . best college of your choice . . .

REBEL. *Her* choice!

INDIVIDUAL. My choice is . . .

REBEL. To show them who I am . . .

INDIVIDUAL. But who am I???

ALL VOICES. Some one tell me . . . please . . .

CONFORMIST. Dates . . . parties . . . friends . . . fun . . .

REBEL. Your own thoughts . . . ideas . . . beauty in poverty.

MOTHER AND TEACHER. How can you see beauty in poverty?

REBEL. I can. I'm different. Not crazy, just different from your stupid idea of doing everything like . . .

REBEL AND CONFORMIST. Everybody else!

CONFORMIST. Live life smoothly . . . without tears . . . yelling . . .

CONFORMIST AND REBEL. Problems . . .

REBEL. . . . come up no matter what you are. No one is completely happy . . .

INDIVIDUAL. Mother?

MOTHER. Have to go to opening night . . . have to meet Ambassador's wife.

204

INDIVIDUAL. Dad?

FATHER. Yes, dear. If you must . . . we must.

INDIVIDUAL. Poor Dad . . .

FATHER. Figure it out for yourself.

REBEL. I'm different . . . a true Cassandra . . .

CONFORMIST. Nobody believed her. She was very unhappy. My namesake.

INDIVIDUAL. I don't want to be unhappy.

REBEL. Won't be unhappy. Know I'm right. Believe in myself.

CONFORMIST. Nobody else will believe me . . . life will be miserable unless I do what they want me to do.

REBEL. Dull . . . quiet, unimaginative . . .

OLD MAN. These people have their own rules and their own society . . .

SINGER. In with the outside . . .

INDIVIDUAL. Does that make any society right?

REBEL. No!

OLD MAN. Don't conform to non-conformity.

GIRL. Hey!

INDIVIDUAL AND GIRL. Can that be it?

CONFORMIST. Society demands . . .

REBEL. That I conform . . .

OLD MAN. You are your poem and your poem is you . . .

GIRL. You mean, that's all there is?

OLD MAN. No. Many, many more poems. One poem is just a small part of what's inside you . . .

GIRL. Then it doesn't matter if no one likes it?

OLD MAN. Do you?

GIRL. I do like it. And it doesn't matter whether anyone else likes it. I wish they would, but they don't. At least not right now.

INDIVIDUAL. It's all right. It's my poem. I like it. If I like my poem, then I must like me . . .

GIRL. I accept . . .

INDIVIDUAL. myself . . .

REBEL AND CONFORMIST. Myself,

GIRL. Cassandra.

ALL VOICES. I accept Cassandra.

CURTAIN

BREAKTHROUGH

A Space Fantasy in Three Acts

written by senior high students

supervised by Emily Jefferson

Breakthrough was written and produced by the Dallas Theater Center Teen Theater in the spring of 1961. The student playwrights were also the original cast.

Norma	GAIL GALVANI
Joe Neat	RAWLEY CARTER
Mother	BARBARA SMITH
Father	CLAUDE CROWE
Nancy	PAMELA STONE
Nelda	DIANE MARSALIS
Philipation	LINDA STOCKSTILL
Abigail (Voice)	JOAN GAYNOR
Girls in Dormitory	
Prima	SUZANNE STEWART
Secunda	MARY NIENDORFF
Tertia	SUSAN HETH
Quatra	VICKI DAVIS
Robotville	
She	MARY JEAN McCULLOUGH
Lady Robots	MIMI COLLIER
	SONDRA SMITH
Science Lab	
XZC	JOAN TROYER
FRJ	CORINNE FREEMAN
BPQ	SINAH LOUISE GOODE
MNU	BRENDA GARTNER
Political Rally	
Speaker #1	JUNE HEROY
Speaker #2	SONDRA SMITH
Speaker #3	SANDRA WINTERS
Speaker #4	JOAN GAYNOR
Someone	MIMI COLLIER
Somebody	JUNE HEROY

About the Play

This play grew out of a class exercise in which the students studied people in four levels of growth. It is called the "growth exercise." Each level of growth was investigated in detail: movement patterns, speech rhythms, textures, colors, lines, and shapes that seemed to best characterize each particular growth level.

The levels are explained in relation to the play as follows:

Group 1: These people are faddists, the conformists, the blind followers of other people's ideas. Group 1 is represented in the play by Nancy—the daughter in college—her state of mind, and the dormitory inhabited by girls who are even further exaggerated into essences of this group.

Group 2: These are the technical people of the world, those who love schedules above all else; those who are devoted to definite forms and ways of approaching problems and who would rather perfect an existing method rather than devise a new one. Although not restricted to the fields of science and technology, prime examples may be found amidst this group. In the play, Group 2 is represented by Father and Nelda, the science-minded daughter.

Group 3: In Group 3 are found the people who are leaders and joiners of clubs and organizations, the back-slappers of the circle in which they move. They often affect knowledge, emotions, and methods which they do not possess or understand in order to gain a result. In the play, Mother represents this level of growth; her ideal state of mind being most productive at a political rally.

Group 4: This group is not represented in the play for it is an ideal level of human existence reached more rarely than any of the other levels. It is the level on which a human being is vitally alive, creating and learning, and trying fresh ideas in whatever his way of life may be. It is the level of true individuality and honesty of mind and spirit, and the one in which all the great and lasting ideas of the world have been conceived.

It is most important that one realize that just as a politician can reflect a level of growth comparable to Group 4, so can the man of technology be found on a Group 3 level of growth. It is not necessarily the vocation which classifies a person's growth level but his attitude and approach to the world and the problems around him.

BREAKTHROUGH

ACT I   SCENE 1

Norma and Joe stroll on stage hand in hand. They are returning from a ride in Joe's new rocket ship.

NORMA. Venus is such a beautiful planet. The atmosphere even feels different. Everything kinda glows, and here it's so ordinary. I love soaring through space in an open rocket. My father would never buy an open rocket, he thinks they flip around in the air pockets.

JOE. *(Laughs)* I like Venus, too. It's such a forward looking planet. For instance, that drive-in where we were was especially built for sports rockets.

NORMA. It's wonderful. I've never been there, but I've always wanted to go. I couldn't before because I've never ridden in a sports rocket.

JOE. You haven't? I'm glad I could be the one to take you on your first ride.

NORMA. So am I. *(She begins to edge toward her front door)*

JOE. *(Taking her arm)* Wait. Have you ever been to that new amusement park, Saturn-under-six-rings?

NORMA. No, I hear it's just fabulous.

JOE. Say, why don't we run over now?

NORMA. Well, uh . . . I'd like to . . .

JOE. Fine, let's go. (Starts to lead her off)

NORMA. I can't go now. Maybe tomorrow.

JOE. Do you have to go in right away?

NORMA. Yes, I really do. We are going on a picnic this afternoon and I have to help pack the pill basket.

JOE. Could I help? Then I'd get a chance to meet your family, too.

NORMA. Thank you, Joe, but I really don't think this is the time. When we're getting ready to go out together it's always so confused. Our family is like that.

JOE. Hey, wait a minute! My family usually goes on a Vernal Equinox picnic, too. Maybe we could all plan to go to the same planet.

NORMA. No . . . We always have to go to the same old place. And my father won't allow us to invite any guests. It's not as if we enjoy each other's company.

JOE. My family picnic is no (Hesitates) "picnic" either. (Laughs) It's the only time in the year our whole family gets together. And even if we wanted to enjoy each other's company, we wouldn't have a chance, because my parents always invite about a hundred other people.

NORMA. Isn't that funny? That would probably be just what we need. We know each other too well.

JOE. For you, then, that ancient axiom "The family that plays together stays together" is no longer true. You know, I really wish we could go off on our own private picnic, Norma. Just the two of us.

NORMA. I do too, Joe. Maybe someday we can. Why don't you call me tomorrow?

JOE. Why wait till tomorrow? I'll call you tonight and we can console each other. But I'm sorry we can't spend the afternoon together.

NORMA. I am, too. (Long pause. They look thoughtfully at each other) I really do have to go.

JOE. Okay. I'll talk to you tonight.

NORMA. Bye, Joe. (She watches him leave, then starts to go into the house. She stops, turns and starts after Joe) Joe . . . Joe . . . (Turns back to the audience) I really wish I could go on a picnic with Joe. Or he could go with us. But I don't know how he would like my family. Or how they would like him. They aren't so hard to like, really. I do love them. They are all interesting people, but somehow they seem so hard to understand. Each one is so wrapped up in his own little world. None of them seems happy. If only I could help them. There must be some way to jar them loose. I'll bet I've wished that nearly a million times. And Joe . . . he's wonderful. I'd love for him to like my family. I just wish there were some way. I wish . . . I suppose I'd better get inside and help with the picnic.

(Fade into living room scene. Nancy is polishing her nails. Mother is talking on the mind machine. Finally Nancy goes over and starts throwing pills into a basket. Norma enters to help her)

NANCY. (Sarcastically) A vernal equinox picnic! Every year it's the same old thing! (Imitating her father) "Everybody ready? Sure you've got enough food? Let's hop into that rocket ship and fly away! Are we all dressed right?" . . . Honestly, I'm sick of it.

NORMA. Oh, I know. Father and his routines! How could he live without them?

(Mother hangs up the mind machine only to have it ring again. The sound is unlike a telephone ring for it is deeper and shorter like an electronic "veep." Mother picks up the mike and begins to talk as the girls continue to pack the basket)

MOTHER. (*Into the machine*) I know it will be hard, but fight the resolution without me . . . Well, it wasn't my idea. You know Sherman!

NORMA. Say, where are the bone pills for Oscar?

(*Mother hangs up the mind machine*)

Father says miniature ostriches must have regular beak exercises.

(*Father enters*)

FATHER. Everybody ready? Sure you've got enough food? Let's hop into that rocket ship and fly away! Are we all dressed right? Come on, everybody . . . let's be off!

MOTHER. Oh, we're getting ready, dear. But I wish you could see what this has done to my club life. Here we have this important convention of Interplanetary Women and I'm on the council. Now I can't even be there to help in the important fight for such a good cause.

(*Father looks into basket, shakes his head, takes a list from the table, dumps pills on the table, and repacks*)

FATHER. Let's see . . . sliced chicken pills, German potato salad pills, frito pills, dill pickle pills, mayonnaise pills, lettuce pills, hot fudge sundae with nuts, cherries and whipped cream pills, salt and pepper pills, oni . . . say, where are my onion pills?

(*Nelda enters with her head buried in a book*)

MOTHER. Well, dear, we hate to have you eat those onion pills.

NELDA. Father, you know how bad those pills are for your digestive system and inner stomach. It says in *Ailments of the Digestive System and Alumenary Tract* on page 1756, paragraph B: "The lining of the inner stomach is affected by the intake of excessive acidity and . . . "

FATHER. I don't care! I must have my onion pills. My father had his. Grandfather had his. And I'm going to have mine. Where's my hand rocket? I'll go across the continent and get some. Of course, according to my schedule for the day, that will throw us exactly two minutes and forty-seven seconds off.

(*Father grumbles as he exits. Mother goes to answer the mind machine and Nancy flops into a chair*)

MOTHER. (*To Nancy*) Don't put your feet on my new chair, dear; it's an antique. (*Into machine*) Yes, Astra, dear . . . Well, I'm sorry but I just can't help it. How did you find out I won't be at the Interplanetary Women's Council meeting? . . . I see. (*To the girls*) I can't stand these mind message party lines! (*Back into machine*) You know how important this is to me, dear. If it were anything else, I would get out of going, but the picnic is part of Sherman's schedule, and you know what that means . . . (*She hangs up*)

NANCY. Mother, what are we going to do about him? I come home from college to get away from regimentation, but school is a breeze compared to this. Everything is so . . . ugh!!

NORMA. Yes, why just the other day, Joe . . .

NANCY. My little sister mentioned a boy's name! Oh, shooting stars! What is this planet coming to? How long have you known him? What does he look like? How old is he? (*Pause*) What about the other day?

MOTHER. Now, now. Leave her alone, dear. Of course we care about her friends, but we don't want to press her. No, of course not. I'm sure that he must be a very nice boy and within her age and intelligence bracket.

NANCY. But, Mother . . .

MOTHER. No, just leave her alone, dear. She'll tell us when she feels the time is right. (*Pause*) (*To Norma*) How do you feel *now*, dear?

NORMA. Not very well, that's for sure!

MOTHER. *(Surprised)* Well, uh . . . that's fine, dear.

(Father bursts in)

FATHER. All right, I have them. It has made us . . . oh, dear . . . three minutes late. I've miscalculated by thirteen seconds. I'll have to replan our route.

NELDA. Remember what happened last year on the way to your Universal University Reunion?

FATHER. We got there on time, didn't we?

NANCY. Nobody goes to the U. U. Reunions anymore. I was glad we got off course.

NORMA. Just because there weren't any cute boys or sorority sisters there . . .

MOTHER. *(To Father)* Sherman, we can't go that way. There's still that detour around the air pockets.

NELDA. Let's drop by the foreign office so I can pick up the new Martian language tape.

NANCY. What do you want to learn Martian for? You already know twenty-seven languages!

NELDA. You'll wish you knew it when they take over our government!

MOTHER. Oh, the Martians can't do that, dear. The girls made a resolution against it.

FATHER. Women and their useless resolutions! Why don't you do something worthwhile? For instance, straighten out this leap year business. If that weren't in the calendar, I could plan more than three years in advance.

NORMA. Oh, I like Leap Year.

NANCY. You dooooo? Does Joe like it, too?

NORMA. Humph!

NANCY. Say, are you talking about Joe Neat? He's that adorable blond with the lovely convertible.

NELDA. Is that the convertible with the extended franaspar and the 48 carbonuclear engine? I have investigated the condition of this engine and its particular sound leads me to believe that the capacitator supplies an over-abundance of Quintle.

FATHER. Quintle! I've found that it synchromeshes too readily. We're having some trouble with it in Machine 3525 at the plant.

MOTHER. The Quintle Auxiliary has asked me to preside over their next meeting, but I just don't see how it's possible. With all the problems facing me, I need a cabinet.

NANCY. A cabinet would be lovely. You could put all my friends in it.

NELDA. Philosophy proves we have no friends, only acquaintances.

FATHER. Is Joe prompt?

MOTHER. Why don't you invite him to come along this afternoon? We'd love to have him, dear.

NELDA. *(Sarcastically)* That's all this excursion needs . . . a boy.

NANCY. Wonderful! The fraternity boys would love to come.

FATHER. There has never been anybody but us on the picnic, and there won't be anybody else now!

NANCY. *(Pleading)* Daddy . . .

FATHER. No!!!

210

MOTHER. *(Trying to change the subject)* Mildred Neat must be his mother . . . which reminds me, she isn't . . .

NANCY. Is he in a fraternity?

NELDA. Fraternity means brotherhood.

NANCY. Is he on the Drazen team?

FATHER. Have you seen his family's schedule?

NELDA. What's his I. Q.?

MOTHER. What does his Father do?

FATHER. I know his Father.

NELDA. I know his brother.

NANCY. He's cute!!

NORMA. Please! Be quiet. I'm sick of it! The whole thing! *(To Mother)* You with your clubs! *(To Nancy)* You and your sororities! *(To Father)* Your schedules! *(Pause . . . To Nelda)* And your science books! Well, I'm through!

MOTHER. Norma, dear . . .

NORMA. And don't call me dear!!

FATHER. *(After long pause)* It's 1400, picnic time. Let's get in that rocket ship and fly away!

(They all rush out, leaving Norma alone on stage)

NORMA. If I've wished it once, I've wished it a million times . . .

PHILIPATION. *(Offstage)* Poof! Poof! Aw, come on, Poof! The darn stuff never works when you want it. Oh, well, I'll announce myself. *(Shouts)* HERE COMES PHILIPATION!!!

(Philipation enters, a strange looking little creature looking half like a robot and a little like an elf. He wears antennas and a gleeful grin)

I vowed the millionth time you said that, I would come no matter what I was doing at the time.

NORMA. *(Obviously surprised)* I'm sure you can find a reasonable explanation for this but as for myself . . .

PHILIPATION. *(Brandishing a chicken leg)* Bite? *(She backs away)* An old-fashioned habit of mine. Couldn't get used to your pills. The audible vibrations emanating from your extra-sensory assets lead me to believe that you have a problem. However, as to its particulars, I am uncertain. Enlighten me. *(Takes out a notebook)*

NORMA. It's not exactly my problem. It's my family. Each one wants everyone else to be just like he is.

PHILIPATION. So this is bad . . . ?

NORMA. Can you imagine a world in which everyone is the president of the PTA?

PHILIPATION. My mother was president of the GTA. GTA . . . Gremlin-Teacher Association. That's a little out of your atmosphere?

NORMA. But were clubs all she was interested in? And try living with someone who must prove the formula for air before she will breathe it. The worst is my sister; she nearly drives me crazy trying to keep up with the latest fads.

(All throughout this speech Philipation is rapidly taking notes)

PHILIPATION. You do have a problem. Luckily, I have been consulted in time. I shall rectify the situation promptly. Actually, it isn't too serious. I've dealt with problems of universal importance. For instance, do you recall the . . .

ABIGAIL. *(From above and offstage)* Philipation!

PHILIPATION. *(Trying to keep Norma from hearing)* Well, I handled that! And then there was the time . . .

ABIGAIL. Philipation!

PHILIPATION. *(Meekly)* Yes, dear.

ABIGAIL. Come back here and finish your supper!

PHILIPATION. But, dear. I'm on an important mission.

ABIGAIL. Well, you didn't sign out.

PHILIPATION. Sorry, dear.

NORMA. I see there are a few problems you can't solve.

PHILIPATION. Ahem! Now on to point four.

NORMA. You sound like my father.

PHILIPATION. *(Writing)* Your father . . . *(Looks up)* . . . runs on a pretty rigid schedule?

NORMA. That's putting it mildly. He wants all of us on it. And I'm off it right now. They're waiting for me to go on a picnic.

PHILIPATION. Oh, don't worry. Time stands still for me. I love picnics. Let's hop in that rocket ship and fly away!

NORMA. *(Turning to look at him curiously)* I'm getting a little dubious about your qualifications.

(Philipation's opening "poof" now poofs. He looks embarrassed)

PHILIPATION. That's what happens when you change brands!

(Lights fade as Norma and Philipation exit to rocket ship)

ACT I   SCENE 2

Philipation and Norma are entering the rocket ship. The family is in a frozen position, seated, and ready to go.

NORMA. What happened to them?

PHILIPATION. Oh, to employ a time-worn cliche . . . time marches on.

(He gestures)

NORMA. Wait! Won't they see you?

PHILIPATION. Nope! *(Now finishes his gesture and the family awakens)*

NELDA. . . . . . . not part of her usual behavior pattern.

NANCY. She can't talk to us like that!

MOTHER. It's just a phase. *(Sees Norma)* Glad you're feeling better, dear.

(Norma and Philipation stand close by. Father starts the rocket and it makes funny noises)

FATHER. *(To Nelda)* Does it sound to you like the left quadritek is lagging?

NELDA. It's merely a faulty timing device.

FATHER. They don't make them like they used to . . .

212

NANCY. Daddy, come fix the picture.

(Father touches a button or two and Nancy seems satisfied with her television picture. He puts the ship in remote control and they all settle down)

NELDA. *(Reading as she looks out the window)* "When passing by a shooting star be careful of your franaspar. Burma Shave." How ridiculous!

NANCY. What's a franaspar? Are we going to stop at a space station?

FATHER. No, we can't stand any more delay.

(All begin to watch television. Philipation makes a cocky gesture to Norma and goes to the controls where he begins to play with them. All kinds of funny things begin to happen. Finally, Mother looks out the window)

MOTHER. Sherman, dear. Wasn't that the Jupiterian Museum? We weren't supposed to be anywhere near it.

FATHER. Nonsense, it's not on the route.

MOTHER. We're headed toward the Milky Way!

NELDA. Yes, Father, perhaps you had better come look. I believe she is accurate in her evaluation of the situation. *(Looking out window with Mother)*

FATHER. *(Now looks out window and rushes to controls, frantically working with them)* This has never happened before. I knew I shouldn't have bought this ship from that new company. The owner seemed rather unorganized.

MOTHER. But his wife is a supporter of my pet charity.

NELDA. *(Reaching for the manual)* It's obviously the billsquid. Let's look it up. *(Looks in manual)* Here it is. *(Reads)* "Adjusting the Billsquid. The automatic advance of the billsquid timing is controlled by the induction manifold unit. In addition, a vernier adjustment is provided to give control over the actual point with varying conditions of fuel."

NANCY. Hurry, Daddy. Dust Valley Days is starting. Don't you want to see it?

NELDA. *(Continuing)* "Turn the milled nut clockwise to retard the squiding or anti-clockwise to advance and note the degree of change of the scale. The rim of the crankshaft pully is marked with a notch which will coincide with the longest of the three pointers of the timing chain. When Number one and Number three are in the up position, note that the Billsquid activating levers must be kept in contact with the billsquid points the whole time of star . . .

(Norma has turned to Philipation looking puzzled. He nods and turns back to the family)

PHILIPATION. Zot! *(Family freezes)* Now for the most difficult part of my task: to make these various personalities see themselves. It's very hard to know yourself. The only way to do it is to look into your own state of mind, to see yourself as others see you. Most people refuse to do this. But whether your family wants to or not, they're about to be projected into their own one-dimensional world. I have no control over their will; what effect this insight will have on them depends on their strength of character.

(Philipation raises his arms as if to begin his signal as the lights quickly fade . . .)

ACT II   SCENE 1

The scene is a girl's dormitory room. It appears that as many people as possible have been crammed into what looks like the remains of a bedroom. Actually, there are only a few extras in addition to the four girls and Nancy in the scene. Everyone is onstage in a frozen position. After a few counts, everyone snaps to life, giving the impression of a madhouse, which of course it is. Girls are yelling and screaming unrelated phrases such as "May I borrow your . . ."; "Isn't he the neatest?"; "Absolutely divine rocket ship"; "Just a marvelous dancer . . ."; "Just not in style . . ."; "Everybody has one"; "Have you heard . . ." "And then I said . . .", etc. Nancy walks in and watches for a fascinated minute, then speaks to the nearest girl.

NANCY. Pardon me, I think I've taken a wrong turn somewhere. Could you tell me where I am?

PRIMA. I think you're in unorganized-and-generally-chaotic-messy-ville. Although I'm not absolutely sure. You can't ever tell whether you are coming or going in this place.

NANCY. Would you mind repeating that name again?

PRIMA. Yes, I would. It takes something out of me every time I say it.

NANCY. Oh. Okay. What do you do all day long? Just this?

PRIMA. We all do exactly what we want to. That's why all the mess.

NANCY. Funny, but this place reminds me of my dormitory back at school. Except we don't do what we want. We have this dumb housemother who broods over us like we were a bunch of chickens. It must be great. I mean doing what you want to all the time.

PRIMA. Oh, it was at first. But, sister, it gets old after a while. I've been here for ages now and I'm still not unpacked. Spent the whole time trying to keep up with the crowd and now nothing I brought is in style anymore. So why unpack?

SECUNDA. Hey, Prima. Get a move on. We'll be late.

PRIMA. For what?

SECUNDA. I don't know. But I seem to remember that we have to be somewhere a half an hour ago. Everyone is going. So hurry.

PRIMA. Well, back to the maddening crowd. Nice to have met you. Although I didn't, really, I s'pose. (Walks away, then turns back) Whatever you do, don't try to get into the bathroom.

NANCY. (To herself) I'll be darned. My Elysium. The heaven I've been waiting for. Now I can do just as I please. I guess I should go make some friends. What's-her-name seemed nice enough. If they're all that nice, I think I'll live here the rest of my life. (Looking around) It looks a little messy, though. Even for me. Maybe I can clean up a bit. Wouldn't Mother be surprised if she could see me volunteering to help with housecleaning!

(Nancy begins to pick up stuff here and there, bumping into people all the while. She makes a few attempts at being friendly, but the girls seem so intent on doing what they please that she gets no more than a few crisp nods. Finally after she has fought her way over to the other side of the room, she sits down desparingly. A girl who is hurled out of the chaos approaches her offering a smile as a sign of good will)

TERTIA. Hi. I'm Tertia. Sorry I haven't gotten to know you before now. You probably think we're a bunch of unorganized-and-generally-chaotic-messy-people.

NANCY. Oh, no. I don't think that at all. As a matter of fact, I don't even know what you said.

TERTIA. Well, at any rate, welcome to our little wonderland of where everybody can do just what they want. What would you like to do to start off?

NANCY. I'd like to kind of clean this place up a bit. But I don't know where to start.

TERTIA. I don't think you want to do that. See that girl over in the corner? With the kind of crazy wild-eyed stares? She had that same idea. Tried to clean this place up when she came. My gosh, how she worked! But after picking up after these girls for years and years when all they did was throw things down that she had just picked up . . . well, it was just too much for her. Sure was a nice kid, too. Oh, well. Was there anything else you wanted to do?

NANCY. Ummmmm . . . not right off hand. Say, wait a minute. Have you got anyone around here in authority whom I can dispute? That's something I've always wanted to do.

TERTIA. Are you kidding? There has been no one in authority around here for about twelve light years. If there were, it would ruin our whole internal economy.

NANCY. Oh. Then I guess I'll just sit here and watch. Tell me, why are you all dressed alike?

TERTIA. That's because we all keep up with the latest fashions. When one gets something new, we all do. So long. And by the way, don't try to get into the bathroom.

NANCY. Oh, goodbye. Nice to have met you.

(Tertia exits. Nancy sits there for a while enraptured by the mass confusion. Pretty soon she gets up and goes over to a dressing table and starts combing her hair for lack of something else to do. Shortly thereafter, she is accosted by another young thing who is yelling at the top of her lungs)

QUATRA. Come on, it's time to go eat.

NANCY. What? Oh, you must have me confused with someone else. I just got here.

QUATRA. No mistake. I thought you might like to go AHHHHHHH eat with me.

NANCY. Oh. Well, sure. Thanks. Where do you eat around here by the way?

QUATRA. Downstairs. Simply everyone eats there. The girls run a cafeteria. Of course, it's all AHHHHHHHHH free.

NANCY. They don't run it like this, I hope.

QUATRA. Sure they do. They run it however they please. It's a great way to live. AHHHHHH.

(Nancy recoils each time Quatra yells)

NANCY. Well, maybe in a bedroom or somewhere like that. But in pill mill or where you eat, that's different.

QUATRA. How's it different? Seems to me it's all the same. If you're going to do something you ought to do it AHHHHHHHH all the way.

NANCY. That's hardly a sound philosophy.

QUATRA. It probably isn't. We don't talk much about things AHHHHHH like that.

NANCY. Sure. Listen, I don't mean to intrude, but would you mind telling me why you periodically yell at the top of your lungs? It is rather noticeable.

QUATRA. If I didn't yell now and then I'd feel like I wasn't doing my part to add to the confusion. I just hate to be left out of things. I'm starved. Shall we go eat?

NANCY. Suddenly I've lost my appetite. You go on without me. I'll be along later. I'm sure I can find it.

QUATRA. Suit yourself. Glad to have you aboard anyway. Have fun. Bye, bye. By the way, don't go into the bathroom.

NANCY. Okay. Now, wait a minute. What if I want to go to the bathroom. As a matter of fact, I'd like to see this place. I'm going to the bathroom right now.

QUATRA. Oh, no you're not! Get her girls!

(The girls rush in on Nancy in a mad frenzy. She is yelling "Let me go to the bathroom" as lights go down on them and up on Philipation who says to Norma:)

PHILIPATION. Perhaps we'd better stop at the next space station.

ACT II   SCENE 2

Lights come up gradually on Robotville. Things are stark and without any human warmth. Around the stage roam two robot women picking up objects as they come to them and setting them down with no apparent reason. Dad enters and stares around marveling at the precision. Several times the robots nearly collide but miss each other as if they were on tracks. A bell rings now and then and they change direction. A young girl, dressed sparsely to show off a good figure, approaches Dad. She is almost normal except for her total color characteristics. Dad is embarrassed at her tight outfit but his manly pride will not let him cower.

SHE. Hello. I've been expecting you. You are no doubt Sherman? Well, I'm glad you're here. Welcome to our little place.

DAD. Thanks. But how did I get here? You see, I'm on my way to a picnic. And I'm already eight minutes late.

SHE. Yes, I know. Phil told me you'd be here. Have a seat. You see, we aim to please. Here, everything works on clock time. You seemed so unhappy at home where nobody was ever on time.

DAD. Now . . . now . . . now wait a second. How did you know my name? And who is Phil? Is this some kind of a joke?

SHE. It's a little too complicated to explain right now. Let's put it this way. Suppose . . . just suppose that there was a place where everybody did everything at just the right time. And nobody ever got off a schedule that was mathematically perfect. And suppose that everybody never did anything to upset anybody else's plans. What would you do? (Her voice has been getting lower and lower and more sultry all the time she speaks until at the last she is almost whispering)

DAD. (Startled by the situation) Well, I'd . . . I'd move there without hesitating a second. Yes siree. Not one second. But then, it's ridiculous to assume that such a place actually exits. But I sure wish one did.

SHE. Well, Mr. Quirk, one does exist. You're in it right now. The place most suited for you.

DAD. Aw, go on. You can't be serious.

SHE. Oh, but I am. Don't think that you are the only person who lives by a clock. Why some of the greatest people in the universe live by a clock. And some of them are right here.

DAD. This all sounds very wonderful. But what about you? You are hardly the IBM type.

SHE. Oh, it's a deal that I worked out with the boss. I'm what you might call the normal factor. I sort of keep things in tow. Good hours, high pay, room and board.

(About this time a robot comes over to her and stops, turns around with her back to SHE and waits. SHE picks up an unusual looking tool and idles with the back of the robot for a minute, then taps it on the seat. It walks off resuming its task of walking about with no coherent direction)

DAD. What was that all about?

SHE. Oh, that's one of my odd jobs. I keep them running.

DAD. How many of those . . . things . . . do you have around?

SHE. Gee, I guess we've got hundreds of them in the other part of the country. I keep those two here in the greeting room with me so I won't get lonely.

DAD. Seems to me that a girl as attractive as you ought to have loads of friends.

SHE. I do right at first, when a new recruit comes in, but after the meta, I just have to wait until another comes in.

DAD. I see. What do you mean "after the meta"?

SHE. It's like this. Say someone comes in. I offer him what I offered you—the perfect world. And if he stays, well, he sort of changes.

DAD. How? I mean, how does he change?

SHE. Let's say you decide to stay. And so you start living by our schedule on your schedule. You have your choice, you know. So, after a while you do the same things every day. This goes on for about four months by earth time. And pretty soon you start doing things automatically. Know what I mean? Without even thinking. Because you don't use your mind much anymore. It starts to die out kind of like the whale's hind legs.

DAD. I beg your pardon.

216

SHE. Oh, no offense. Just a general simile. Nothing specific. Anyway, that's what happens and when it does, we call it the meta . . . remember?

DAD. Yes. Metamorphosis.

SHE. See that girl? The one that just came over? She just recently went over to automatic timing. Oh, sorry. I didn't explain that either. You see, in order to make things more convenient for you, we have a machine which switches your material organisms, et cetera, over to a mechanical function. That way you don't have to worry about your body. You said yourself once that worry was a waste of time.

DAD. Now, wait a minute. You mean to tell me that everybody who stays here eventually turns into a robot?

SHE. I hate to put it quite so bluntly but I guess that's what you call it.

DAD. If that's the case, why doesn't it happen on earth? I know some people that never break a schedule.

SHE. Ah, but on earth you have mediating devices. Such as your wife and daughters. Those are the ones that keep you from going over the line. You really ought to be grateful, you know. I mean it's not very pleasant living with a robot. I should know.

DAD. You know something? You might be right. There is one thing that troubles me, though. How can you stay here and not go crazy? I mean with all these nuts and bolts running around.

SHE. Oh, I'm used to it by now. It gets hard at times, I'll admit, but I manage. That's the reason for this wild outfit. It helps me remember I'm a girl and not a machine.

(Lights dim on scene during the last sentence and come up on Philipation on the edge of the stage, watching)

PHILIPATION. It helps me remember too, honey!

ABIGAIL. (Shouting from above, offstage again) Philipation! I thought you were working! Stick to the job!

PHILIPATION. (Looking meekly at the audience) Yes, dear.

(Blackout)

ACT II   SCENE 3

The science lab. This set simply bristles over with test tubes, gadgets, testing equipment, etc. There are three lab assistants working feverishly on something that the audience can't see. They are in smocks. Seated at a desk with some apparatus and piles of papers is a young lady very efficient looking. She is examining some papers and frowning ever so often. Nelda enters.

NELDA. (Looking around) A most impressive place. A scientist's wonderland.

XZC. Over here, Miss. Right over here.

NELDA. Oh, hello. I'm at somewhat of a loss to explain just how I got here. I was on my way to a picnic. I don't mean to interrupt anything.

XZC. You aren't interrupting anything. If you were, we wouldn't have let you in.

NELDA. I see. Would you mind . . .

XZC. Shhh. I'm busy. What are you doing in here without a mask?

NELDA. Mask?

XZC. Are you trying to ruin our experiment? I suppose you are thoroughly sanitary? You know what germs can do.

NELDA. Yes, I am. But I don't think that is any of your . . .

XZC. Your smock is over there. Put it on and go to work. Hurry, science means progress.

NELDA. To work on what?

XZC. To find out the answers.

NELDA. The answers to what? I really don't understand.

XZC. Don't you love science with all your heart and soul? We had you listed as an exceptionally good risk. You have always forsaken everything for science. Your family life, your social relationships. Well, why don't you do that now? Why won't you help us find the answers?

NELDA. I'd love to help. But what answers are you looking for?

XZC. It's your job to find the answers to everything. Now stop wasting time. As a scientist everything is your business.

NELDA. But I really don't see the reason . . .

XZC. There is a reason for everything. Now be quiet and get busy. Any more smart remarks and I'll turn you over to FRJ. She'll handle you.

(At that moment FRJ enters and beckons to XZC. They talk quietly, pointing and nodding. Nelda tries to hear but can't. XZC leaves and FRJ approaches Nelda)

FRJ. I hope XZC didn't upset you. She is really a devoted worker and not half so bad after you get to know her.

NELDA. I was a little bewildered. She is rather disagreeable.

FRJ. True, but enough of personalities. Let's discuss the reason for your visit.

NELDA. Quite frankly, I'm not sure what I'm doing here. You see, I was . . .

FRJ. Yes, yes, I know. I meant I would discuss the reason for your visit. You see, we have a proposition to offer. Look around. You see the world's most complete laboratory. See the labels that are on everything? These describe the composition and life history of the object in miniature print. If you ever wish to find the answers to anything, just look at its tag and read it with a special glass issued you when you sign in. Here everything is science.

NELDA. Mind if I ask a question?

FRJ. Of course not. Go ahead.

NELDA. Are those tags on everything? (FRJ nods) And do you have files on everything? (FRJ nods again) Then what are you looking for?

FRJ. The most important thing in life is mind advancement. We must forever be probing. For instance, over here . . .

BPQ. (Entering and speaking to FRJ) FRJ, you're needed in Greesger research. The neucleus has been reacting favorably with the protons.

FRJ. Wonderful, BPQ. (She exits without looking at Nelda)

NELDA. Well, that was rude. What am I supposed to do now?

BPQ. Probe!! (She exits. Nelda wanders to a corner of the room where a lab technician is working. She looks over his shoulder. She is ignored)

MNU. (Finally) Yes?

NELDA. You're doing this the hard way. If you pour liter one into liter five, you'll find the solution faster.

MNU. (Handing over equipment) Show me.

(*Nelda starts to perform the experiment and MNU watches. Eventually all the technicians, FRJ and BPQ and XZC, enter and crowd around her saying in chorus "probe, probe, probe, probe . . . " Until the stuff blows up. Blackout*)

ACT II   SCENE 4

A political rally. Many people are waving banners and wearing large campaign buttons. They are carrying signs with various slogans and shouting. Mother enters into this chaos and is quickly handed a banner and told to wave it. She does for a while. Then the people begin to march around a platform and finally make a semi-circle as someone jumps up on the platform to speak. At various intervals during the speeches the group in favor of each candidate yells "Hooray!" Mother looks from group to group and yells with each one of them.

SPEAKER #1. Fellow lovers of democracy! I stand before you today to present the facts.

CROWD. Hooray!

SPEAKER #2. (*Pushing #1 away*) You don't know the facts! My friends, I appeal to your intelligence. The cultural level of our lives today . . .

CROWD. Bravo!

SPEAKER #3. (*Jumping in front of #2*) How can we worry about culture when half our people are starving?

CROWD. Yeah!

SPEAKER #4. Re-elect me and you will have another prosperous year like those we have had for so many . . .

CROWD. Yea!

SPEAKER #5. We need young, new ideas! A new frontier!

(*As they yell this time, Mother pulls someone out of the crowd. The noise subsides while they talk but there is an occasional burst of applause or cheer during the conversation*)

MOTHER. I beg your pardon, dear. These all sound like wonderful ideas but what are they running for?

SOMEONE. It's an important election for an important office. Actually, I prefer the first speaker; she has such an attractive hair style.

SOMEBODY. (*Emerging from the crowd to join them*) But Bendon and Butterfly have such a beautiful new rocket ship.

MOTHER. There seem to be so many candidates.

SOMEONE. At the last count, there were 105.

MOTHER. How are you going to choose from so many?

SOMEBODY. Oh, we don't care who wins. It's the campaigning we like.

MOTHER. You don't care at all?

SOMEONE. Of course not. Once the election is over, we start planning next season's parties, rallies and barbecues.

MOTHER. What do the officers you elect think about that? (*Aside:*) I'd hate to think all my offices had been won in a case like that.

SOMEBODY. All we ever elect is the chairman of the nominating committee.

MOTHER. You mean, the campaigning goes on forever?

SOMEONE. Certainly. Don't you just love politics?

SOMEBODY. Why don't you run for office? We've all held it at least seventeen times.

MOTHER. I hate to take on more responsibility. After all, I have offices in several clubs already. President of the Interplanetary Women; secretary of the U. U. Mother's Club; Sergeant-at-Arms of the Quintle Auxiliary . . .

SOMEONE. Fine. You should be able to make a good speech. We'll be your campaign managers.

(Mother is shoved onto the platform. No one listens at first)

MOTHER. Friends, fellow citizens of . . . Thank you for the opportunity of being allowed to speak to you on this lovely afternoon. I, Mary Quirk, know that I am the best qualified for this position. Honesty, integrity, humility are a few of my many assets. If elected, I will do, not try to do, but do . . .

CROWD. What should you do? *(Marching and slogans start all over again and Mother is shoved off the platform and off the stage. Lights out)*

ACT II   SCENE 5

Back in the rocket ship. The family is still frozen in positions as before. Only Philipation and Norma are speaking.

NORMA. That's really something!! I'm glad you're on my side; I'd hate for my mind to be opened to the world.

PHILIPATION. Ah, yes. It was enlightening, but one of my lesser accomplishments. Why, once I even . . .

(From above and offstage)

ABIGAIL. Philipation!

PHILIPATION. Yes, dear.

ABIGAIL. It's time for your tonic.

PHILIPATION. *(Pulls out a bottle labeled "Nature's")* She's right this time, after a strenuous day of miracle-making, it rejuvenates me.

NORMA. *(Reading the label)* Nature's?

PHILIPATION. Serutan spelled backwards. *(He takes a long drink, has an immediate reaction and performs a magic trick)* Always makes me do that.

NORMA. *(Looking at her family)* Don't they get tired staying that way?

PHILIPATION. Oh, yes. Yes indeed. *(Starts to unfreeze them)*

NORMA. Did it work?

PHILIPATION. Please! Well, I never guaranteed the results of our little experiment. Win a few, lose a few!

NORMA. Don't be rude or I'll tell Abigail.

PHILIPATION. *(Remorseful)* Terribly sorry. Shall we go on with it?

NORMA. I've wanted to see this change for so long. Yet, now I'm not so sure.

PHILIPATION. Well, we can't leave them like that.

NORMA. All right.

PHILIPATION. Time marches on. *(He gestures and the family begins to unfreeze)*

NELDA. *(Still reading the manual)* If not, the fly wheel will become jammed in the mesh and can be freed only by turning the billsquid armature with a spanner applied to the shaft extension at the commutation end.

FATHER. We're back on course. But look at the time we've lost.

MOTHER. I just knew we'd get lost, dear.

NANCY. Now the picture is out of focus again.

NELDA. Did you check the ellipsoidal tube?

(Norma glares at Philipation who shrugs and takes out his notebook)

NORMA. Any more brilliant ideas?

PHILIPATION. Let's see . . . . . . failures, failures . . . that would be right under the last summit conference.

(These next lines provide the family change. They each go through three cycles, taking on the characteristics of each other, even vocally. By the last lines they are as if in a trance and the lines clicked off like a metronome. Philipation makes a gesture)

NANCY. Father, did you decide to stop by the foreign office? I think I'd like to learn to speak Martian.

FATHER. Wonderful, dear. That will make you eligible for the U. U. Likeable Linguists Club.

MOTHER. We can't stop. We'll ruin our schedule.

NELDA. Daddy, is it time for 3005 Moonbeam Strip?

NANCY. Don't you think we need a new rocket ship? In my position I need to keep up appearances.

FATHER. Let's do. Everybody's getting a new Excess 5 model.

MOTHER. Technically the engine is unbalanced. The differential distributor deviates.

NELDA. Excess 5? But we've always had an Excess 7.

NANCY. Off schedule.

FATHER. Technically speaking.

MOTHER. Nobody does that.

NELDA. Of course, dear.

(Like clockwork, they exchange attitudes and physical positions—and maybe even bits of costume if they were exchanged to begin this sequence. They return to normal)

FATHER. There's the foreign office. Shall we stop?

NANCY. Oh, not just for me. I don't want to cause any bother. Why don't we wait and stop on the way back.

MOTHER. Isn't this near the place where we usually stop?

FATHER. Yes, but I heard there's a better place just the other side of Orion.

NELDA. I'm hungry. Did we bring enough Sundae pills?

NANCY. Norma, you've been awfully quiet. Do you feel all right?

NORMA. I'm all right now. Mother, may I call Joe and ask him to meet us for the picnic? I'd like him to meet my family.

NELDA. Why don't we invite his whole family. It will be fun to meet some new people.

FATHER. Probably won't have enough pills. Shall we go back for more?

NANCY. We don't all have to go back. Why don't Nelda and I do it?

MOTHER. Well, if you don't mind.

FATHER. Here we are.

MOTHER. This looks like a lovely spot.

NANCY. We'll help unload before we travel back.

(All busy themselves. Norma turns to Philipation)

NORMA. You really are wonderful. Please stay and come to our picnic.

PHILIPATION. Why I'd love to . . .

VOICE OF ABIGAIL. Philipation!!!!

(Blackout)

A LIST OF ORIGINAL PLAYS

The following plays are mentioned in the text or included as photographic examples of original productions. They are listed here with names of the student playwrights and their teachers.

THE PATCHWORK SKY   written for television by 8- through 12-year-olds (1956)

TEACHER. Ruth Byers

STUDENT PLAYWRIGHTS. Anna Kay Petty (author of original story idea), Bobby Bowden, Michael Kelly, Carol Ann Wizig, Jean Smith, Judith Lynn Wizig, Judy Jolley, John Mac Ousley, Linda Lutz, Debbie Wimpee.

POLWACKIT, THE MAGIC CAT   written by 6- through 9-year-olds (1957)

TEACHER. Ruth Byers   ASSISTANTS. Jearnine Wagner, Brad Harris

STUDENT PLAYWRIGHTS. Laura Brown, Cynthia Cashion, Krissy Park, Timmy Reed, Joette Hudson, Debby Sikes, Mary Susan Bird, Beverly Ann Neal, Natasha Geren, Elizabeth Lacy, Lu Ann Goswick, Nancy McGehee, Linda Lutz, Lacy Taylor, Harriet Easterling, David Shellenberger, Skippy Whitcraft, Juliana Geren, Deborah Wimpee, Lisa Ann Deamer, Alva Jean Ayers, Taffy Bartha, David Fried, Mike McEver, Carl McIntosh.

CAST IN PHOTOGRAPHS OF A LATER PRODUCTION IN 1965. Paul Amundsen, Lisa Brachman, Timothy Robinson, Stephen Robinson, Darren Davison, Jill Roberts, Barbara Murchison, Sarah Jester, Mary Wynn Wicker, Judy Burke, Holly Hexter, Cynthia Williams, Lisa Foster, Brett Willard, Lisa Brachman, Sharon Torrence, Sawnie Aldredge.

AN EGYPTIAN ROMANCE   written by 8- and 9-year-olds (1961)

TEACHER. Emily Jefferson

STUDENT PLAYWRIGHTS. Mike Stewart, Scott Davison, Pamela Martin, Robin Dubin, Mimi Portocarreo, Bruce Kilburn, Greg Ashton, Nancy Cohen, Victoria Stewart, Gail Fairleigh, Wynne Pauly, Ruth Birchall, Barbara Woolf, Michelle Armstrong, Sherry Wessel, Kathi Marcher, Mark Phillips, Lynne Williams, Devon Fisher, Randy Chud, Suzy Bourland, Clemens Kessler, Craig Wycoff.

CAMEA   a Greek tragedy by 10- through 12-year-olds (1965)

TEACHER. Barbara LeBrun

STUDENT PLAYWRIGHTS. Susan Smith, Stephanie Widener, Lori Zuckerman, Meredith Moore, Gail Gault, Sonnie Waldorf, Cindy Clarke, Amy Hook, Carol Crabtree, Allison Wood, Beth Mims.

PERSEPHONE   a Greek tragedy by 10- through 12-year-olds (1965)

TEACHER. Everetta McArthur

STUDENT PLAYWRIGHTS. Sara Lindsay, Patty Blalock, Kathryn Cowan, Carol Blalock, Lisa Powers, David Jenkins.

HILORSITY   a Greek tragedy by 10- through 12-year-olds (1966)

TEACHER. Barbara LeBrun

STUDENT PLAYWRIGHTS. Mary Cox, Monica Healey, Cathy Baker, Molly Moroney, Lucia Guerriero, Paige Rippey, Cynthia Crowley, Linda Frazer, Mac Brachman, Denise Galvani.

PROMETHEUS BOUND   a Greek tragedy based on the Greek play by Sophocles. Written by 10- through 12-year-olds (1965)

TEACHER. Don Davlin

STUDENT PLAYWRIGHTS. Mitzi Lynn, David Turner, Gilbert Travis, Bruce Hendricks, Susan Rosenfield, Darren Davison, Carol Lancaster, Diane Lancaster, Mary DeBolt, Teri Tynes, Janet Tapley, Becky Jones, Carla Jo Costello, Denise Campisi.

THE CURIOUS KOMEDI   an unwritten Roman comedy created by 10- through 12-year-olds (1965)

TEACHER. Synthia Rogers

STUDENT PLAYWRIGHTS. Kim Pauley, Celia Cook, Linda Hayden, Jena Sue Morris, Renee L'Hoste, Mary E. Mitchell, Molly Houston, Sally Dacus, Darlene Davison, Barbara Pope, Karen Krafft, Cissy Humphrey, Bill Woodburn, John Valez, Lisa Kahn, Art Greenhaw, Jackie Dear.

PREPOSTORIA   a Roman comedy by 10- through 12-year-olds (1966)

TEACHERS. Sue Finley and Synthia Rogers

STUDENT PLAYWRIGHTS. Meredith Moore, David Turner, Becky Jones, Teri Tynes, David Jenkins, Denise Campisi, Carol Crabtree, Lisa Powers, Carla Jo Costello, Sara Lindsay, Carol Blaylock, Janet Tapley, Susie Rosenfield, Cindy Terry, Cathleen Carter, Darren Davison, Gilbert Travis, Joseph Fuller, Mary DeBolt.

WHERE IS MY GOLD?   a Roman comedy based on *Pot of Gold* by Plautus. Written by junior high students (1966)

TEACHER. Synthia Rogers   ASSISTANT. Don Davlin

STUDENT PLAYWRIGHTS. Lisa Caldwell, Tracy Achor, Carolyn Jeffords, David Gernsbacher, Sally Steger, Edward Bock, Trudi Williams, Adrienne Giller, Valerie Mowrey, Pamela Kay Karlen, Kathy Zilbermann.

FRACTURED FAIRY TALES   written by junior high students (1966)

TEACHER. Sally Netzel

STUDENT PLAYWRIGHTS. Clint Venable, Laura DeBolt, Becky Block, Scott Davison, Judy Leedom, Allatia Harris.

MAKE ROOM FOR FRANCIS   original plot by junior high students with dialogue by Miskit Airth (1962)

TEACHER. Miskit Airth

STUDENTS. Laureen Humphreys, Elena Esteve, LeBau Bryan, Jeff Phillips, Linda Kogin, Bill Younger, Marianne Wesson, Judy Lindley, Cathy Manning, Joan Grossman, Venetia Hobson, Martha Sue Richardson, Cheryl Anthony, Kathleen Humphreys, Ann Holbrook, Jeni Henderson, Marjorie Heitman, Laurie Geibel, Michelle Murdoch, Linda Kogin.

THE GOLDEN TEARDROPS   written by junior high students (1958)

TEACHER. Jearnine Wagner

STUDENT PLAYWRIGHTS. Roy Butler, Jimmy Harris, Larry Mahon, Barbara Cashion, Barrett Moore, Cynthia Ridgeway, Fred Bean, Serena Cleveland, Michael Kilian.

CAST IN PHOTOGRAPHS OF A LATER PRODUCTION IN 1966. Kim Shaw, Celia Cook, Darlene Davison, Debbie Brand, Marilyn Matthew, Lisa Arnold, John Hagen, Heidi Huber, Susan Jones, Paul Robinson, Suzy Wheeler.

THUNDER N' BLUE BLAZES   written by junior high students (1960)

TEACHER. Holly Hill

STUDENT PLAYWRIGHTS. (playwriting committee) Sue Danwill, Margaret Mitchell, Susan Nagle, Linda Poole, Joan Skelton.

XANADON'T YOU DARE!   written by junior high students (1961)

TEACHER. Holly Hill

STUDENT PLAYWRIGHTS. (playwriting committee) Cynthia Hull, Jennie MacKenzie, Bart McCarthy, Jackie Pinsker, Linda Poole, Nancy Tunstall.

PHOTOGRAPHS OF ORIGINAL CAST. Alan Hill, Barbara Barbat, Cynthia Hull, Bill Bickley, Pam Martin, John Scurry, Bart McCarthy, Jennie MacKenzie, Nancy Tunstall, Susan Martin, Joan Skelton, Jacqueline Pinsker, Gwen Isles, Julie Lambert, Cathy Potter, Becky Patton, Linda Poole, Betsy Buzzini, Wilson Pietzsch, George Mirsky.

PHOTOGRAPHS OF SECOND PRODUCTION IN 1965. Bill Maquire, Wendy Schneider, Jackie Burke, Gretchen Moser, Michael McKinney, Scott Davison, Glen Owen, Kristi Wheeler, Barbara Cromwell, Suzy Wheeler, Elise Eriksson, Linda Williams, David Lyons, Michelle Tycher, Lyssa Ann Jenkens, Bill Bekins, Shelly Blake, Marlene Skaggs.

BEWITCHED   a magical musical in Prologue and Two Acts. Written by junior high students (1961)

PLAYWRIGHT SUPERVISOR. Glenn Allen Smith   TEACHER. Jayne Randolph

STUDENT PLAYWRIGHTS. (playwriting committee) Carol Miller, June Pauley, Meryl Lee Pauley, Diane Sawyer, and Carol Smith.

LUFU: DEFINITION PLEASE   written by senior high students (1966)

TEACHER. Claudette Gardner

STUDENT PLAYWRIGHTS. Susie Cox, Karen Dodson, Clyde Evans, Irene Hodgson, Mark Hudnall, Elynn Jones, Joan Kaim, Lisa Metcalf, Peggy Morrison, Ivett Quattlebaum, Judy Rodriqez, Margaret Rose, Debbie Pond, Lee Zimmerman.

WHEN GABRIEL BLOWS HIS HORN   a musical comedy written by senior high students (1958)

TEACHER. Ruth Byers   MUSIC CONSULTANT. Virginia Cannaday

STUDENT PLAYWRIGHTS. Bob Wilson, Bill Hunter, Kay Dennard, Pat Nash, Diane Wilson, Penne Percy, Harriadene Johnson, Emily Cravens.

THE MAGICAL WORLD OF MINE   unwritten mime by senior high students (photographed in 1966)

TEACHER. Ric Slocum

STUDENTS. Scott Davison, Michaelyn Hawkins, Elida Hodgson, Tommy Nicholson, Eddie Richburg.

THE GLASS TUNNEL   written by senior high students (1967)

TEACHER. Claudette Gardner

STUDENT PLAYWRIGHTS. Sara Taubman, Debbie O'Brien, Ginny Burgess, Becky Ebner, Bonnie Lovell, Jane Olson, Sally Cole, Taffy Mills, Sharon Hill, Elizabeth Ritz, Sharon Smith, Judi Miller, Jami Harrison.

I learned that
I *can* write something!

Sally Reid